Advance Praise for *Into the Cold Blue*

"John Homan has gifted us with what will surely stand as one of the definitive eyewitness accounts of the Second World War: a tale filled with nostalgia, romance, and unflinching examples of terror in aerial combat. A book that encompasses the whole of an exceedingly eventful life, *Into the Cold Blue* is an invaluable addition to the canon of World War II literature."

—**Matthew Algeo,** author of *Last Team Standing: How the Steelers and the Eagles—"The Steagles"—Saved Pro Football During World War II*

"*Into the Cold Blue* achieves that perfect balance of intimacy and breadth of vision, the personal and the global, as it guides readers on a tour of the air war. John Homan's truth-telling is delivered with candor on every page. Tales of missed targets, bad planning, failed equipment, senseless waste, and varying acts of cowardice complement stories of sacrifice, heroic leadership, and grim determination. Anyone curious about life in a B-24 as it roared over occupied Europe must read this book."

—**Todd DePastino,** author of *Bill Mauldin: A Life Up Front*

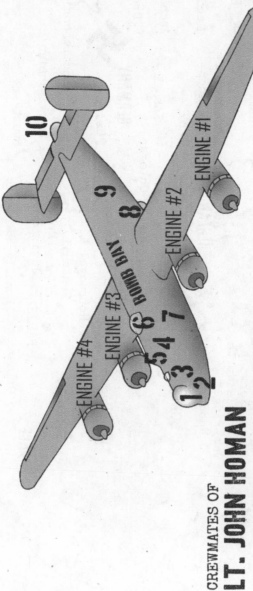

CREWMATES OF
LT. JOHN HOMAN
845th SQUADRON, 489th BOMB GROUP

1. Nose Gunner: Sgt. George W. "Bill" Puska
2. Bombardier: Lt. John K. "Pup" Dalgleish
3. Navigator: Lt. Charles E. "Chuck" Reevs
4. Pilot: Lt. John L. "Predge" Predgen
5. Co-Pilot: Lt. John F. "Sam" Homan

6. Engineer/Top Turret Gunner: S/Sgt. Louis J. "Lou" Wagner
7. Radio Operator: S/Sgt. Dean A. Leonard
8. Ball Turret Gunner: Sgt. Richard H. "Dick" Bunch, Jr.
9. Waist Gunner: Sgt. Marion J. "Bo" Cochran
10. Tail Gunner: Sgt. Vernon R. "Vern" Long

Into the Cold Blue

INTO THE COLD BLUE

MY WORLD WAR II JOURNEYS WITH
THE MIGHTY EIGHTH AIR FORCE

JOHN F. HOMAN
with JARED FREDERICK

REGNERY
HISTORY

Regnery History books may be purchased in bulk at special discounts for sales promotion, corporate gifts, fund-raising, or educational purposes. Special editions can also be created to specifications. For details, contact the Special Sales Department, Regnery History, 307 West 36th Street, 11th Floor, New York, NY 10018 or info@skyhorsepublishing.com.

Regnery® is an imprint of Skyhorse Publishing Inc.®, a Delaware corporation.

Visit our website at www.regnery.com.

Please follow our publisher Tony Lyons on Instagram @tonylyonsisuncertain.

10 9 8 7 6 5 4 3 2 1

Library of Congress Cataloging-in-Publication Data is available on file.

Cover design by John Caruso
Cover image credit: background and smoke by Shutterstock, B-42 photo courtesy of the US Air Force, John Homan portrait by Charlie Wade and enhanced by Jakob Lagerweij of Colourised Piece of Jake

Print ISBN: 978-1-68451-515-8
eBook ISBN: 978-1-5107-8172-6

Printed in the United States of America

For James.
Learn from the past.

CONTENTS

PROLOGUE

July 7, 1944

The cold blue sky was spattered with red bursts and puffs of anti-aircraft fire. Downward streaks of black smoke to our front marked the demise of both Allied and Axis aircraft. Chaos drew closer and closer as our B-24 bomber hummed onward. Vast formations of American squadrons ahead of us were under fierce enemy attack. Then came the uneasy realization that the German airmen were coming for us next. From my co-pilot's seat, I leaned toward the control panel and squinted through the windshield to gauge the approaching whirlwind. Distant enemy planes were at first no larger than tiny specks whizzing through our advanced formations. Having just kicked the enemy's nest, we were soon to be engulfed by an angry swarm.

Moments prior, we had dropped our payload on the morning's target—a Junkers aircraft plant in Aschersleben, located in the north-central region of Nazi Germany. Both the Royal Air Force and U.S. Army Air Forces (USAAF) pummeled the area multiple times throughout that year, but the enemy remained persistent in its productivity. Additional bombardments were therefore ordered. Our division dropped over 200 tons of incendiary and high explosive bombs on that plant. Ordnance plowed into the factory with devastating impact. On a larger scale, more than 1,100 American heavy bombers took off that morning to strike eleven priority targets throughout the Reich. The assault was the biggest aerial blow since D-Day.[1]

The heavens were hazy and lit by a faded glow. Our eyes remained watchful for fighters—both the enemy's and our own. We were anxious to welcome American escort planes to render support. Intermittent flak up to the target posed sporadic danger, but we had yet to confront the day's greatest menace: the Luftwaffe.

A voice shouted over the intercom, "Bandits! One o'clock!"

Rapid flashes of yellow and orange suddenly appeared to our front. In a matter of no time, the enemy was among us.

Our first encounter with the semi-dormant but still formidable German air force had at last arrived. Little could have emotionally prepared us for the sudden rush.

My mind raced. "Stay focused," I told myself. "There's no time to be scared up here. Do your job."

With incredible speed and lethality, the enemy took us on face to face. As many as 200 Messerschmitt fighters engaged us in a death struggle four miles above earth. They spewed red sheets of fire in swift succession. My heart pounded at the sight. Veteran crews quickly realized the Germans had changed their tactics. Rather than charging at us obliquely, the enemy sped to the front of our formation and charged head-on— going down our line of four or five air groups at 400 miles per hour, twice the speed of our planes. The scene resembled a massive domino effect. Squeezing the triggers of their powerful 20mm cannons with each pass, oncoming Germans could hardly miss. Minus brief pauses for cooling, their heavy guns could unleash 700 shells per minute. The enemy put these weapons to shocking use.

One of my comrades later referred to the sudden onslaught as "a huge ball of German fighters." There was no discernable formation, just a well-armed mass hurtling straight at us. Bandits screamed forward at closing speeds of 600 miles per hour. It was the stuff of nightmares. White gun flashes dotted the sky. Deathly volleys had the capacity to shred our 64,000-pound Liberators to pieces. With crazed determination, Jerries sometimes pressed their assaults within yards of our aircraft. I maintained a tight grip on the controls, doing my best to concentrate amidst the struggle.

In hot pursuit of the enemy was an array of American fight-ers assigned to protect those of us in the heavies. Among the support squadrons were vaunted P-51 Mustangs, now known as "Cadillacs of the Sky" for their sleek design and astounding velocity. The arrival of these long-range fighters we referred to as "little friends" was a form of deliverance. When Mustangs emerged, Nazi fighters sometimes dispersed to prey on vulnerable bombers with less protection. These prompt reinforcements helped level the playing field and led to a swirl of dogfights. Flyboys corkscrewed in and out of the clouds at a dizzying pace.

Lt. Richard Stenger, a fellow co-pilot in my outfit, expressed lasting memories of these aviator duels in that mission. "Our P-51s had seen them," he recalled of the Messerschmitts, "and were right on their tails just as they went through the formation. And then started the greatest melee and fastest action that I ever thought possible. P-51s were chasing them all over the place. . . . The bombers and fighters were dropping like flies in a Flit-sprayed room."[2]

Germans tried shaking off the Mustangs with impressive acrobatics, but the Americans were too fast. Planes swooped in and out of sight in the blink of an eye. Imagine a typical race car circling the Indianapolis 500, then double or triple its speed. That's how fast this rate of action was. Aircraft 1,500 yards out zipped over our ships in a heartbeat. The experience was surreal.

At the nose of our plane, Sgt. George "Bill" Puska blazed away at oncoming intruders with hefty twin .50 caliber machine guns. Tracer rounds fired in short bursts allowed for aiming correction and served as targeting markers for five fellow gunners onboard. The cabin floors were littered with small mountains of spent, sizzling brass. I hardly heard any of the racket with the constant whir of Pratt & Whitney engines outside my window. In this frenzied environment, gunners set their targets with extreme precision to avoid instances of friendly fire. Our Mustangs or P-47 Thunderbolts could be misidentified even at close range. The ability to distinguish friend from foe was essential.

During these tense encounters, I was more concerned for my gunners than for myself. They had nothing to focus on but the enemy. All they could do was worry and shoot.

As engineer officer (my official title as co-pilot), I also kept watch on other planes in formation. If my skipper was wounded or killed, command passed to me. I hoped that would never be the case. The administrative officer (the main pilot) carefully observed instruments and control panels. His primary duty was to take our plane to a target and back safely. Both our jobs in the cockpit were exceedingly technical. The operation of our equipment required constant attentiveness. If I made a mistake, it could be fatal.

I spoke into my throat microphone, "How's everybody doing?" If one of the crew didn't answer, I sent another man to check on him. Communication and teamwork were fundamental to our endurance. The emergence of the Luftwaffe that summer morning put us to the ultimate test.

The killing was rampant, the chaos complete. I witnessed a desperate German pilot bail from his crippled bulk of machinery with his parachute aflame. The entangled web of canvas and burning silk hopelessly plummeted to the ground. Meanwhile, our tail gunner reported a German fighter going down in flames just behind our squadron. Its fiery debris sliced through the thin air.

The fight lasted perhaps eight minutes. Despite the tempo of combat, time seemed to slow as we endeavored to escape. One by one, Jerries eventually peeled from the engagement. No longer hunted by German interceptors, many a battered ship staggered the 450 miles back to base. Surviving aircraft rumbled through Holland, toward the sea, and on to England. Thankfully, I somehow remained cool and composed through it all.

Our crew was luckier than many. A group flying adjacent to us lost all eleven crews of its lower squadron. Over 100 men were gone in a matter of minutes. To our immediate right was Lt. Frank Fulks, piloting the high squadron's lead plane. His aircraft suffered several hits on the nose and top turret from 20mm cannons. His ship was a shambles. Fulks's navigator and bombardier were seriously wounded as well. The pilot fell out of formation for a brief time and then took position on our wing, remaining there until we reached home.

During this stretch, we fell into dire straits ourselves. Our number-three engine failed just before we crossed back over the German border, possibly due to battle damage. Although the B-24 could still fly with one engine out of commission, the malfunction made a difficult day even more harrowing. We were certainly not alone in our predicament. The bomb group endured many difficult landings that afternoon.

During the stressful return flight, my eyes were drawn to the top of Fulks's battered plane. The sight has never left me.

The turret was shattered and caved in. Its gunner's head was ripped away by the brute force of the explosion that claimed his life. The wind of the slipstream had siphoned his blood across the plane's exterior surface. The top fuselage was painted with ghastly red streaks all the way to the tail.

It was the goriest sight I've ever seen in my life.

To cope with this horror, I tried erasing the memory. My job required so much concentration that I couldn't dwell on such scenes. When I arrived back at base, I was too exhausted to contemplate matters of life and death anyhow. I collapsed into my bunk and promptly fell asleep. Only decades later did I learn the full extent of that turret gunner's tragic demise.

That operation marked just my second journey into combat. When we returned to quarters that night, we discovered our names listed on the board for the next day's mission. "Oh, Jesus Christ," we collectively moaned. "Let's get to bed." The deathly cycle was already reset for morning. Over the next four months, there would be many more missions to fly, many more targets to bomb, and many more friends to mourn.

Telling My Story

War is misery. I never enjoyed the sting of battle. I never experienced an exuberant rush in combat. I never relished dropping high explosives on people. War is not a game. This is the story I must share. Nobody should experience the hell I suffered during my thirty-four missions over Europe. I want future generations to avert such hardship and wholesale ruin. I have dedicated this book to my great-grandson, James, with the hope that he inherits a kinder and more peaceful world than mine. The story of the Second World War reveals the best and worst of human nature. I witnessed my fair share of that conflict's drama and devastation. Now is the moment to reflect upon what it all means.

Allow me to begin with a consideration of the big picture: How and why did we fight the air war as we did? Japan's domination of Asia and Germany's conquering of Western Europe prior to the attack on Pearl Harbor underscored the centrality of airpower to any military pursuit. In the months after America's entry into the Second World War, the U.S. VIII Bomber Command (later renamed the Eighth Air Force) arrived in England in 1942 with just a few groups of B-17 bombers. This air force grew to be the largest and most powerful of the conflict. The learning curve and growing pains were long and severe. Since the B-17 had been named and promoted as the "Flying Fortress," a decision was made that fighter escorts were not needed for daylight bombing. This proved an overly optimistic assessment.

During 1942 and into 1943, losses were distressingly high, despite some fighter protection by P-47s and P-38s. This led to serious, high-level discussions about abandoning daylight bombing. At that time, only one out of every three crews could be expected to complete twenty-five missions. Gen. James Doolittle took command of the Eighth as the number of groups increased. Doolittle's new strategy was to destroy both German industry and airpower. The Luftwaffe needed to be neutralized before the invasion of France sometime in 1944.

Simultaneous with these conversations, the P-51, a new and much-needed fighter, was designed, tested, and entered service at the end of 1943. The plane was a superior, high-altitude, and long-range plane. Now the heavy bombers would ideally have excellent fighter escorts on long missions into the heart of the Third Reich. Our bombers began to hit German fields, and fighters would attack enemy planes in the air and on the ground. Accompanying the Fortresses were B-24 "Liberators," dependable heavy bombers I flew on dozens of training, transportation, combat, and supply missions.

The strategy changed again in May 1944. Almost all German petroleum was converted from coal, which was shipped by rail to many small refineries. This new approach emphasized restricting fuel production by concentrating on bombing refineries, plus all-out widespread attacks on rail centers and equipment. This latest scheme proved a massive success. By the end of the year, only one out of every thirty German oil refineries were in full production. The Luftwaffe and other military operations were measurably curtailed. I participated in several of these missions that helped diminish the enemy's capacity to wage war.

During these months of trial and error, the "Mighty Eighth" often sent up one thousand bombers in daylight raids, while the Royal Air Force did the same during night operations. The acts were the most devastating practices of modern, total war. Hundreds of thousands of German civilians perished because of American and British bombs. Perhaps just as many structures were ruined. These dreadful results were inflicted at a considerable price for my fellow airmen of the Eighth. Some 47,000 total U.S. casualties were inflicted, including 27,000 killed in action. Our fatality numbers were higher than Marine Corps losses in the entirety of the Pacific War. Over 5,000 planes were likewise lost. Many of them and the crews within remain missing to this day. An additional 28,000 airmen were captured and incarcerated until war's end.

But there is a certain danger to boiling down the tolls of war into black and white statistics. All who study and attempt to understand armed conflict must never forget the human element and personal costs. We did not comprehend the war as an endless progression of maps, charts, data tables, and tactical summaries. We measured losses by tallying our friends and comrades who never returned from missions. This was our war in all its grim realities.

In learning my story, I trust readers will gain an appreciation of the many challenges and complexities of air operations. The combined logistics, maintenance, intelligence, and combat of bomber groups is a saga forged by thousands of GIs. Big missions were prepped, planned, and executed by common citizen soldiers. Whether a serviceman was a base cook or flight navigator, no role was small or insignificant. The joint effort was massive in scope and helped pave the way to Allied victory. I pay tribute to the many unsung individuals who made that achievement possible.

This book is the result of years of research stemming from my quest to understand and convey my exploits to loved ones and neighbors. I saved my flight logbook from the war, attended veteran reunions, wrote newsletter articles, pored over unit records, participated in oral history interviews, and have presented at museums. These activities have kept my memories of the war vividly alive and have served my co-author, Jared Frederick, and me quite well in our desire to impart a compelling story.

To help advance the narrative, we occasionally invoke the words and accounts of my fellow veterans of the 489th Bomb Group to clarify and contextualize key military situations. This formula will hopefully provide the reader a fuller range of perspective and deliver essential insights on 1940s airmen's life. Anecdotes of camaraderie also offer a touch of levity to my storyline that is often somber and contemplative.

I never thought, then or now, that war should be glorified, varnished, or sanitized. This book has been written with that conviction in mind. I disdain unnecessary warfare. Let this book serve as a warning, as our democracy faces grave dangers equal to those I witnessed eight decades ago.

I am among the last of the generation who waged World War II. At the urging of friends and family, I am ready to share my experiences.

Yet I must insist on this: In no way should it be construed that I believe we airmen had a rougher time or did more than other branches of the Allied forces. For instance, pilots in the South Pacific contended with malaria and monsoons—challenges I was thankfully spared. Though my generation is not without its shortcomings, ours was a collective effort in the name of a collective good. Perhaps that too is a lesson to absorb. A momentous task was placed before us, and we set to work as best we could. The profound impacts of violence, love, legacy, and the fragility of life are chronicled via my personal experiences in the following pages.

But the story does not begin in the flak-filled skies of Germany. To fully comprehend my life's journey, I must take you further back in time, to the windswept shores of Raritan Bay.

CHAPTER 1

Roamer

I was a child of the Great Depression. Although I couldn't have realized the fact at the time, limitations posed by the 1930s fueled my creativity, prudence, ambition, and endurance. Coming of age in this era of economic constraint, combined with my affection for the outdoors, deeply influenced my future as a military officer. Hindsight is a powerful force to be reckoned with. With this philosophy in mind, I wish to revisit the places and personalities that had major bearing on my evolution as a citizen and soldier.

My parents hailed from England. Theirs is a classic story of emigration and overcoming the odds. My paternal grandparents resided in Hull, England, which I later visited during the war. At that port city in East Yorkshire, my grandfather served as a ship's carpenter. A hulk of a man, he played with vigor on Hull's rugby team, for which he gained quite the reputation. His spouse, my grandmother, was a lively Irish-Catholic lass, as I would colorfully witness firsthand in 1944.

My father, Samuel, was schooled for only eight years until he too entered the shipyards. To support himself, he labored on a three-man riveting crew, helping construct and then unload countless boats. My mother, Lillian, was raised by a family of Episcopalian shopkeepers. She had a lifelong love of music, an endearing trait that graced our household during my boyhood. A well-versed student of literature and history, she instilled in me an appreciation of the arts and the past. Because of my parents' different religious affiliations, however, my grandmother would not approve their marriage unless the couple wed in the Catholic church and raised their children accordingly. The lovers assented to the compromise and married in July 1920 in the Hull suburb of Sculcoates. My older sister, Hilda, arrived two years later.

Following World War I, working-class families in the United Kingdom sometimes found themselves in dire economic troubles. The recent conflict cast a pall of uncertainty over industry, labor, and commerce. Wishing to enhance their livelihoods, some of my aunts emigrated to the United States. My parents followed in February 1923, with little Hilda in tow. I recall my mother telling me she was deathly seasick during the family's lengthy voyage from Liverpool. In fact, she was so ill that kindly sailors helped babysit my infant sister.

At the conclusion of that trip, my father landed in Boston with no immediate prospects of a job. Early on, he found employment in Boston's shipyards and embarked on numerous test trials for new vessels. He was no stranger to maritime tradition. At the outset of the First World War, he lied about his age and attempted to enlist in the British Army at fourteen years old. His worried mother scurried to the family's parish priest and convinced the clergyman to prevent such an outcome. Instead, by 1917, my father sailed away in the stifling confines of a boiler room on a British minesweeper. According to military records, he sailed on the likes of *Victory II* and *Dreel Castle*. Dad later informed me his international travels carried him to the United States and as far away as Russia. He remained in the Royal Navy until 1919. I suspect his sense of adventure rubbed off on me. Later in life, I resumed the family's sailing traditions with my own seagoing travels.[1]

My father eventually gained employment at the Bath Ironworks in Maine. There, I drew my first breaths on January 5, 1924. For supplemental income, my father trekked deep into the recesses of Maine's spruce forests as a lumberman. While riding on a train, he picked up a discarded newspaper and spotted an advertisement for an opening at the Hercules Powder Company in Parlin, New Jersey. There were no personnel departments in those days; he just ventured to Parlin and showed up at the company gate alongside fellow jobseekers. A foreman appeared and announced that he needed a pipefitter. My father—who was not a pipefitter—raised his hand. He stayed there for forty years, becoming a mechanical foreman.

With the move to New Jersey at age three, I made the first of several relocations in my long life. We resided in South Amboy until my family resettled in a comfortable middle-class dwelling on Henry Street in nearby Parlin. My earliest recollection stems from those days in South Amboy, perhaps in 1927. The first memory of gazing upon the blue vastness of Raritan Bay and across to New York when I was a preschooler is my furthest extent of reflection. I was lucky to have survived childhood since I suffered a near-fatal case of pneumonia at age three. I remember our frugal Irish landlord taking pity and purchasing candy for me during recovery. It is both strange and humorous that I recall these simple gestures. Never underestimate the lasting power of a kind act.

I survived another close brush with death the following year. A young friend from across the street named George Pietruski joined me for playtime in a woodlot near our homes. We noticed a piece of metal sticking out of the soil. Intrigued, we excavated the mysterious object, lugged it to my father's garage, and commenced banging on it with a hammer. Dad soon entered to investigate the racket. His eyes bulged and he yelled, "That's an artillery shell! Get out of here now!" In 1918, an earthshattering explosion at the Morgan Munitions Depot several miles away rained shells all over the county. George and I had discovered one of the projectiles. Authorities quickly arrived to remove the round. I was a curious young

man who (almost) had a blast. Some of the ordnance from the
World War I era disaster was unearthed as recently as 2007.
Little wonder the Sayreville high school team name is "The
Bombers."

Our former Parlin home still stands today. The neighborhood appears nicer than at any moment I resided there.
At that time, the street was graveled and bordered by a
small farm. No fences or manicured lawns were to be found.
Although many women of this era embraced the liberation
of the "Roaring Twenties," Mom remained a devoted house-
wife and lovingly cared for her children. My little brothers—Frank and Edward—respectively arrived when I was
five and six years old. We were a cheerful clan, often uplifted
by the musical talents of my parents. Mom was a stellar
piano player and father was a tenor. I fondly recall their
Irish melodies echoing throughout the house on many an
evening. Mothers on the block also developed "leather
lungs" for a two-street shouting range to beckon us home
for dinner.

Mom excelled at parenting. She raised each of her four
children differently, accommodating their individual personalities and interests with affectionate patience. Mother allowed
her sons and daughter to grow as fast as they were willing to
mature. Her pragmatic outlook on life prepared us to be self-
reliant and realistic. Meanwhile, father was not a strict disci-
plinarian. He was a fun-loving guy but established boundaries
for the kids to the extent that we all knew how much we could

get away with. "There are more horses' asses than horses in
this world," was one of his quaint English sayings. Above all
else, he was our provider. Both he and my mom were arrows
on a compass, continuously pointing their children in the
proper direction.

These commendable traits proved especially valuable during the arduous days of the Great Depression. Resulting from
the upheaval of the 1929 stock market crash, Dad's hours at
the plant were rolled back to a measly three days per week.
Supporting four children on such a limited schedule was very
rough. Economic woes of the era were recognized daily in the
Homan household. Mom sold off her beloved piano as well as
her jewelry. Price tags were placed on anything to spare, resulting in a rather spartan lifestyle. The house was refinanced so
we wouldn't lose our home—a fate that befell so many during
those hard times.

We implemented numerous penny-pinching tactics to make
ends meet. In short, we did more with less. One pair of sneak-
ers had to last the summer. When they wore out, a thick piece
of cardboard was inserted for lining. When regular shoes fell
apart, we used leather, glue, tacks, spare heels, and a lathe for
repairs. If a car tire succumbed to a puncture, a cardboard
patch was placed inside to extend its life. Each child owned
one set of fine clothes, worn exclusively for church or special
functions. We each received one Christmas gift. Children were
often presented fruit or nuts for the holiday since such items
were delicacies. Because we couldn't afford bubble gum, we

picked fresh tar chips off the streets and chewed those instead. Quite the after-dinner flavor.

I never visited a dentist until after high school. I did not have pediatrician checkups. My first appointment with a physician resulted from being randomly struck with a rock while playing softball. The doctor shrugged off my injury, declaring, "No one is ever going to hurt a Homan by hitting him on the head." He shaved a spot on my skull, installed a few clamps, and sent me back to school with a bloodied shirt. Little wonder I thought myself tough stuff.

Mother took on additional work by folding and boxing ornate lace handkerchiefs. We all pitched in as time allowed. Another pastime to help fill our family purse was scouting the neighborhood for empty bottles to receive one-cent return credits.

Community solidarity helped stave off hunger. Hunting and fishing buddies often delivered fresh game that lasted several meals. Peculiar to these years of privation, baked squirrel, rabbit pies, and codfish were frequent household menu items. We could have been worse off. By the time I was eight years old, one-sixth of the country faced starvation on a weekly basis. We purchased potatoes by the bushel at the farmer's market. Fair shares of beef heart and beef tongue were consumed. We did not eat high off the hog, but we ate. All the Homans were blessed with good health and a roof over our heads. The kids in our family had so much fun growing up that we never truly realized we were poor. I accredit this to good parenting.

The Borough of Sayreville, in which my home of Parlin was located, was emblematic of industrial communities during those interwar years. We had one town doctor, who I think removed every set of tonsils in the vicinity. The place was steeped in the folklore of the American Revolution and was a major production hub for DuPont gunpowder. On more than one occasion, the town was rocked by accidental explosions emanating from nearby ordnance depots and plants. Dangerous jobs there paid well but obliged many employees to disregard inherent risks. Overlooking the Raritan River, the borough of some 8,000 residents included many first- and second-generation citizens who predominantly lived a non-union, blue-collar existence. Most of them trudged to the DuPont or Hercules plants for a living. Both facilities boasted their own housing developments and athletic facilities, creating a quintessential company town. Until I joined the Army Air Forces, there were few places in the world I knew so intimately.

In these environs, pals and I enjoyed an endless playground in the abandoned clay pits on the town outskirts, wonderfully devoid of adult supervision. Some of the finest clay in the Mid-Atlantic was once mined from these locations. There, an inquisitive youngster might have been lucky enough to discover ancient fossils preserved in the earth. Prior to any environmental or safety considerations, the clay mines were left accessible to anyone with a mind for curiosity or adventure. Neglected craters evolved into man-made ponds seemingly ideal for swimming and exploration. The terrain was swampy, prompting us to christen New Jersey the "Mosquito State."

Among my favorite swimming holes was a site adjacent to the Hercules plant. Resting in the depths of Duck's Nest was a wondrous relic from the early days of the motion picture industry. Many people are unaware that New Jersey was a moviemaking mecca prior to Hollywood's ascendence. In 1914, Sayreville was in this spotlight when used as the setting for a silent film entitled *Juggernaut*. For one grand sequence, a railroad trestle was constructed across Duck's Nest. It was blown up when a train filled with a few dozen mannequins rolled halfway across the span. Dummies onboard were mistaken as corpses floating in the water for weeks afterward. The pond was both large and deep. For those of us strong enough, the rusty locomotive greeted us at the bottom of our descents. The engine was salvaged in 1938 when I was in high school. I heard the scrap was shipped to Japan.[2]

My childhood quests fostered a fascination with the Boy Scouts, of which I was an avid member for several years. When the moment arrived to register, however, I didn't even have the requisite nickel for the fee. I was urged to scrounge for the necessary amount. Likewise, I had no funds for the uniform shirt and was forced to locate a passable knockoff. When I finally joined the organization, my love of the outdoors blossomed. I was awarded every conceivable merit badge for outdoor challenges, including mapping, hiking, cooking, and signaling. Looking back, I now recognize how foundational those endeavors were to my subsequent military service. Solid navigational skills and good instincts for survival were undoubtedly formed during adolescence.

Alongside Parlin chums, I savored leisurely summer hikes that took me a dozen miles or more. Ice skating and sleigh riding were common winter diversions. By our teenage years, we were all in robust shape and swaggered with self-confidence. At the time of my enlistment in the Air Forces, physical training consisting of running, pull-ups, sit-ups, and push-ups had little bearing on my transformation into a fighting man. I was already in peak condition. All that said, my youthful ego was to become a casualty of the coming conflict. I was not as invincible as I once thought.

Pre-war escapades with friends offered splashes of color during that otherwise drab period. I proudly belonged to a rebellious gang known as "The Roamers." We sported distinct jackets as a means of identification and pride (not unlike the leather jackets later worn in my squadron). My nickname was Sam. Hailing from a relatively small town in which there were few boys our age, the cadre of eight or ten young men was practically inseparable. That camaraderie did not come without occasional consequence, as we naturally became embroiled in juvenile shenanigans. One such amusement was the invention of "knuckle poker." The winner was permitted to hit a knuckle of the loser with a full deck. The game ended when all the knuckles of a player bled.

As a matter of course, a female equivalent of the Roamers soon emerged. Not to be outdone, the group named itself "Phi Dighting" (as in Die Fighting). My future wife was among the sprightly members. (Her spirited personality did not dissipate with age.)

Roamer antics demanded constant vigilance. Before zippers, trousers had four or five fly buttons. The object of one prank was to see how many buttons you could rip off a pal's pants with a single swipe at the crotch. To use baseball terminology, one button was a single and four buttons were a home run. Our mothers resewed trousers often.

We constantly harassed each other to demonstrate bravado. For instance, when one member threw a short punch and the would-be victim flinched, the assailant earned two free shots. Another gag involved discarded nitrocellulose film we salvaged from the DuPont junkyard. The highly flammable trash made ideal stink bombs. We giddily left them on front porches throughout town.

One Roamer was wilder and more aggressive than the rest. A few of us were walking down a backstreet one evening when a police car halted us. A cop emerged to reprimand the gang for not using a sidewalk. Our untamed member responded in a calm voice, "Officer, I don't mean any disrespect, but f--- you." We froze, wide-eyed, expecting harsh retribution. Perhaps mildly amused by this articulate demonstration of the First Amendment, the officer waved us off and sped away.

The hellion who defied the police once smuggled red wine into one of our basketball games. During halftime, the team secretly indulged in the intoxicating spirits. It made for one hell of a fourth quarter as scuffles on the court became brutal. Following the game, the wine provider was as drunk as a skunk. In a useless effort to sober him up, we shoved him into the backseat of a car and drove him around with his head wedged in an open window. Laying him atop the ice of a frozen lake also failed to stir him awake. Hauling him to a late and lively poker game likewise produced no beneficial results. We ended the night by abandoning him on his front porch, leaving him to the mercies of his parents. The gang didn't see him for three days as he recovered. At a high school reunion many years later, I reconnected with this Roamer and learned he became a junior executive at General Electric. He sure cleaned up well.

Roamers didn't always evade punishment for their transgressions. When I was sixteen, five of the gang formed the habit of breaking into the back window of the DuPont commissary to steal candy and cigarettes. One night, a guard caught them red-handed. The culprits knocked him on his can and fled. Even though the community had only three police officers, the mystery took only two hours to solve. Everybody knew everybody in a town so small. The law quickly descended on the juvenile fugitives and the Roamers met stern reprimand. They had to report to the police department every Saturday. We called them the "Commissary Five." Knowing of my association with the crew, my father accordingly interrogated me.

"Did you have anything to do with this?" he asked in a grim tone.

"No!" I avowed. As mentioned, I knew my limits. Thievery and assault were well over the line.

"Good!" my father said with a swipe of his hand. That was the end of the questioning. This brief encounter was the perfect representation of our trust in each other.

Despite the infinite troubles of the age, I did my utmost to enjoy a carefree life. I generally dodged worrisome adult matters. I swam constantly, collected stamps, and enjoyed the likes of *Buck Rogers* and *Dick Tracy* on our console radio. To support my hobbies, I accepted an array of odd jobs. For a spell, I patched used tires for thrifty motorists. Elsewhere, I worked as a furnace stoker at a new apartment building. I even ran errands for a young mother and her newborn. For each run, she awarded me a nickel. For years, I couldn't afford haircuts that cost a quarter. Monetary shortcomings instilled a valuable lesson in me: budget yourself responsibly.

My ultimate displays of pragmatism were best exhibited during summer sojourns to the movie theater in an adjacent town. Tickets were twenty-five cents. We could purchase three whole candy bars with a dime. Roundtrip bus rides were also ten cents. However, the travel fare cost only five cents if one walked half the distance. We typically chose this cheaper option. In the 1930s, theaters were among the few air-conditioned venues available to the public. The tactic was a wise business ploy to attract ticket buyers anxious to escape the heat. Once in the theater, we gravitated toward Westerns and *Tarzan* features.

These films had a major impact on our senses of adventure and imagination, inspiring us to carve toy rifles and construct rudimentary tree huts in the woods. Double barrel rubber band guns were hastily manufactured with scrap wood, strips of tire innertubes, and clothespins. Such was the weapon of choice for playing cowboys and Indians. I tried swinging from tree to tree in Tarzan style with mixed success. I once fell and could not breathe for a disturbingly long time. I kept this act of stupidity to myself. In any regard, many of these movies promoted the same principles professed by my mother: responsibility and self-reliance. Be the hero and not the villain. Stand up for the little guy.

Although our favorite motion pictures were typically preceded by newsreels showcasing current events, I sadly paid little attention to world happenings. Hardly could I have imagined the global storm soon to consume us all. By contrast, my mother was quite informed of the latest news. Perhaps her family connections in Europe and her husband's experiences in the Great War nurtured this awareness and civic literacy. She worried for the future as I remained blissfully unaware of terrors unfolding overseas.

I was soon to receive quite the education on the matter.

One particularly exhilarating means of entertainment was my odyssey to the 1939 New York World's Fair. I saw numerous Disney displays, corporate exhibitions, Jimmy Lynch and his Death Dodgers, Sonja Henie ice skating, and swimmer Eleanor Holm. The experience was rather magical, but not without a degree of collateral damage. I tried replicating Lynch's madcap stunt driving in the clay banks and royally screwed up my father's Willys car. I sped off a ramp and the vehicle's front smashed into the ground. Ker-plunk! Both front wheels bent inward. I peeked under the car and was terrified to discover the tie rod practically touching the dirt. A friend and I retrieved the jack out of the trunk, dug a hole under the car, and delicately lifted the vehicle to correct the rod. Our efforts were futile. Those wheels were never properly aligned again.

Attending the Ice Capades at the World's Fair also provided zany ideas as to what audacious amateurs might achieve on skates. We attempted to simulate many moves until we earned grotesque hip bruises the size of grapefruits. We Roamers thereafter concluded there was a major difference between figure skates and hockey skates.

As I matured, I developed an eagerness for travel. During junior high school, several friends and I became Explorer Scouts. A new scoutmaster planned a weeklong hike on the Appalachian Trail. The entire 2,200-mile path was finished in 1937. Its completion spurred a longing for discovery in young men like me. We commenced building custom wooden frame backpacks and trained by conducting fourteen-mile hikes. Three of us even headed to an Abercrombie and Fitch store in New York to purchase provisions such as dehydrated food. I was appointed the first-aid man and obtained medical supplies, including a snake bite kit. Mother Nature would not catch us off guard.

The day finally arrived when we were transported to High Point, New Jersey, to begin our momentous hike. Youthful boldness misled us into ignoring trail markers the first two days. More affluent travelers in our merry little band sported new hiking boots. Meanwhile, I developed excruciating foot blisters the size of half dollars. At the conclusion of day three, we rested at a small but inviting lake. We decided to strip down and take a refreshing dip in the placid waters. Shortly thereafter, the local sheriff and deputy paid an inhospitable visit. They surmised from our wet hair that we had illegally swum in a community reservoir. The subsequent fine drained our treasury, thereby squashing dreams of hiking the Appalachian Trail.

Such disappointment was trivial in contrast to the greater setbacks of the era. In 1937–38, another economic recession gripped the nation. My family looked to the president to rally our countrymen. I distinctly recall listening to several of Franklin Roosevelt's iconic "Fireside Chats" on the radio. FDR possessed the unique ability to simultaneously convey information and inspiration over the airwaves. The man was an absolute hero to us. His unwavering optimism and swift government intervention buoyed our sagging spirits time and again. Our new school, a product of the president's Works Progress Administration, was a tangible reminder of Roosevelt's commitment to a modernized and enlightened America.

When war erupted in Europe in 1939, other local facilities became even more significant. The production of nitrocellulose (a key ingredient in explosives and artillery shells) dramatically ramped up at the Hercules plant. My father was thirty-nine at the time and had never completed his naturalization papers. Back in England, eligible men up to age forty were being conscripted. Dad was therefore qualified for the draft in his native country 3,000 miles away. When pondering the possibility of forced enlistment, he promptly pursued the final steps of attaining American citizenship. Ironically, he was obliged to register for the United States draft in March 1942. Luckily for him, the War Department was rarely desperate enough to conscript middle-aged foremen.

My mind still drifted elsewhere as I anticipated the next passage toward manhood: In 1940, I prepared for my driver's license examination. When Dad returned from work, he often took me out for a driving lesson. The old man cruised us to the local tavern on a gravel backroad, exited, and instructed me to retrieve him at a designated time. Now that's multitasking. While in a pub, Dad always watched bar patrons to see which ones might engage in a fight. When brawls broke out, he quietly relocated to a corner and enjoyed the show.

The family automobile was a heavy 1936 Pontiac with a straight-eight-cylinder engine and a long stick shift. When I at last obtained my license, father was very liberal in allowing me to make use of the car. I secretly pushed the vehicle to its limits. If I was on an open road, my heavy foot often bested me. I found that the Pontiac could exceed ninety miles per hour.

Police eventually became aware of my leadfooted tendencies. On a Sunday afternoon, a few buddies and I were joyriding when a Sayreville cop pulled me over with the accusation of speeding. It just so happened this was one of the rare occasions I was not. The officer ordered me to follow him to borough hall, where he planned to run me in once and for all. Knowing the cop's reputation as a boozer and smelling liquor on his breath, I plotted a daring escape. At the first intersection, he turned left toward Sayreville, and I turned right in the direction of the neighboring town. I never heard another word on the matter. I presume the officer was too woozy to recall my sly getaway.

Perhaps the best part of my high school years was the prospect of romance. I was fortunate to spend time with an attractive young lady named Irene Piech. The ambitious daughter of a nitrating operator at the plant, she sported thin spectacles and was graced with a thick crown of brown hair. Both smart and spunky, Irene was something special. Every Saturday night, we visited the Hercules Club together so we could listen to *Your Hit Parade*, a popular radio music program. I called her "Peaches."

When we met, she was a sophomore, and I was a junior. We clicked. Swimming and playing tennis together became routine. Soon enough, I took her to proms and various formal socials. Irene was a true scholar. She frequently traveled to the

Wearing my one good suit for a high school portrait. *John Homan collection.* (3)

Rutgers University Library to conduct research for high school reports. Academic excellence earned her a scholarship to the New Jersey College for Women—today known as Douglass College. She was a freshman there when I eventually left her for war. Thoughts of her sustained me through many dark days ahead. I penned numerous, heartfelt letters. But I never asked her to wait for me, as I didn't know when—or if—I would ever return. Even so, there was a hopeful, quiet assumption that we would reunite when hostilities ceased.

As I embraced youthful love and rebellion, my father remained hard at work while America segued into war production. His profession was not without perils. At a sister Hercules powder factory an hour's drive north of Parlin, disaster unexpectedly struck on September 12, 1940. Some two dozen buildings at the Kenvil plant were obliterated when nearly 300,000 pounds of gunpowder exploded with devasting fury. Fifty-one workers perished and another 200 sustained injuries. The reverberation was felt nearly 100 miles away.[3]

Even today, some allege that pro-Nazi Americans or German agents were responsible for the catastrophe. In response, one congressman called for the shutdown of New Jersey's Nazi party camps and declared the plant explosion "didn't happen through any miracle." After all, Hercules provided critical materials to Allied nations via Roosevelt's Lend-Lease program. Rumors of sabotage made the once-distant conflict seem all the closer. Americans remained torn on the issue of intervention. I recall one keynote speaker at a local commencement ceremony delivering a fiery speech professing isolationism.[4]

Then the fateful year of 1941 arrived. Most of us were oblivious to the fact that all our lives were about to change. That spring, I was a senior at South River High School. The almost whimsical contents of my yearbook now seem far removed from the reality of that gloomy hour. Paging through the publication nonetheless fosters nostalgia for my days on the tennis team, track team, and in the Etiquette Club. The lighthearted description of my personality, composed by yearbook staff, still brings a smile to my face:

> As a freshman, John proved himself to be one of those few more accomplished boys who could actually "trip the light fantastic." That in itself is an accomplishment. As for Mr. Hankinson's verbal debates, no one enjoys them better than John. Anyway, he always seems to find a shrewd answer to anything put before him.[5]

Despite the high opinions of classmates, I did not think myself capable of many profound thoughts. By contrast, family today might claim my shrewdness has not diminished over the decades. I've never been one to back down from an engaging conversation or hot debate. However, intellect did not earn me any immediate rewards in 1941. Following graduation, I found myself working in the miserable conditions of a genuine sweatshop at Metalfield. At a ramshackle hole-in-the-wall factory, cosmetic powder cases and lipstick tubes were manufactured in large quantities. The mostly female staff toiled endlessly, pushing old-fashioned foot pedals to churn out products.

For my own labors, I earned a pitiful thirty-five cents per hour (or $7.25 in 2023 dollars). Short of unemployment, my wages could hardly have been lower. I was too young for a position at the Hercules plant, and few other worthwhile jobs in the area were to be had. I was stuck. On my feet all day, I carried boxes of heavy brass from the foot press department to the shipping dock. During many shifts, I wasn't even spared a moment to visit the john. Worst of all was the monotony.

Not even the tragedy of Pearl Harbor could directly alter my predicament. On the chilly afternoon of December 7, 1941, the Roamers were lounging in the local ice cream parlor. All were in a state of unrecognizable shock when news of the Japanese attack on Hawaii emanated from the shop's radio speakers. I was seventeen years of age. All the other Roamers were eighteen and eligible for military service. They all signed up within days. I was the odd man out and felt left behind.

There was temptation to follow in my father's footsteps and lie about my age to enter the ranks. Surely, I was not alone in these thoughts. Bob Angle, later an ordnance man in my bomb group, claimed to be the youngest man in our outfit. "Fifteen and a half when I first joined the Eighth Air Force," he later confessed. "Fourteen when I first joined up in August 1941. Lied about my age and never have been able to shake the extra four years to this date." Though Angle's motivations were purely patriotic, I could not bring myself to be dishonest to recruitment officers.[6]

Harsh memories of the previous global conflict lingered in the minds of my parents. Mom was adamant in her refusals to permit my enlistment when I came of age. She couldn't bear the thought of her sons in uniform. But I was determined to serve my country. I quietly devised a plan and bided my time.

The war we avoided for so long was suddenly inescapable. Sensations of unity and insecurity swept the country in the wake of Pearl Harbor. Whether an individual was seven years old or seventy years old, all were expected to contribute to the burgeoning military effort. All the while, wartime mysteries and threats lingered on the domestic front. German U-boats sunk several cargo ships and tankers off the New Jersey coast. Worries over spies and saboteurs intensified.

In January 1942, I finally turned eighteen and landed a position at Hercules. Around this same time, I recall well-dressed "G-men" arriving at the plant to interrogate and remove German nationals employed on site. Some of these workers were never seen or heard from again. To what extent any of them were guilty or innocent of collusion, I may never know. Now that the Third Reich had declared war on our nation, little was left to chance on issues of industrial security. None of us were terribly surprised. After all, the German American Bund did have a presence in the area. The previous June, the state legislature had outlawed the Bund's charter. Several of the Hitler sympathizers were indicted on "racial hatred" charges. Most New Jersians were no longer neutral or indifferent on the matter of Nazism in their midst.[7]

Prior to the war, I sometimes conversed with an "old rummy," the town drunk. Despite his shortcomings, the aged drinker was surprisingly astute on world affairs. Before President Roosevelt placed economic embargoes on Japan, the imperial exploits of that island nation were partially powered by oil and scrap iron from the United States. On this trade issue, "Rummy" offered a dark prognostication: "One of these days, you're gonna get hit right in the ass with your old bedstead," he warned.

International affairs were well beyond my comprehension. All I knew is that I desired to be in uniform. My aim was to become a pilot in the Army Air Forces (AAF). I would like to think there was some profound or inspirational logic involved in my decision, but at seventeen, what the hell did I know? While some contemporaries may have been allured by aviator romance promoted in movies such as *Flight Command, A*

Yank in the RAF, or *Flying Tigers,* my rationale was quite practical.

I was a fit but skinny kid, weighing approximately 140 pounds. I was prepared to accept any physical challenge placed before me. But I had no desire to be like my father—stuck in a boiler room below deck and not seeing anything during the whole war. Therefore, I ruled out the Navy. Nor did I wish to slog out the conflict in mud with the infantry. My penchant for outdoor adventure did not equate to a love of perpetual filth. Although I had never been near an airplane, I knew the Air Forces required a higher degree of specialized skill. Aerial warfare was barely older than me. The AAF was the youngest of the branches and bound to be on the cutting edge of technological advancement. I wanted to familiarize myself with the future and avoid the many privations of frontline doughboys.

My hopes were dashed when I discovered that entry into a pilot training program required two years of college or the equivalent. Having just graduated from high school the previous June, and knowing my mathematical abilities were lacking, I returned to school. An arduous lineup of geometry courses awaited me. I enrolled in enough classes to attain the technical requirements for the AAF. I altered my schedule at Hercules. Balancing heavy shifts of work and study required an incredible level of discipline I was unaccustomed to.

Knowing well my mother would not permit me to enlist, I conspired to be voluntarily conscripted. The head of the local draft board was a father of one of the Roamers and worked at Hercules. I maintained contact with him as I developed a strategy to enlist and keep the fact a secret from my family.

"How are you fixed for volunteers?" I asked the draft officer one day.

"Oh, we are three months ahead." In other words, he had three months of volunteers already in queue and had met his quotas. I found myself in another round of the waiting game.

I figured, "Okay, I have three more months to work and go to school then." The more courses I took, the better the chance I had of obtaining my desired status in the Air Forces. This process of back and forth continued several months. In the interim, America's war dramatically accelerated. The Philippines fell to the Japanese, the Battle of Midway turned the tide in the Pacific, Operation Torch paved the way toward victory over Germans in North Africa, and the Eighth Air Force commenced widespread bombings of Western Europe. With all this news splashed on the front pages, my itch to enter the fight only worsened. When I finally attained an acceptable level of education, I approached the draft chairman again in early 1943.

"I want you to draft me," I confessed. "My mother doesn't want me to enlist, and the draft is my only way in." He said he would accommodate my request as soon as slots became available. I was quietly elated.

In preparation for my eventual entry into service, I visited a local physician's office for a blood test. The doctor was ancient. I recall him paying visits to my class when I was in grammar school. He had one eye, having lost his other when he walked into a barn peg while on a nighttime house call. He used no stethoscope and simply placed his quivering head up against my chest. One week after he drew a blood sample, I received notification from his office that the doctor had not obtained a sample large enough for examination. I begrudgingly returned and endured repetitive stabs in both arms as the partially blind physician probed for a sizable vein. I departed with sore black-and-blue marks on my limbs. The doctor's many inefficiencies further delayed my quest.

I achieved my long-desired objective of enlisting in the United States Army on January 19, 1943. I remained well ahead of the slow conscription process. Many don't realize how heavily the government relied on forced enlistment during the war. In fact, 60 percent of the sixteen million Americans who served in the conflict were drafted. I take a degree of pride in being among the minority who volunteered of their own free will. Even so, I naively attempted to conceal that fact from my mother. I asked the draft board to falsely inform her I had been called up. For a time, I thought I succeeded in my bureaucratic deception.

My designs disintegrated when Mom read of my intent to enlist in the weekly periodical entitled the *South Amboy Citizen*. The editors did me no favors when they announced, "Five men were withdrawn from the list of those to be sent to Newark by the local Draft Board Tuesday for examination. John F. Homan, of 16 Henry Street, Parlin, who appeared before the Board requesting that he be admitted to the Army at once, was added to the list."[8]

The cat was out of the bag. Suffice it to say, mother was not pleased. Father had little to say on the matter. He knew I was not going to evade the war. In any case, I was in the Army now.

CHAPTER 2

High into the Sun

I trudged alone in the snow, soaked and frustrated. This was not the soldier's life I had envisioned for myself.

Following induction, I reported to Fort Dix, New Jersey, and immediately applied for the Air Force Pilot Cadets. Dix was undergoing massive expansion as I arrived. The week of my enlistment, newspapers reported the government had purchased over 800 surrounding properties to enlarge the camp, now composed of clapboard barracks and tarpaper shacks. Shortly after I entered, I received notice to report to McGuire Air Force Base, which is adjacent to Fort Dix. I walked by myself during the five-mile roundtrip between the sites for a series of in-depth physicals.[1]

After I returned to McGuire, I was ordered back to Dix the following day for an additional round of written tests. The day was a cold and miserable one, full of sleet and freezing rain. By the time I arrived at barracks, I felt like a popsicle. My heavy wool uniform was drenched by the wintry mix.

An amused sergeant approached. When he saw me walk in from the storm dripping wet, he inquired, "Where have *you* been?"

"I've been walking back and forth between here and McGuire!"

"Well, hell, Homan. You could have asked for a ride!" My shoulders slumped.

The incident instilled in me an important lesson about the Army: Never hesitate to speak up. When in doubt, ask questions. Think smarter rather than work harder. This new approach to military life immediately served me well. Within two weeks, I was promoted to barracks chief. Under my supervision were a bunch of street toughs from Brooklyn, previously full of hot air and overinflated egos. Army barbers had shaved off their beautiful hairdos and the boys became docile. Removed from their natural habitat, the ruffians were now meek and deferred to me as "Sir," even though I was not yet an officer. This was a satisfying power dynamic.

Fort Dix was little more than an indoctrination center. When I first arrived, my personal belongings were dumped into a box labeled with my address. That's the last I saw of civvies

A gift for Irene: A photo of me—cold but smiling at Fort Dix. *John Homan collection.* (4)

for some time. I was then marched in procession with a herd of bare-ass men for awkward health inspections. A quartermaster who accurately guessed my dimensions just threw a pile of uniforms at me. Worst of all were the Army dentists, a rough bunch. One declared, "We are having a contest to see who can fill the most teeth in one day!" This was quite the welcome.

The repetitiveness, standards, and hierarchies of Army life were endlessly drilled into our heads. Strictness was draconian. One man was discharged for wetting his bed.

For me, physical training in the dreary ugliness of the season was an inconvenient bore. Sergeants and officers yelling at us for no apparent reason was a point of constant aggravation. In my view, quiet dependability is the most efficient style of leadership.

Equally vexing was the lack of communication. Despite all the testing and red tape, I had yet to receive notification regarding my application to the Pilot Cadets. I grew increasingly leery as winter progressed. Had my efforts been in vain? Were my dreams of becoming a flyboy squashed? The issue seemed hopeless. My despair heightened when we were summoned to a chilly nighttime formation.

Our outfit was instructed to unpack its gear for inspection in the darkness. Wool shirts, caps, socks, mess kits, tools, and haversacks were soon spread atop our heavy overcoats on the frozen ground. A sergeant conducted a prompt inspection, we repacked our gear, and then proceeded to a nearby train depot. I felt rather forlorn while I was herded into the passenger car and took a seat. Edgar Latham, who grew up two blocks from my home and enlisted the same day as me, was at my side. The locomotive whistle screeched as the final troops boarded.

But then something incredible happened. A lone clerk entered our car and shouted down the crowded aisle, "John Homan!"

Surprised, I quickly gazed up.

"Your transfer has come through!" the man yelled. "Grab your kit and follow me!"

I was astounded. This well-timed notification of my acceptance to the Air Forces had arrived not a moment too soon. The hypotheticals of life are too numerous to count, but this one ranks among the most intriguing of my story. What would have happened had I not been yanked off that train at the last minute? What if the messenger had failed to reach the car in a timely manner? Would my orders have ever caught up with me? When I encountered Latham again after the war, he told me the train took him to artillery school at Camp Edwards, Massachusetts. In an alternative outcome, I might have become an artillerist shipped overseas.

In a matter of days, I was stationed at Mitchell Field on Long Island. The installation started training pilots in a new stratospheric altitude chamber, a sealed space in which airmen could grow accustomed to variations of air pressure while wearing oxygen masks. I was not assigned to such procedures, however. Mitchell Field was nothing but a holding cell until I could transfer to flight school in Nashville, Tennessee. In the intervening weeks, I was designated to casual duties such as Kitchen Patrol and guard posts. My comrades and I were quartered in an uninsulated hut warmed with a single cast iron stove. Water froze ten feet from the fire.

One frosty night, I was assigned the illustrious duty of guarding the base coal pile. I carried a strange rifle, probably a leftover from World War I. No ammunition. I paced back and forth in the biting temperatures and wind. I became numb. The result was ten days in the infirmary with pneumonia. This was an inauspicious beginning to my tenure in the Air Forces. Hospital life was much like barracks life. Everything was very regimented. If you were told to drink a certain amount of water then, by God, you were going to drink that amount of water.

After I was released for light duty and heading back to barracks, a sergeant forming a detail spotted me and hollered, "Fall in!" I tried explaining I was still weak, but to no avail.

My justifications were greeted with louder and angrier demands. Still frail and lightheaded, I spent the day shoveling remnants of the previous day's blizzard. This was not what the doctor ordered.

Among the sparse benefits of being stationed at Mitchell Field was the fact I was only two train rides from home. Bunkmates sometimes hailed from distant places and could not find temporary solace with family as I could. Securing leave nonetheless posed difficulties. I visited the lieutenant's office one afternoon to inquire about a brief trip to Parlin. The man was a fat slob and a pathetic excuse for an officer. He was incapable of showing respect for his men because he lacked respect for himself.

I entered, popped a salute, and stated, "Sir, I respectfully request a weekend pass."

He failed to return my salute, refused to look up, and kept his feet propped on the desk. "No," was his curt reply. With a scowl, I offered another unreturned salute and departed. I hoped to later encounter that "gentleman" after I received my commission. Luckily for him, I never did.

Soon I learned there were other ways to procure a pass. A buddy informed me the Military Police at the gates were lenient. All one had to do was wave a piece of paper at the base checkpoint. MPs didn't bother inspecting the slips. This simple scheme worked beautifully. Visits to Irene and family over the following weekends offered a great boost in morale. (I suspect the statute of limitations for my infractions is past.)

In late spring 1943, I finally escaped the doldrums of Long Island and set out for Nashville. The railroad journey from New York to Tennessee took three days. This was the farthest I had ever been from home. The trip seemed interminable. Anytime we encountered a freight train, switchmen moved our cars off the main line. We would-be aviators were not high priority on the rails.

Our Nashville classification center was nestled in a steep valley, cloaked by a constant pall of black smoke from various base facilities. The polluted air and heat were suffocating. There was no time to experience Nashville's flamboyant music scene. I was put through two hectic weeks of rigid, rigorous tests covering an endless spectrum of technical topics. They were the most complex exams I've ever taken. Perfect eyesight was a requirement for candidates. Depth perception was measured. Booklets filled with shapes of every conceivable shade were distributed to detect colorblindness. Those who were colorblind were immediately rotated to non-flight duties.

Some gadgets used for testing resembled arcade games. Certain contraptions evaluated concentration, speed, dexterity, and vision. One device, reminiscent of a lathe, required the left hand to complete one task while the right did another. Elsewhere, a machine had the appearance of a record player. At the edge of the turntable was a copper insert the size of a penny. The object was to hold a hinged stylus on the copper as the unit rotated. A different test consisted of a numbered board with corresponding switches. As a number lit up, I had to quickly turn it off by using the proper switch. Simultaneously, a GI behind me tested my concentration abilities by firing a starter pistol and reciting numbers I was to memorize. The process toyed with the mind.

Exam results determined a student's next assignment: pilot training, navigator courses, bombardier instruction, gunnery school, or none of the above. I scored well on the aptitude tests, but an unexpected health concern arose. While stationed in Nashville, I learned I had a rapid heartbeat. In a worst-case scenario, such a condition could have rendered me 4F and physically ineligible for flying or military service entirely. The thought of shipping home under those circumstances dampened my spirits. To obtain a clean bill of health, I had to visit the camp medical office three days in a row for extensive checkups. (In contrast to the examination conducted by my hometown physician, an actual stethoscope was implemented.) Fortunately, the results alleviated the doctor's initial worries. Thankful to avoid an early return ticket to New Jersey, I proceeded to the next round.

Enhanced training awaited me at preflight school at Maxwell Field outside Montgomery, Alabama. Selected by Orville Wright as the country's first civilian pilot training station in 1910, the installation already had a fabled place in aviation history. There, according to one reporter in April 1943, "Uncle Sam has set up a material and human apparatus designed to give our boys their first academic and physical approaches to the strenuous work of making an airplane a

death-dealing instrument of warfare." All cadets (our designa-
tion until graduation) wanted to be pilots. If a cadet lacked a
pilot's skill or intuition, he often became a navigator or bombardier. That way, the government didn't completely waste its
investment in that individual. Still, not all were destined to
depart the station with wings on their chests.[2]

Our cadre arrived at Maxwell Field by train around 1 a.m.
on a humid spring night. Gung-ho upperclassmen were ready
to pounce on our fresh batch of greenhorns. As we disembarked, senior cadets immediately locked us in a brace, an
extreme and unforgiving form of attention. Verbal abuses
flowed like water. We then double-timed to barracks while
wearing full packs. Little sleep was had that first night. At 5:30
a.m., the unpleasant shock of reveille sounded over the loud-
speakers. Cadet training had begun.

As underclassmen, we were subjected to academic work
and training six days a week for the next nine weeks. Of this
regimen, one officer boasted, "Our men can snap into any
occasion that requires physical stamina and endurance." He
wasn't lying.[3]

On arrival, each cadet was administered a comprehensive
physical fitness test. The PT (Physical Training) instructor's
goal was to enhance overall fitness, even if a cadet like myself
was already in stellar condition. There was always room for
improvement. Following a strenuous session of calisthenics,
we ran the "Burma Road," a torturous route with obstacles,
and then back to barracks. The red dirt road (nicknamed for

the rugged, 700-mile military supply route that connected Burma with southwest China) was a hilly track consisting of large pipes, ropes, and other hurdles to overcome. I sometimes doubled over with excruciating side stitches, a transient abdominal pain that often affects runners. But I couldn't stop. Dropping out for any reason meant automatic placement on sick call. This would have been bad news. Doctor visits had delayed my military advancement far too often, so I soldiered on and coped with the aches.

All were subjected daily to West Point–style military discipline. The honor system and chain of command dictated our every move. Hazing from upperclassmen was severe. Men were made to stand at attention in the Alabama heat for excessive periods. Exhausted GIs were thrown into the showers and taunted. Ridicule was commonplace. In many ways, the experience was dehumanizing. The process was designed to rid the system of weaklings. It worked.

If a cadet was caught breaching the honor code, he was submitted to a humiliating "Drumming Out" ceremony. For this embarrassing formality, the ranks were awoken at midnight and placed in parade ground formation. The accused was then hauled in front of his peers. His transgressions were read for all to hear. After a drumroll and a declaration of charges, the cadet was evicted and dispatched to the "Russian Front." Now I knew the true meaning of being "drummed out of the Corps."

When I rose to upperclassman, I was entitled to inflict cruelties on new cadets. I refrained from the mean-spirited antics. I nonetheless recognized the bullying as an effective means of intimidation. Following orders is often driven by fear as much as respect.

My original Aviation Cadet patch. *John Homan collection.* (5)

Anytime we were not in barracks, we were required to be at attention. Even in the chow hall, we had to eat a "square meal." This meant using our utensils at right angles, sitting in erect postures. We memorized the proper placement of dishes and silverware because we could only look straight ahead as we ate. Lowerclassmen were not granted leave from base, but upperclassmen were. The latter often smuggled in "nips" from town. These one-shot whiskey bottles were easily tucked into socks and covertly made available during meals.

I flew no planes at Maxwell Field. Learning was limited to ground school and physical training. In the classroom, education was all encompassing. I heavily studied mathematics, physics, the fundamentals of aerodynamics, meteorology, navigation, aircraft recognition, code signaling, map and chart reading, and the dangerous nature of high explosives. These subjects were the basic building blocks of creating an airman.

In early July 1943, I entered primary-flight training at Souther Field near rural Americus, Georgia. The installation, today one of the oldest continuously operating airports in the country, was once a vast peach orchard. There was a large grass field, a small cluster of buildings, only a handful of officers, and no control tower. Despite modest facilities, Souther had at least one claim to fame. In 1923, aviator Charles Lindbergh purchased his first plane there for $500 and spent the next several weeks on site learning to fly. In fact, Lindbergh's engineer was still on the staff twenty years later, teaching aircraft mechanics. Following my eventual retirement, I revisited Souther Field and was amazed to discover the old-timer still roaming the hangars, serving in an informal advisory capacity while in his nineties.

I remember him because he always said, "You pronounce it 'Car-bure-a-ter,' not 'Carburetor.' It's 'Car-bure-a-ter.'"

When I was young, Lindbergh was a man I looked up to—literally! During my childhood, whenever a plane flew over town, friends and I gazed skyward yelling, "Hey Lindy!" After Lindbergh's baby was kidnapped and murdered in 1932, my father drove to the nearby scene of the crime to satisfy his curiosity regarding the publicized tragedy. Amid isolationist fervor prior to the war, Lindbergh accurately attested to the strength of the Luftwaffe. I eventually witnessed that aerial might firsthand. Only later did I discover the depth of Lindbergh's role in the antisemitic America First Committee.

A Yankee in the shadow of Jefferson Davis in Montgomery. This was Irene's favorite photo of her flyboy. After the war, she showed it to me to exhibit how much I had aged. Her ring is on my pinky finger. *John Homan collection.* (6)

Speaking of intolerance, my journeys through the Jim Crow South offered a startling glimpse of racial segregation. Prior to enlistment, I had never crossed the Mason-Dixon Line, never ventured west of Philadelphia, nor above New

York's Bear Mountain State Park—where I had once visited
during a class field trip. When stationed near Montgomery,
Alabama, then a major troops mobilization center, I toured
sites around the legislature building. (Some internal distress
that day limited my sightseeing range to the capitol and its
public restrooms.) There, I gazed up at the statue of Jefferson
Davis on the statehouse lawn, where he became the first and
only president of the Confederacy. I gained the impression
white southerners never accepted the defeat of their Civil War
ancestors.

In Americus, the sad legacies of that fratricidal war were
quite evident. The main streets were dotted with large antebel-
lum homes. I distinctly remember the curfew set in place for
African Americans. They were not permitted in the streets
after nightfall. All the while, I was invited to fancy cotillions
with young ladies channeling their inner Scarlett O'Hara.
Little wonder the community became a focal point of the civil
rights movement in the 1950s.

Later, outside Bainbridge, Georgia, I saw the conditions of
impoverished sharecroppers who resided in a state of semi-
slavery. Even at age nineteen, I found the circumstances
abysmal.

That August, 500 German prisoners of war arrived at
Souther Field to harvest peanuts and cotton on surrounding
plantations. There are tales that such inmates were treated
better in southern communities than the African American
populace.[4]

No Black flyers were permitted to be my wingmen at home or overseas, despite the fact that they were more than able and willing. But as a rookie cadet, I had little time or inclination to ruminate on these injustices. Mastering flight remained my greatest priority. Souther Field was essentially a large green pasture with a windsock at one end to indicate landing direction. A small pictorial yearbook I own explains why the unassuming Georgia crossroads was an ideal location for a base: "The reasons for this fact are exceptional air conditions and almost perfect drainage. There is no record of a windstorm of any consequence in the past one hundred years of Americus's history." The installation served many pilots well, including scores of Royal Air Force cadets temporarily transferred to America for training. I followed in the footsteps of many a brave and daring airman.[5]

Pilots received experience in Link Trainers, also known as Blue Boxes. These were early flight simulators on moveable platforms in which I could sharpen my ability to assess and react to cockpit instruments. An instructor watched at a nearby plotting table as a mechanical pen charted my progress. The teacher established airspeed, direction, and altitude before assigning a mock flight plan. "The first few tries were pretty sloppy," fellow pilot Wilmer Plate recalled, "but it didn't take long for us to conquer the beast and begin to gain confidence in our ability to fly on instruments."[6]

Enthusiasm mounted when I was introduced to my first plane, a silver Boeing PT-17 Stearman. The bi-winged, fabric-covered aircraft featured two open cockpits with inertia starters. A flywheel had to be hand-cranked to supply starting power. The Stearman was the primary trainer for the Air Forces during the war. The plane could practically fly itself. My activities were aided by an excellent teacher named William D. Bradley. Quiet and patient, he was a superb mentor. While in flight, he'd shake the controls if he wanted my attention. Most instructors were civilians who gained experience as crop dusters and barnstormers in the Twenties and Thirties. The privately operated venture at Souther Field was categorized as a Contract Pilot School under an entity known as Graham Aviation.

Taking flight in a Stearman trainer over Americus.
John Homan collection. (7)

Even with solid guidance, I foolishly pressed my luck at the outset of training. The night before my first aerobatic session,

SOUTHER FIELD, AMERICUS, GA.   56ᵗʰ ARMY AIR FORCES FLYING TRAINING DETACHMENT

On the reverse side of this postcard I wrote to Irene, "Left is the barracks. And right is the Academic Area. Very small but a perfect setup." *John Homan collection.* (8)

fellow students smuggled champagne into the dry town. We liberally partook in the beverage simply because we were not allowed. My inaugural takeoff commenced the following morning with a mild hangover that worsened with altitude. After the first aerial stunt, I shook the stick to get the instructor's attention. Looking into the wing mirror, I rapidly pointed at my mouth and then downward, signaling I was about to be sick. The softspoken Bradley landed and never uttered a word on the matter. He was an ideal leader. I admire a person who knows what the hell they're doing and gets it done efficiently without too much fuss. Bradley never grew mad and was always forgiving. If I made a mistake, he kindly corrected the

I stand at left as we cadets prepare for a busy day of flight.
John Homan collection. (9)

error and quietly urged me to have another go. It was refreshing to be under the tutelage of a man who was not at all
judgmental.

My first solo climb into the wild blue took place on July 6,
1943. Exactly one year later, I embarked on my first combat
mission.

At Americus, all cadets were expected to fly solo after ten
hours of instruction. They then advanced to aerobatics. The
clock was ticking. My second day in the cockpit was no more
gallant than the first. As my instructor demonstrated a loop,

I blacked out on the pull-up. When we were back to altitude, he said, "Okay, now you do one." I was too embarrassed to admit I had passed out in a trainer, so I put the plane in a dive, pulled up, and did a loop.

We were scheduled for solo practice sessions after each new lesson. Aerobatics training consisted of spins, stalls, slow rolls, snap rolls, loops, and more. Learning to fly in the military meant doing everything with precision. Students were to climb at a precise rate, at an exact airspeed, and level off at a specific altitude. Aerobatics required total accuracy—or else.

One perk of these rigid demands was a spike in salary. Once I started flying, my private's pay was more than doubled. When I entered the Army, the amount was a paltry $22 per month. The War Department then upped my pay to $50 per month (or $906 in today's dollars). One GI adage declared, "Money may not make you happy, but it does help you to be miserable in comfort." The situation was not terrible since the military provided all my necessities and I had no dependents.

Less appealing was the small band of lieutenants and captains conducting periodic check rides to measure cadet progress. Anyone who failed a single review was immediately scrubbed from the program. The washout rate was approximately 50 percent during the first month. Twenty percent of trainees couldn't take off or land by themselves while 30 percent failed to master the required aerobatics. Soon enough, our evening formations were reduced to half the original number after twenty flying hours. The ongoing dwindling of ranks motivated me to persevere in face of the odds.

My inner drive forced me to conquer my greatest fear: I am terrified of heights. Hanging upside down in an open cockpit, secured only by canvas straps, can be a daunting trial. Even today, I couldn't visit the Grand Canyon and peer over the edge of a cliff. This is a strange confession for a pilot. Oddly enough, high altitudes never bothered me while I was at the controls. I was so intent on the tasks at hand that I erased anxiety from my mind.

Unlike some pilots, I never developed a spiritual connection or sense of wonderment while soaring through the clouds. A training session on a sunny day was pure escapism. In the South's sweltering climate, I suffered from a terrible case of prickly heat. Stinging red blisters triggered by humidity made me one unhappy camper. All the pores on my back were inflamed. The outbreak felt like a million pin pricks in my skin. Wearing sweat-soaked wool or stiff khakis undoubtedly contributed to my misery. Gliding 5,000 feet above the earth in an open-air cockpit greatly alleviated the discomfort. I also welcomed a degree of autonomy once I learned to fly solo. For a few brief moments, nobody could order me to do anything. I was a man unto myself.

While solo-practicing short-field landings at a remote auxiliary post, I was so absorbed by my newfound freedom that I failed to notice a rapidly approaching thunderstorm. The dark clouds were ominous and fast. I promptly landed as best

I could, tied down the plane, and sought shelter under a wing. The sudden downpour made me sopping wet, and I couldn't shut off the engine because I lacked a crank to restart the aircraft.

As soon as the storm passed, I climbed into the saturated cockpit and hustled back to home base for an appointment with an officer. A little on the soggy side, I dashed to the office, delivered a crisp salute, and reported in.

"Cadet Homan reporting, sir!"

"You're late."

Mildly proud of my recent actions, I started explaining.

He cut me short and coldly asked, "What's your excuse?"

Of course, the proper answer was, "No excuse, sir."

He then penalized me. I was ordered to march for ten hours on my own time, across a hot concrete ramp at 120 cadences while shouldering a rifle. That's military discipline—unsympathetic and unforgiving. This incident reinforced another key principle of Army life: Always be on time.

Attentiveness was further ingrained in us at daily retreat, a 5 p.m. flag-lowering ceremony. This required standing in dress uniforms at strict attention in scorching heat. The sandy parade ground soaked up the warmth something awful. On occasion, a dehydrated cadet passed out and pitifully lay where he fell until the ceremony concluded. In addition to prickly heat, I constantly suffered from chigger bites, which left scratchy red blotches on my skin. These ailments made formation an ordeal. When I wasn't enjoying lower temperatures while flying, the only means to relieve the pain was calamine lotion and cold showers. Everyone loathed the pomp and circumstance of retreat, but I now interpret the ritual as a supplemental measure of discipline. We did what we were told to do.

Well, most of the time. We now and then ignored the minimum-required altitude of 5,000 feet while practicing chandelles (steep, tight-turning climbs) around a local water tower. One cadet, while thus engaged, must have pulled his turn too tightly. His plane stalled out and spun through a two-story garage. Miraculously, he walked away from the wreckage with only a sliced knuckle. All we airmen in the vicinity that day were summoned to testify at an inquiry investigating the pilot's conduct. No one knew or saw a thing. This act of willful ignorance was a fine demonstration of the buddy system. The pilot in question graduated in the next class.

In September 1943, I arrived at Bainbridge Army Airfield in southern Georgia, a 2,000-acre tract just a few miles north of the Florida border. The remote base opened the previous summer and left much to be desired. Due to wartime necessity, most structures were hastily built out of temporary materials. Several large hangars with curved roofs extended the span of the flight line. The grimy mess hall was infested with cockroaches. I purchased packaged food at the camp post exchange to avoid the unkempt facility. Eventually, the chow hall conditions were brought to the attention of the Inspector General. The kitchen was soon shut down until it could pass scrutiny. Bainbridge was a poor example of a military installation.

Par for the course, I flew an equally lousy plane there—the BT-13. The aircraft had more horsepower, was all metal, larger, heavier, and much more complicated than the typical trainer. The plane had no hydraulics and lacked retractable landing gear. I had to place a pillow against my back to reach the rudder pedals. This cushioning also eased the consistent vibrating. Pilots thus derisively nicknamed the single-engine craft the "Vultee Vibrator."

Don't think the Vultee's deficiencies were a laughing matter. The first morning of preparation at Bainbridge, while readying for camp inspection, we pilots watched a plane take off, stall, flip over, and crash on the runway. Our formation stood in shocked silence. We were immediately given an about-face order. Several airmen were killed on routine missions at both Souther and Bainbridge that summer. By January 1944, the War Department revealed to the public that one out of every fifty air cadets was killed in training. I learned to cope with tragedy and persist in my duties. There was little else I could do.[7]

My inept instructor was a far cry from the dignified William Bradley. The officer was a shaky, chain-smoking, foul-mouthed son of a bitch angered by his assignment to a "hell hole." He complained about instructing "idiots" and missing his shot at glory as a fighter pilot. His favorite expression when you goofed was, "Grab your left ear with your right hand and grab your right ear with your left hand and pull your head out of your ass!" Mean-spirited management rarely benefits those intended to be strengthened by it. My speculation was that this officer earned a spot on a commander's shitlist and was accordingly exiled to the base as punishment.

The first session at Bainbridge was held at an auxiliary field. There, I learned how to operate the cumbersome Vultee. After a few rounds in the air, the instructor ordered me to drop him off, complete a series of takeoffs and landings, and then return to pick him up. When he eventually climbed back into the cockpit, he yelled over the engine, "Who the hell do you think you are? Barney Oldfield?"

I had no idea who Barney Oldfield was. When I inquired back at base, I was informed he was a celebrity race car driver in the early 1900s known for his high-speed stunts. I therefore deduced from my instructor's snide exclamation that I had taxied too fast. Reflecting on that first excursion at Bainbridge, a sign that hung over the door of the base's ready room comes to mind. The board announced THERE ARE OLD PILOTS AND THERE ARE BOLD PILOTS, BUT THERE ARE NO OLD BOLD PILOTS.

One of the most perilous moments arrived during my first night landing session at the auxiliary field. My lieutenant instructor did a few touch-and-go "shoot" landings. On each approach, I could feel him on the controls. He finally shouted, "Get the hell off the stick!" We circled around a few more times, repeating the same routine until he told me to taxi over to the sideline. He exited and waved, "Go ahead—but don't kill yourself." This was hardly an assuring farewell.

I taxied, took off, went around the pattern, and began my approach. Over the radio, I heard the ground controller inform a pilot ready for takeoff to maintain his position. A fatal mis-understanding occurred. The plane flying to my front was already on the approach. The aircraft on the ground, rather than standing fast, unknowingly veered into the landing area. The taxiing pilot was killed when the incoming aircraft crushed him and his plane. The latter then careened into an adjacent light truck. I frantically pulled up to evade the entan-glement below. All planes in the air were ordered back to main base and I had to leave my teacher behind. The whole experi-ence was shattering.

I was so shaken by the collision I had just witnessed that I'm surprised I found my way home. Nerves then got the best of me when I attempted my first solo night landing. I overshot the runway by a fair margin, forcing a second try that verified the old saying, "Any landing you walk away from is a good one."

Still, my primary instructor once told me that if I was in the vicinity of an accident, I should consider myself partially at fault. That was the mentality of training. Such a sentiment can tear away at a man's soul after he's seen a crash. Again, the only way I could overcome fear and guilt was through concentration. If a pilot can't focus while operating an aircraft, he's a dead duck. We all have an emotional switch, and some-times it must be turned off.

Danger was ever present, both in the air and on the ground. One night about midnight, a Women in the Air Force (WAF) flight scheduler, another cadet, and I awaited planes in the ready room. Suddenly, a bright orange glimmer shuffled past the window. Something was on fire. To our horror, a mechanic was consumed by flames and wildly running about. His screams echoed through the buildings. A couple of us quickly grabbed cockpit cushions, knocked him down, and beat out the blaze. I later learned the repairman was cleaning parts while smoking, with gasoline all around him. This was an important lesson on situational awareness.

Only minutes after we extinguished the fire, we were summoned to our planes for additional nighttime maneuvers. Imagine how difficult it was for us to fly after seeing that poor mechanic suffer painful burns. But if we didn't remain conscientious, we could end up in a fiery mess ourselves.

Regardless of distress, training proceeded at a rapid pace. Advanced education continued with more aerobatics, landings, and takeoffs, but now included increased nighttime and instrument flying. Each phase became more advanced and difficult. By the end of basic training, I had 130 hours of flying time under my belt.

In October, I entered the final phase of schooling, known as advanced flying. The location was the immense Moody Airfield outside Valdosta, Georgia. Moody was a far superior operation that was a welcome change after the dreary setting of Bainbridge. The sprawling complex included a wonderful chow hall overseen by a Women's Army Corps officer whose cooks custom-prepared eggs for breakfast. The grounds were nicely maintained and there was a sense of comparative refinement.

Our aircraft were more efficient as well. The plane was a Beechcraft AT-10 Wichita, a twin-engine, dual-controlled trainer. Constructed of plywood, the AT-10 featured retractable landing gears and advanced navigation equipment. This sleek, gray plane was easy to operate and proved ideal for airmen like myself about to advance to multi-engine bombers. In the Wichita, two pilots flew side by side. As part of Element E in Squadron B, my days and nights were consumed with simulator training, instrument flying, formation flying, and cross-country trips.

Anyone scheduled for a nighttime cross-country flight chose a co-pilot to serve as navigator. I was seemingly proficient at navigation and was therefore chosen often, which meant I flew as co-pilot many evenings. During one journey deep into Florida, I tuned in to an Atlanta radio station. When the pilot asked me for the heading back to base, however, I told him I didn't have a clue. This ended my frequent stints as a night navigator.

An additional element of our education was learning Morse code by using the old key system. Cadets walked around base talking in "dits" and "dahs" for practice. Having previously received a signaling merit badge in the Boy Scouts, this process came easily to me. Despite this background, I never actually used Morse code overseas.

The field at Moody had dual runways, right and left. Tower operators indicated which to use. One cadet was instructed to use a specific runway but was too close to the plane ahead. He thus switched runways on the approach and cut off an instructor. The teacher angrily radioed the tower to hold that cadet in custody. The student received a royal chewing out and walked around base for a week with a sign around his neck advertising I AM BLIND.

I learned to expect the unexpected in this environment. On a routine training flight, for instance, my left engine lost some power and ran rough. I called the tower, was instructed to land, and taxied to a maintenance area. A mechanic emerged with his ladder, reached into part of the engine cowling, removed a handful of dirty, dislodged cylinder pieces, and nonchalantly plopped them in my hands. Luckily, the plane could fly on a single engine.

Another day, when acting as co-pilot, the administrative officer started unevenly applying brakes on landing. He then overcompensated, causing the plane to veer off track.

"Get off the brakes!" I yelled. Instead, he applied both brakes. The plane violently nosed over and ground both propellers into the runway. I knew we were in major trouble. A loud tongue-lashing awaited us in the ready room.

Minor setbacks aside, the finish line for training was within sight by Christmas 1943. That holiday season was my first away from kin. Feeling rather homesick, I noticed a welcome announcement on a base bulletin board. Pilots far removed from family were invited to enjoy Christmas dinners in local households. Seeking a dose of yuletide cheer, I jumped at the opportunity. On December 25, I arrived at

Left: Irene and I in January 1944. Right: My best Clark Gable impression. *Charlie Wade photos from the John Homan collection.* (11 and 12)

a designated home in a picturesque neighborhood, ate a hearty meal, and enjoyed the company of the family's attractive daughter. She even joined me at a holiday social that evening. I was on my best behavior. My civilian flight instructor lived next door to the young woman and was likewise present for some of the festivities. The community was a small one after all.

By New Year's, I had accumulated approximately 200 flying hours. In anticipation of graduation, I was fitted for my beautiful Class A officer's dress jacket. The chocolate brown uniform was wonderful quality, made of the finest material.

Lighter than enlisted men's wool, the clothing could be worn
in winter or summer. Though today a bit weathered and missing an original gold button, the garment hangs in my closet
with pride alongside my beaten up "crusher cap." Someday the
items will be bequeathed to my great-grandson so descendants
might have a tangible link to my service. Graduation itself was
to be a simple affair, but boy, I was thrilled with the new
uniform.

Commencement took place at Moody Airfield on January
7, 1944, just two days following my twentieth birthday. Along
with a certificate, I received an instrument rating card autho-
rizing flights at less than 500-foot ceilings. Silver wings and a
commission as a second lieutenant were likewise conferred.
"Butter bars" now graced the shoulders of my immaculate
uniform. I realized I wouldn't be guarding any more coal piles
and fewer sergeants would be screeching at me. The rank
ensured a level of respect and authority I previously lacked. I
was pleased to look the part of an officer.

My highly coveted aviator wings. *John Homan collection.* (10)

Following graduation, I was granted a ten-day delay en route to Salt Lake City for further assignment. The trip was my first leave in a year, and I was anxious to hit the road. There was no time to waste, so I booked a commercial airline reservation from Jacksonville, Florida, to Newark, New Jersey. As I waited in the ticket queue, a well-dressed man barged to the front of the line and demanded a seat to Washington on a priority basis.

The attendant glanced at me, as if to ask if such an arrangement was acceptable. Standing behind the agitated customer and not wishing to lose my seat, I shook my head.

Getting my drift, the clerk stalled the aspiring passenger by questioning his priority status. They were still going at it hot and heavy as I boarded the plane.

A brief but meaningful reunion with family in Parlin was a welcome reprieve. Eager to model my uniform, I sought out one of Irene's colleagues, Charlie Wade. He was the photographer at the newspaper she wrote for. In addition to a photograph in which Irene and I embraced, I asked for a set of individual portraits. An accompanying photo features the federal eagle emblazoned on my headgear and a tobacco pipe in my hand. I like to think I achieved the debonair Clark Gable style I aspired to. I gifted the solo portraits to my parents and presented the couple's shot to Irene as a token of remembrance. This was the only time I was home during aviation training prior to embarkation overseas.

I made the most of my brief leave, but not without some misadventure. Irene and I hit the town every night. She was a college freshman residing with a "house mother" and adhered to a strict 11 p.m. curfew. Irene usually drank only one alcoholic beverage during each of our nightly excursions. One evening at a club along Route One, she doubled her normal limit and was flying high. Energized by her second drink, she refused to leave as curfew approached. Not wishing to incur the wrath of the house mother, I nudged Irene into my Buick and put the pedal to the metal. Our drive was further delayed when a state trooper pulled us over for speeding at eighty miles per hour and chewed me out. Since I was in uniform, he gave me a stern warning and let me off the hook. Despite all the drama, Irene was home on time.

Before I turned in, I opted to visit a local bar for a nightcap. There I encountered a former classmate named Benny Traska, who was in the Navy. We took turns buying each other drinks. When I offered him a lift to a diner up the road for a midnight snack, he respectfully declined. Instead, a young couple in the bar joined me for a late meal. The three of us had a splendid conversation at the diner until the man arose to visit the restroom. As my guest responded to nature's call, Benny entered the restaurant and noticed the good-looking woman and I seated together. When her partner returned and exhibited affection, a tipsy Benny swung into action.

"What do you think you're doing, making time with my friend's gal?" he barked.

Benny knocked the young man to the floor and all hell broke loose. Our efforts to clarify the situation to the rambunctious sailor were unsuccessful and the cops were called. I then explained the confusion to the officers. The police had no interest in arresting the local enlisted man and they promptly left when Benny calmed down. As I saw twice that lively night, wearing a uniform could be a fine Get Out of Jail Free card when a serviceman was in trouble.

When leave came to an end, I departed from New York City's grand Penn Station by sleeper car to Chicago, and then to Salt Lake City. During the war, Penn Station was a vast sea of humanity. Thousands of rushed voices and footsteps echoed off its high arched ceilings. Servicemen and women scrambled throughout the massive, ornate halls. Mountains of baggage accumulated outside as passengers hailed overburdened taxis. Customers piled into the automobiles by threes and fours. One journalist from 1943 summed up the environment best: "It's the time and place where railroading, hot as a Bessemer furnace, meets holiday crowd psychology in one of wartime's critical transportation tests." Perhaps the most evocative scenes were the many tearful farewells between servicemen and their sweethearts. So many of those couples never reunited.[8]

Union Station in Chicago was no less frantic. My next train was delayed a few hours, so I decided to play tourist. Luckily, I saw an advertisement for an Andrews Sisters performance beginning at the Chicago Theatre in a few minutes. The venue was only a mile away, so I hitched a cab ride and was fortunate to nab a ticket. The Andrews Sisters were a close harmony trio who leapt to fame with hits such as

"Boogie Woogie Bugle Boy" and "Bei Mir Bist Du Schön."
Their lively tunes became optimistic wartime anthems. That
day, they performed alongside Mitch Ayres and his orchestra,
who appeared in several films with the sisters. I took great
enjoyment in the show and made it back to the station just
in time to catch my train. The performance was a fine interlude in my travels.[9]

The transcontinental journey by rail offered me a finer
glimpse of the country I was soon to fight for. I arrived at my
destination eager to commence the next stage of military service. My time in Salt Lake City turned out to be little more
than another transition point, however. I was lumped into a
ten-man crew of strangers and dispatched some 400 miles east
to Casper Army Air Base in Wyoming. Nestled along the
North Platte River, Casper was a true Wild West town run by
cowboys and oilmen. All the decent businesses were located
on side streets while saloons and parlors were readily accessible
on the main drag. The previous May, singing cowboy-turned-
sergeant Gene Autry entertained troops and townspeople.
Residents barbecued moose meat. The place reminded me of
the many Westerns I had watched in theaters during childhood. We arrived at that former frontier outpost during the
most inhospitable time of year. The weather was downright
harsh. Consequently, I went into town only two or three times.

The airfield itself was manned by the 211th Army Air
Force Base Unit, which trained some 16,000 bomber crewmen during the war. From January through March 1944, my

crew quartered in tarpaper barracks heated by potbellied stoves. We wore fur-lined jackets, pants, and boots to keep from freezing. Flight conditions were equally miserable. The temperature drops two degrees for every 1,000 feet of altitude. Some days, the ground temperature hovered near zero. This meant our flying temperature at 20,000 feet was forty degrees below zero. Plane cabins were neither pressurized nor heated.

My future as a combatant hinged on that plane: the Consolidated B-24 "Liberator." The B-24, the largest U.S. bomber at that time, was a giant step in size and complexity. In fact, I thought the plane was too large at first. The prospects of a ten-man crew in a four-engine plane with tricycle wheels were daunting to some. There was so much to learn. Beyond the basic characteristics of flight, there were many mechanical, electrical, radio, and emergency systems to master. The instrument panel in the cockpit was a sight to behold. There was an endless spectrum of switches, indicators, gauges, wheels, and buttons. I committed them all to memory.

Keith Turnham, later to join my bomb group overseas, had a lukewarm reaction to the plane. "The roar of the engines and the size of the plane astounded us all," he remembered of his first encounter with a B-24. "It looked like a flying coffin to me and the more I watched this plane the more I was convinced that it was. We watched in awesome anticipation at each maneuvered act, but they didn't make sense to us."[10]

B-17 pilots similarly ridiculed our B-24s for their cumbersome shape. Certainly, the B-17 is a notable plane of greater visual appeal. The "Fortress" could sustain heavy punishment and remain operable. The B-24 was flimsier yet dependable. The plane was certainly not without considerable flaws, but it could still take one hell of a beating and reach home. That's what mattered most. The Liberator was constantly tested, evolved, and modified throughout the war. Although "an ungainly-looking ship on the ground," contends author Stephen Ambrose, the B-24 "had a grace of its own in the air." While the adequacy of our crew could not be fully evaluated until we applied our educations in combat, I believe the end results proved the effectiveness of training.[11]

Like Morse code workshops, though, not all lessons were implemented. Many hours were spent on aircraft recognition—identifying black silhouettes of Axis planes flashed on a screen for a split second. However, at our first orientation session overseas, we were instructed to ignore everything we learned on that matter. "Just shoot at any strange plane that comes close," was the advice.

Practice missions progressed to bombing and gunnery runs. For these purposes, we made heavy use of desolate ranges in the Texas Panhandle. There, we dropped 100-pound bombs with five-pound charges of black powder. Cameras recorded the results for later analysis. The practice bombing range was marked by light patterns for nighttime use. One crew accidentally bombed an oilfield with similar lights on the wells.

Photographic evidence revealed our plane as the culprit. The mishap could have been much worse. That April, an aircraft dropped two practice bombs on a Gulf pump station in Beaumont, Texas.[12]

The B-24 was an exceedingly well-armed war machine. The Liberator could haul a maximum payload of 8,000 pounds of bombs. Its top range was farther than any other American aircraft—3,000 miles. Additionally, the plane carried two .50 caliber machine guns in the nose, two in a top turret, two in a tail turret, two in a belly turret, and one on each side of the waist. The firepower a single bomber could unleash was tremendous. During one ground firing run, a plane inadvertently obliterated a flock of grazing sheep. We ate mutton for several meals thereafter.

Gunnery practice typically took place via tow target planes or billboard-sized targets mounted on the sides of a valley. We were briefed to link with tow target planes in a certain quadrant at a specified altitude. Those aircraft were usually B-26s or B-25s flown by pilots of the Women in the Air Force. My group never saw one of those planes in the designated time or location. I suspect WAF pilots may have feared friendly fire during these target practices.

Standing orders were for gunners to clear their weapons before entering the landing pattern. In one unfortunate instance, a tail gunner forgot to check his pieces. When the plane parked on the ramp, he accidentally triggered his twin .50s with an unforeseen burst. The errant rounds sprayed into the bomber behind him and set it aflame. Far down the field, a soldier was wounded in the leg by the same volley. The gunner was rightfully court-martialed with severe penalties. There is a big difference between messing up on the job and messing up because someone *didn't* do their job.

As winter slowly thawed into spring, we set off on a one-plane practice mission to mock-bomb an industrial site near St. Louis, Missouri. The roundtrip was over 2,000 miles. A camera recorded our progress. On the return, over the Rocky Mountains in pitch blackness, we were consumed by a heavy rainstorm that wrought severe turbulence. The situation grew dire. We were rattled around like pebbles in a tin can. Visibility was nonexistent. We had quite a scare when we saw the air speed indicator gradually drop. The skipper and I both pushed the sticks forward, pressed the throttle on, and roared through the sky. Still, the indicator headed toward zero. We simultaneously reached for the pitot tube heat switch. In seconds, our airspeed was near redlining. If this rate was exceeded, the result could be fatal structural failure.

Ice was forming on the plane—an ingredient for ultimate disaster. With this gloomy realization, both the pilot and I concluded, "Let's get the hell out of here!" There was no way we could safely proceed through the mountains in those conditions.

I called to our navigator, "Give us the coordinates to the nearest air base." We undertook a quick 180 and eventually set down in Grand Island, Nebraska, until daylight. I am very glad we erred on the side of caution. We may otherwise not have survived the night.

At veteran reunions many years later, our navigator often reminded us that our altitude that stormy evening was well below the mountaintops when we pulled up. We were fortunate to have avoided a collision into some tall rock face.

Brief brushes with death aside, training persisted with activities both exciting and dull. Back at base, we conducted minor physicals every morning before flying. Now and then, I was granted brief reprieves from the bothersome routines of military life. One night before a physical, I was out quite late with the doctor assigned to conduct the examination. We had a swell time on the town but were out carousing well past acceptable hours.

Reveille came very early the next morning. The bleary-eyed physician stood before me in formation at 5:30 a.m. He did not look so great, and I probably appeared no better.

"How many hours of sleep did you get last night?" he inquired.

"Eight hours, sir." An obvious fib. "But I don't feel so good."

"Open your mouth," he ordered. The doc applied a tongue depressor.

"Hhhmmmmm," he slowly hummed. "You have nasal pharyngitis. Go back to quarters and get some rest."

The command was music to my ears! It's great to have empathetic friends in high places.

My bunk was the closest one to our quarters' old-style telephone attached to the wall. An earpiece was held by a hook on the side. Given my proximity to the phone, the duty of answering calls was relegated to me. This chore became old in a hurry. To make life slightly easier, I implemented some GI innovation. I installed two screw eyes in the ceiling and ran a wire from my bunk to the earpiece. When I didn't feel like arising from bed, I simply pulled the string.

Officers from three crews barracked in our building. My bunkmates hailed from many walks of life—a glimpse of the American melting pot. Many of these fellow lieutenants confronted various trials and tragedies down the road. One of them—William F. Palmer—would be assigned to my bomb group in Europe, was eventually shot down, and became a prisoner of war. Another, "Red" Squires, was transferred to the Fifteenth Air Force in Italy and was likewise shot from the sky. We all had heavy flying and fighting ahead of us.

In April 1944, my crew relocated to Pueblo, Colorado, as a final phase of preparation for overseas deployment. Snow still covered the ground. On April 23, we received a fitting parting gift before leaving the Centennial State—a brand-new silver B-24, hot off the assembly line from the Ford Motor Company's Willow Run plant in Michigan. That bomber factory located outside Detroit was an impressive wartime operation. The facility stretched a mile long and churned out a B-24 every fifty-five minutes. (Each of those Liberators had over 1.2 million parts.) Just weeks before we received our new plane, Willow Run

announced the completion of its 3,000th bomber manufactured since May 1942. Ours came with a sales receipt for
$285,000, along with an equipment manifest listing everything
from a Norden bombsight to radios to heavy machine guns.
We were quite enamored with our new ride.[13]

One of the veterans from our outfit later summarized the
materials necessary to produce a single B-24: enough steel to
manufacture 160 washing machines, enough aluminum to
make 55,000 coffee percolators, enough alloy steel to churn
out 6,800 electric irons, and enough rubber to recap 800 car
tires. Although the plane is simple by modern standards, the
B-24 was cutting-edge technology for its time. America's
industrial capacity was put to the ultimate challenge.[14]

Our crew naturally babied and scrupulously examined the
Liberator. From nose to tail, seemingly every gleaming inch
was analyzed. We treated the pristine aircraft with tender loving care. All were under the impression that this was to be our
combat plane. With this aircraft, we'd do our part—or so we
thought.

CHAPTER 3

The Wash

The long-awaited command at last arrived. On May 27, 1944, our crew received orders to proceed by air for assignment to the Eighth Air Force. In hindsight, the timing of the orders was revealing. The colossal buildup of troops throughout the United Kingdom, combined with the incessant bombings of Western Europe, portended the amphibious assault on France. We were called to Britain rather than the Pacific due to Gen. Dwight Eisenhower's plea for fresh crews. Summons to an English air base underscored a chilling fact: We were needed for the forthcoming fight.

As men soon to engage in combat, we were mindful that current happenings overseas determined our future odds. Military operations in late May were indicative of what was to come. The day we received our stateside flight orders, a great aerial offensive consisting of thousands of Allied bombers and fighters thundered against German transportation systems in occupied France. Across the narrow strait of Dover from Calais, according to the Associated Press, the English coast received "one of its greatest joltings of the war—houses shaking, furniture bouncing, and doors banging again and again from the vibrations of the cross-channel explosions." In a matter of weeks, bombs dropped from our plane would contribute to the ongoing chorus of destruction.[1]

Energized by the swift call to action, we quickly assembled our gear, prepared our plane, departed Casper, Wyoming, and pushed east. The prolonged flight that followed was executed in steppingstone fashion. We flew first to Lincoln, Nebraska, where we briefly rested before proceeding. Our crew took off from Lincoln at 1:35 a.m. on May 29. On the way to Grenier Field in Manchester, New Hampshire, we passed over Des Moines, Toledo, Cleveland, Erie, Buffalo, Rochester, Syracuse, and Albany. At Grenier, we received our last bit of processing before departing the States. Our next stop was an unknown site referred to only as "X." We were not provided with a precise location, only coordinates to reach that destination. The travels took us into Canada and over a wide swath of the St. Lawrence River.

The site turned out to be the burgeoning air base at Goose Bay in Labrador. Since 1941, the site had mushroomed from a relative wilderness into a vital transportation hub. A steady cycle of heavy bombers started using the location as a launch point to Europe only six months after construction began. This installation afforded crews like ours the straightest possible path across the imposing North Atlantic. Concurrently, the use of Goose Bay significantly lessened the casualty rates of transatlantic flyers. Shorter routes accounted for fewer crashes and easier air-sea rescues. These fair fortunes notwithstanding, we were grounded by poor weather for two days before proceeding from Labrador at 10:30 p.m. on the second of June.[2]

Destination: Prestwick, Scotland. During the short period of visibility, I saw nothing but ominous-looking ice floes blanketing the ocean in solid white. For most of the next fourteen and a half hours, however, we stared at little more than thick cloud cover enveloping the plane.

Some might consider an inaugural transatlantic flight an adventure, a daring new chapter of military exploits. In actuality, the journey was boring as hell. Over 2,000 miles of pure nothingness. We lacked the oxygen tanks to cruise at high altitude for the duration. Therefore, we zoomed past the first two layers of clouds and soared to approximately 8,000 feet. (Airmen do not require supplemental oxygen until 10,000 feet.) When we reached the desired altitude, the navigator provided a heading. The pilot and I trimmed the plane up, thereby synchronizing the engines. We placed the trim tabs on the controls and then flipped to autopilot mode. From there, we essentially flew on automatic the entire span of the sea. Fuel tanks in the bomb bays were used to extend the aircraft's range.

Radio silence was practiced due to safety precautions. As airman Keith Turnham recalled, "The Germans had installed radio equipment and were using our own frequencies to misdirect American planes into false fjords where they would crash." Several aircraft had apparently gone down because of this ploy, and nobody wished to entangle in a huge ice floe. For now, we were on our own.[3]

Our trustworthy navigator gained only a few celestial fixes during the entire crossing. Whenever possible, he quickly gazed through the clouds to spot stars against the dark blue sky. When necessary, he radioed slight heading corrections over the mic system, and we simply adjusted knobs on the controls. To assist crews like ours, the English transmitted a powerful radio signal from Northern Ireland for planes to home in by radio compass. We were warned the Germans broadcasted a decoy signal from Norway to lure or misguide American aircraft. Vigilance was our watchword.

Although we professed alertness, remaining awake during that journey was damn difficult. We were very tempted to fall asleep as the engines hummed outside the cockpit windows. Our heads bobbled with fatigue. At one point, our navigator found everyone aboard asleep while the ship was on autopilot. We had no coffee, no candy, no caffeine. Crewmates had only each other to remain awake and engaged. Neither the pilot nor I left the controls the whole night. The flight was one of our first great tests of mental stamina.

Given the extended periods of time spent with my nine fellow crewmen, I quickly learned their names, backgrounds, and personalities. In some ways, they became my brothers away from home. Through rigorous training, we collectively demonstrated the proficiency and willpower to master some of the advanced technical standards of the age. We felt confident in our abilities.

Lt. John "Predge" Predgen was the administrative officer, our skipper. He towered over all of us. His tall stature, thick eyebrows, and long nose lent themselves to his position of authority. Hailing from Illinois, John had a family story like my own. His father was a housepainter who emigrated from England. Now, Predgen and I were bound for the land of our ancestors. He received his commission at Blytheville Army Airfield and was only one month my senior in military rank. The lieutenant was a good and capable man. One could sense his love of flying. "I was up in these cumulus clouds today looking through a hole at the scenery below," he wrote to family a year prior. "It reminds you of a valley in the mountains, Shangri-La." The admin officer was usually the oldest man on the plane, but such was not the case with our crew.[4]

Navigator Charles "Chuck" Reevs was four years older than the skipper, making him the eldest man aboard at age twenty-seven. Blond-haired and blue-eyed, Reevs worked as a bookkeeper for a liquor company prior to the war. Chuck enlisted in the peacetime Army six months before Pearl Harbor. He transferred into the Air Forces following a stint as a grunt in the 6th

Infantry Division. The man was only 5'2" and he joked that his short stature was what made him an airman. Earlier in life, he was initially accepted onto his high school basketball team, but his coach feared that he might be killed by larger players. The disappointed youth was cut from the squad. His coach's warning nearly became prophetic after Reevs joined the Army. His left humerus was fractured during a basketball game at Fort Leonard Wood and a screw was installed in his arm. He teasingly referred to his broken limb as his "war injury." Only the coming of Pearl Harbor and a subsequent reappraisal of his physical abilities earned him a transfer to the Air Forces. He wanted nothing more than to become a P-38 pilot, but he was ultimately shipped to navigation school instead.[5]

Chuck wrote frequently to folks back in Rhinelander, Wisconsin. Periodically, his letters appeared in his community newspaper. Two of his brothers were in the Navy. He was very smart, mature, and had a good head on his shoulders. I palled around with him often.

John "Pup" Dalgleish served as bombardier, the man who sighted targets and unleashed payloads. Born in New Rochelle, New York, he had spent most of his life in Meriden, Connecticut, where he excelled as a letterman on his school soccer and baseball teams. Following graduation, he attended Northeastern University for a few semesters, but joined the Army before he could complete his degree. Twenty-two years of age, he had a round face and a wide smile. He was a loner of sorts and did not mix well with crewmates.

Nineteen-year-old flight engineer Louis J. Wagner already boasted ample experience with planes despite his youth. In the Baltimore area, he had been employed at the Glenn L. Martin Company, which was a major manufacturer of aircraft during the World War II era. He was a fine engineer and a precise tech sergeant. He knew his business on an airplane. Whenever he predicted complications in flight, his estimations were always on the mark. When he spoke, we listened.

Radio operator Dean Leonard was a twenty-two-year-old carpenter's son from Minneapolis. He'd been promoted to staff sergeant about two weeks before we departed Casper. Coincidentally, his brother, Wayne, was also a radio operator—in a tank soon to storm Utah Beach in Normandy. Only five days after our crew's first combat mission, Wayne was wounded in France and evacuated to England. Dean ended up visiting his little brother in hospital as the GI recuperated. I was glad my own brothers were too young to fight in the war.

George W. Puska, nose gunner, was a burly Arkansan who had labored on big oil rigs with a company called Seismic Exploration. On base, he had occasional flashes of genius. When assigned to Kitchen Patrol duties, he inexplicably dressed to the nines, opting to sport his Class A uniform. Everybody knew they were to wear fatigues when sent to scrub pots at chow hall. Puska had other plans. Mess officers couldn't make sense of the sly sergeant's appearance, so they always made him an usher or tasked him with mild clerical assignments. That man never peeled a potato. Pure brilliance. Sadly, George survived the war only to perish in a boating accident at age thirty.

The youngest crew member was tail gunner Vernon R. Long, who came from the small city of Norfolk, Nebraska. Long was rather quiet and played the violin when he was in high school. He was very boyish, so much so that I thought he had lied about his age to enter the service. He enjoyed playing golf and frequently became ill during flights. Unfortunately, I recall little else about him, other than he worked for Sears and Roebuck for many years. Reevs indicated Vern had nine children after the war. Long seldom attended veteran reunions even though he outlived all his crewmates other than me.

Like Wagner, waist gunner Marion J. "Bo" Cochran of Conley, Georgia, possessed experience as a civil air mechanic. For a spell, he was employed by a Pennsylvania outfit at Middletown Airfield before returning home and enlisting. He demonstrated a high capacity for merriment and frequently showcased a signature "shit-eating grin." Marion was a downright funny guy who never failed to provide quality entertainment. The emotional value of triggering a good laugh is a virtue not to be underappreciated by men at war.

Cochran was a suitable partner in crime for Richard "Dick" Bunch, our belly gunner. He manned a retractable Sperry ball turret mounted to the bottom of the fuselage to protect us from fighters below. The position was claustrophobic and vulnerable, factors that later compelled Dick to drink as a coping mechanism. In any case, the pressures of war failed to constrain this Baltimorean's love of women and a good party. He was quite the heller.

"What a crew that Uncle Sam put together for our enemy," Reevs joked.[6]

Front row, sergeants, left to right: Richard Bunch, Dean Leonard, Lou Wagner, Marion Cochran, George Puska, and Vernon Long. Back row, lieutenants, left to right: John Predgen, John Homan, John Dalgleish, and Chuck Reevs. *John Homan collection.* (13)

These men composed our team. In countless ways, our lives depended on each other's skills and judgment. This fact was quite apparent when our journey to Scotland neared its end. Anticipation of the moment soon morphed into anxiety. As we headed across the Irish Sea, our cockpit radios failed and, as luck would have it, there was complete low cloud cover. With daylight now upon us, our navigator eventually informed the crew we were over the country. The problem was that the terrain was fully cloaked. We were unable to pick up the Prestwick tower or range, therefore, we couldn't locate the field. The radios failed to reach the airport presumably below. We asked radio operator Dean Leonard to hop on his equipment and renew attempts at communication. Anticipating the worst, the rest of the crew donned parachutes and were lined up near the bomb bay. We nervously circled in the general area, running critically low on fuel. This was far from the triumphant European arrival we had hoped for.

When all seemed lost, Leonard finally contacted a station. The control tower instructed us to count to ten and back over the airwaves. By doing so, the ground team determined our location with radio compasses, vectored us out over the Irish Sea, and provided headings to shepherd us in. We broke out of the clouds with the runway dead ahead, quickly dropped the wheels and flaps, and then finally touched down. The crew breathed a sigh of relief. Upon exiting the plane, we immediately noticed the airfield was situated between impressive hills. Without the skillful controllers as our guides, that foggy flight very well could have been our last.

Despite all the uncertainty, Reevs was always a half-glass-full type of guy. He remembered of our flight, "It was a great experience for a group of guys heading out across the ocean for the first time to join the fighting forces in Europe."[7]

A shaky but safe arrival at Prestwick on June 3 lifted our spirits, but that satisfaction was tempered by an unpleasant surprise. Our nice, new, shiny, silver plane went one way, and we went another. My comrades and I had been used as little more than aircraft delivery boys. So much for all the attention and care we showered upon that bomber.

The crew had scant opportunity to enjoy Scotland's scenic splendors. Immediately following our grueling flight, we were bussed to some beds and hot meals in the vicinity of Glasgow. That ancient city was bombed no less than two dozen times throughout the war. As far as I could tell, these hardships scarcely dampened the sprightly attitudes of the citizenry. During our commute, the bus driver spotted a ragged panhandler begging a pedestrian for a handout. The driver abruptly stopped the vehicle, pulled the parking brake, exited, and commenced with a genuine tongue lashing.

"Dinna give this man a thing!" the driver barked. "He can work!" This unexpected public service announcement remains one of the few colorful memories from my short time in Scotland. We shortly thereafter boarded a train for a long ride to Stone, England.

The country buzzed as anticipation mounted for D-Day, the much-prophesized invasion of Western Europe. The German propaganda mill whipped up a hodgepodge of fact and fancy, proclamations devised to instill fear in Allied combatants. In one Nazi pronouncement, "a roundabout and suspect report told of the killing of five American airmen in

Germany 'by agitated people.'" Joseph Goebbels, Hitler's chief propagandist, claimed he could no longer guarantee the safety of captured airmen if unrelenting campaigns against German cities persisted. These verbal tirades generally evoked little concern among flyers.[8]

Yet, latrine rumors were spreading simultaneously with propaganda. At the ground level, I sensed the invasion was imminent because everyone on base was suddenly ordered to wear sidearms on their hips or chests. Each officer had to qualify with a Colt .45 before heading overseas. On the firing range, I had much difficulty hitting a man-sized target only yards away. After many futile attempts to improve my marksmanship, I found a note pinned to my blanket one morning with instruction to again report to the range. The day was so cold, my hands shook, and my fingers went numb while clenching the grips. I was thereafter informed I qualified. I'm not sure I did. Perhaps the instructor merely demonstrated mercy.

Word of D-Day arrived on the overcast Tuesday, June 6, 1944. Our crew did not participate in this endeavor, which Gen. Eisenhower referred to as "the great crusade." To our dismay, we had not yet been issued a replacement aircraft or assigned to an outfit. The bomb group we were soon to join, however, did fly into Normandy that hectic morning. Tom Baker, a GI assigned to base defense, recalled the day's episodes in a journal. His brief account emphasizes the operation's biblical scale: "I could hardly sleep last night for the planes overhead," he wrote of D-Day's opening. "When I woke up, our planes were still taking off. They went to France, but it was so cloudy they couldn't see to drop their bombs. . . . Our gunners said they could see landing barges by the thousands and said the sky was filled with planes. We didn't know for sure the invasion was on until we went to chow this morning. I'm glad it is."[9]

The air was so congested with clouds and Allied aircraft, many of the group's planes returned with full bomb bays. The disappointment of the crews did not last. They flew thirty missions over the next month, striking dozens of targets with consistent accuracy. At the end of June, our crew would join them for the air war's next destructive phase.

Like Baker suggested, a sense of uneasy optimism pervaded in the wake of D-Day. There was a realistic hope that the successes of June 6 would domino toward broader victory. Six days later, we boarded another train and were then flown by B-17 to a base in Newcastle, Northern Ireland. "We had to cross the Irish Sea," Chuck Reevs remembered of our roundabout journey. "We all loaded onto a plane—at least fifty well-trained pilots, navigators, bombardiers, and other crew. I was sure it was overloaded." Had our plane crashed in transit, Reevs concluded, the wreck would have been a terrific waste of trained airmen. "I guess war is hell and sometimes we lose sight of the consequences."[10]

Our temporary post in County Down served as a replacement center for the Eighth Air Force. As various groups suffered losses, replacements were thus rapidly available. There, we were subjected to further training. Fazed combat veterans-turned-mentors scared the hell out of us in the process. They were tired men who demonstrated little patience with inexperienced newcomers. We were told to forget all about aircraft recognition training, and to shoot any unrecognizable planes swooping at us. Our learning procedures underwent perpetual reinvention as the war progressed.

While awaiting assignment in Great Britain, some "how to get along with the English" sessions were also administered. A booklet distributed to American servicemen, entitled *A Short Guide to Great Britain*, presented strong advice on reinforcing the Anglo-American pact. "The British will welcome you as friends and allies," the text advertised. "But remember that crossing the ocean doesn't automatically make you a hero. There are housewives in aprons and youngsters in knee pants in Britain who have lived through more high explosives in air raids than many soldiers saw in first-class barrages in the last war." Regarding British women in uniform, the booklet's tone sharpened: "When you see a girl in khaki or air force blue with a bit of ribbon on her tunic—remember she didn't get it for knitting more socks than anyone else in Ipswich."[11]

The educational sessions were well-intentioned, but they failed to minimize many surprises awaiting us in that foreign land. An important lesson was to maintain a steady sense of goodwill with our allies. As I was later to see firsthand, this was sometimes an overly hopeful expectation.

Lingering at a Reception Center, also known as a Replacement Depot or "Repple Depple," could be a tedious and lonely affair. Many soldiers who were tossed into these logistical purgatories felt forsaken. We fared better than conventional infantrymen in this setting. At typical facilities, GIs entered as individuals and were thrown into the divisional mix as strangers. By contrast, we were fortunate to remain with crewmates during the waiting games.

Now and then, we were even treated to regional delights. At one of the depples, I was pleased to discover that beer was being served at a makeshift bar prior to departure. I eagerly grabbed my tin mess cup and poured a hearty pint of mild. As I swallowed, I immediately spit out the beverage. Warm beer! This was my first dose of culture shock. As time passed, I found bitters to be an acquired taste. Predgen complained to folks, "This beer over here is okay, if they would only cool the stuff it would compare with our beer." Thankfully, alternative forms of intoxicating spirits were to be located and consumed elsewhere in large quantities.[12]

Ireland was rainy, green, rustic, and quaint. Showers frequently pattered on the corrugated steel roof of our lodging. The inherent dreariness of base hardly diminished the enchanting ambiance outside the gate. A local woman circled the camp selling fresh eggs out of a basket. We ate plentiful shares of eggs in Ireland because we knew they had long been rationed in England. Many Brits concocted protein-rich ration recipes with dried peas, beans, and lentils to compensate for the lack of meat, cheese, and eggs. We ate high off the hog while we still could.

Our location was slightly above the border separating Northern Ireland and the Republic of Ireland. Keep in mind the former was and is a province of the United Kingdom while the latter proclaims itself a sovereign nation. During World War II, the Republic of Ireland officially remained neutral to avoid blatant pro-British policy. "Between 1939 and 1945, Ireland was able to preserve its non-belligerent status," writes historian Bryce Evans. However, "Ireland's outward neutrality was counterbalanced by the state's secretly pro-Allied stance." I was not well versed on foreign policy at the time, but I can informally attest to this sentiment. My crewmates and I determined this fact during a slightly ill-conceived quest for liquor.[13]

Guard dogs, observation planes, and armed sentinels kept watch on the border. Our dilemma was that the nearest pub was across that border. All I can say is that international politics were not about to deprive us of some well-deserved drinks.

In search of libations one evening, we approached a military policeman at the boundary. We were perfectly candid. "Look," we assured, "all we want to do is visit the pub across the way. We're gonna hop the fence. Now don't go shooting at us."

Our persuasive powers proved convincing. We walked back and forth without a whiff of difficulty. The guard very well may have bent the rules himself from time to time. Our drink of choice that evening was anything wet. Recognizing we were thirsty and well-paid Yanks, the bartender exhibited no partisan grievance regarding our presence in his establishment. Perhaps we did our small part to win over some Irish hearts and minds that night.

That week, Predgen wrote to family and shared his cultural observations. "Could tell you about all the political and religious difficulties between Ireland and England, but not being used to that subject, the only difference I found was in the homes," he observed, "Ireland with their thatched roofs and the British with their tile roofs."[14]

On June 29, we departed for our new home: an English airfield, Station 365, at Holton (also known as Halesworth). The extent of our recent travels underlined the dramatic evolution in air travel in the seventeen years since the first transatlantic flight. As the Army newspaper *Stars and Stripes* astutely noted that summer, "When Lindbergh flew the Atlantic in 1927, there were 100,000 people on hand when he landed in Paris. Today when a pilot with less than 300 hours of flying time drops his four-engine bomber from the U.S. down on a runway in England, he is greeted by a lone mechanic who tells him where to park his ship." How times and technology change.[15]

We were quickly assigned as crew number 2937 to the 845th Squadron, in the 489th Bomb Group, within the 95th Combat Bombardment Wing, of the Second Air Division in the Eighth Air Force! One could feel small and insignificant when considering the enormity of the enterprise. I assume we were hasty replacements for one of the group's four planes shot down four days earlier. Because we were a replacement crew, superiors were going to fly the hell out of us.

All our travels and destinations were intended to be confidential. However, maintaining secrecy was sometimes difficult. When pilot Wilmer Plate arrived in the outfit, he recalled a German propagandist jamming the radios and announcing, "We would very much like to welcome the men of the 489th Bomb Group to England. We hope to see you over Germany very soon."

"So much for secret orders," Plate complained.[16]

With little time to settle in or grow acquainted, we conducted a few practice missions, attended orientation sessions, and prepared for our first dose of combat. Last-minute formation, bombing, and navigation training were additional elements of the transition process.

While completing these maneuvers, we were reminded of a disaster that struck the group exactly one month preceding our arrival. Two B-24 crews were lost in a fiery mid-air explosion while attempting to dodge B-17s on a near collision course. Flight Officer Arthur Shay had just returned from a mission and was in his hut when he heard the Liberators smash together. He dashed outside with his camera and captured the final horrific seconds of the planes as they whirled to the ground. "Twenty seconds, twenty men," a witness gasped as he saw the flames spurt skyward. Shay's photos later appeared in the September 19 issue of *Look Magazine*. The airmen in that crash were so badly mangled and charred that only the group's dental officer could identify the corpses. As I had witnessed in Georgia, accidental deaths were not at all uncommon. Our crew aspired to avert that fateful tally.[17]

Left: My original Eighth Air Force patch. *John Homan collection*. Right: Flight and ground personnel near the Halesworth control tower. *Air Force photo*. (14 and 15)

Excluding these grim realities of war, Halesworth was an otherwise idyllic spot. Allow me to share particulars of this setting as well as staples of airman life. The lush pastoral scenery was overlapped by the sprawling base. As I walked the grounds, I absorbed the airfield's relatively short history. Constructed in 1943, the site was previously occupied by Col. Hubert Zemke's famous "Wolf Pack" of P-47 pilots. This fighter group became one of the most accomplished and celebrated of the war.

The first planes of the 489th landed at Halesworth on May 1, 1944, less than two months before my own arrival.

Stories were plentiful regarding the unit's debut in England. One comical yarn concerned a pilot named Chuck Harkins, who stocked up on bourbon from stateside liquor stores prior to departure for Europe. He meticulously cared for the precious cargo. As soon as his plane was parked at Halesworth, he and his crew were scurried off to a designated squadron area. When he returned to the flight line the following morning to retrieve the stash, his plane was gone—flown off to a modification center. Upon the aircraft's return, the bourbon was missing in action. "That's when I learned to drink Scotch," he confessed. Meanwhile, some men in the outfit sought refuge at a nearby pub named the Queen's Head, a popular watering hole that became a favorite spot for playing darts.[18]

Quests for booze were not the only challenges during the group's earliest days at Halesworth. The logistics behind forming routines, assigning quarters, and coordinating with fellow units caused many a headache. Additionally, frustrated maintenance men discovered no available tools in England. Fortunately, these mechanics had the strong foresight of stealing the necessary equipment from their previous post at Utah's Wendover Field. Our crews might have been in a heap of trouble had not good and dependable men stooped to thievery.[19]

The airfield was in an area blandly known as "The Wash," located approximately six miles from the North Sea, between Ipswich and Norwich. The base's closeness to the Suffolk coast rendered it a perfect region to accommodate escort fighters. In fact, our base was the nearest of any to the sea. The airfield was carved out of rich grain and barley farmland. Many of the intersecting country lanes remained open to locals despite the influx of war machines.

Many amusing and sometimes heated interactions occurred when Americans inevitably drove on the wrong side of the roadway. One story goes as follows: A young English woman collided with a U.S. Deuce and a Half truck, and her vehicle was pushed off the lane. When a constable arrived to investigate, the female motorist declared, "I was Yanked into a ditch!"[20]

In contrast to American military bases today, security seemed rather lax at Halesworth. Military Police officers were posted at each entry point, but no fences were erected. Cattle sometimes wandered onto the grounds and left pungent evidence of their presence. The nearby town of Halesworth itself dated back to Roman times and had apparently seen its share of conflict and tumult since then. Our new environment ushered in many changes, including culinary options. Rather than hot dogs and burgers, newspaper-wrapped fish became common grub among GIs.

A small office for the squadron commander and clerical staff was the operational nerve center of our outfit. There were four squadrons to a group. I never knew where the other three squadrons were located. They were apparently scattered throughout adjacent woodlots and pastures. I had little time or inclination to venture beyond my own neighborhood.

The Halesworth base was nothing less than a militarized city, a sprawling complex attached to an even larger wartime apparatus. The logistics were fueled by a remarkable balance of bureaucracy and brawn. Overall, the installation consisted of several squadron areas, an officers' club and mess, an enlisted club and mess, a headquarters, an air control tower, briefing rooms, equipment storage, a base hospital, a motor pool, and maintenance facilities including a hangar. Heavy bombs were stored at a remote site due to safety concerns and were delivered as ordered. A modest ablution facility served as our wash station.

All these years later, I occasionally revisit my old stomping grounds via Google Earth, zooming in and out of the vicinity to explore my former post. Today, all seems quiet and peaceful. The rural landscape is dotted with solar panels, windmills, and a few industrial plants. A humble museum operated by a dedicated team of locals honors my comrades. The mess halls remain as a small construction firm. The headquarters building and Norden bombsight storage areas are semi-dilapidated brick structures overgrown by brush. These weathered survivors of time hardly illustrate the mammoth efforts that once unfolded on those green meadows.

Squadron areas were scattered away from the airfield. Each section consisted of Nissen huts for crews and ground personnel. These structures were made of corrugated sheet metal with no insulation. The simple dwellings featured blackout shutters on the windows so we could conceal lights in case of nighttime enemy air raids. A meager cast iron stove heated each barrack, hardly enough to warm us on chilly spring mornings when we were roused for missions. Quarters, though far superior to those of frontline doughboys, were primitive.

An aerial view of Halesworth Field. *Air Force photo.* (16)

We were tucked away in a pleasantly shaded tree line serving as our countryside refuge. An earthen bomb shelter was located only yards from the front door. We followed a slight dirt path to reach the mess hall. Crewmen hopped on trucks, bicycled, or walked to the flight line. Believe it or not, my first Willys Jeep ride would not come until seventy-eight years later.

Reflecting on the many gray days we quartered in barracks, I fondly recall a little pooch adopted by the occupants of our shack. Feeding and care provided to the pup was a collective effort. Animal mascots and related critters were ubiquitous in the European Theater of Operations. Their presence was a matter of morale and unit pride, not to mention the obvious therapeutic attributes. Four-legged companions like ours were heralded in the British press that spring as full-fledged members of the war effort. Servicemen went as far as to organize pets in a multinational guild. "One of the most unusual wartime clubs in the world, founded last July, has 500 members—not one is a human being," reported a Lincolnshire newspaper. "Any animal or bird officially attached to any branch of the Allied forces is eligible for membership. Each must be serving as a mascot, guard dog, or carrier pigeon."[21]

To my knowledge, our pooch could not boast affiliation to such a prestigious organization, but he did stir the ire of the commanding officer at least once. The CO of the 845th Squadron was a twenty-five-year-old captain named Lewis W. Tanner. The Texan was a square-jawed, former high school football star who lacked height but not muscle. His grit was demonstrated on the gridiron then over the Atlantic when serving on anti-submarine patrols earlier in the war. By the

end of 1944, he was a major. He did have the tendency, however, of pulling surprise inspections to maintain attentiveness.
Tanner decided to do so one day when no mission was scheduled. All were fast asleep that late morning, blissfully snoring
away in the darkness provided by blackout shutters. No one
had arisen to let the dog out, so the pooch relieved himself in
the entryway. Enter the scrupulous captain, ready to spring his
ambush. The tables quickly turned. He stepped squarely in the
puddle of piss.[22]

Recognizing he was outdone by a puppy, the captain simply
threw up his hands, huffed, "The hell with it," and walked
out. A lesser man might have inflicted retaliation on us. In high
school, Tanner had been chosen "Best All 'Round Boy" in his
senior class. We could certainly see why. Like parenthood,
military leadership requires patience and discipline alike.[23]

Fellow officer Charlie Freudenthal acknowledged these
generally unwritten human qualities as key to understanding
base life. "Though the 489th's stay in England was short when
compared with some of the others," he observed, "there was
packed into that time the hopes, fears, tears, laughter, anger,
and frustration of several thousand men. But records are flat,
and they don't tell about this." Each man tended to operate in
his own distinctive circle. Our squadron rarely mingled with
other squadrons and, within those units, "the aircrew, ordnance, armament, photo, maintenance, medics, admin types,
and others all mixed for the most part with their own." There
was a sameness to our existence, yet our experiences were

simultaneously different. The same might have been true for
sailors on a massive aircraft carrier.[24]

The officers' club was by far the best venue to cultivate
fellowship within our modest network of friends and associ-
ates. The retreat was housed in a large Nissen hut, although
not as luxurious a spot as depicted in the movie *Twelve
O'Clock High*. A pool table was a fixture of the room even
though we had no billiard balls for matches. Rather than waste
the baized surface, airmen transformed the space into an
improvised card table. Meanwhile, one could hardly walk
across the room without putting a foot in the middle of a crap
game. I participated in these chancy gambling rituals perhaps
twice per week. A bad roll of the dice could financially wipe
out a soldier. To reduce transportation costs, GIs were typically paid with the largest denominations available.
Consequently, crap game stakes could be exceptionally high.
I occasionally fancied myself as a poker player, but that naïve
notion proved costly. Making use of the nearby tennis courts
and softball field proved a far less expensive or risky recreational pursuit.

Liquid courage was readily available at the officers' club.
Beer was easily procured from local pubs via large kegs and
consumed as if water. The purchasing of alcohol by the glass
or by the barrel presented us an education in British currency.
A pound was worth about four dollars back then. Luckily,
there were not many places to empty our wallets around
Halesworth (minus the crap games of course). Men got a big

kick out of the pubs since the establishments provided all manner of entertainment and culture shock. A pint of beer cost six pence, or about one American dollar by today's standards. This affordability was fine by us.[25]

The most prized and expensive beverage of all was Scotch. Some soldiers likened the tonic to an overpowering medicine with the capacity of melting enamel off their teeth. But after long days of flying, nothing quite satisfied one's thirst or nerves as much as a solid malt whiskey. High demand necessitated constant resupplying. Whenever there was a shortage, we sent a B-24 to Scotland on a high-priority special mission to restock. There was considerable excitement on base when that plane returned with its prized freight.

Even our base chaplain, Charlie Wakefield, was involved in the distribution process. A Baptist pastor previously in charge of a church in Providence, Rhode Island, he flirted with sin like the rest of us. Before the outfit had departed the stateside Wendover Airfield, the padre stockpiled Listerine mouthwash in large quantities. Once in England, he emptied the bottles and then filled them with Scotch. That's one sharp "Holy Joe."[26]

Although I was raised Roman Catholic, I don't consider myself a religious man. While in the service, I neither prayed nor attended mass. I figured my odds for survival depended on skill and pure chance more than divine intervention. However, many airmen on my base did seek spiritual solace. "Overseas, the serviceman's interest in religion is sincere and realistic," Chaplain Wakefield noted in an address following his nine-month tour of duty in England. "Attendance of the men in the United States at chapel services is small, only 10 percent on average," he stated, "but this jumps to well over 50 percent in Europe, with the men attending religious services regularly and displaying a genuine spirit of faith." Crewmen sought answers to the questions of life as they confronted potential demise. They were not pursuing faith for faith's sake alone, but they sought some sort of deeper meaning from their experiences.

Wakefield told a tale of one bomber crew being shot to pieces and ditching into the North Sea. Clinging precariously to rubber dinghies, the exhausted Yanks were eventually pulled from the drink by an English patrol. The men's first act after reporting in was to attend religious services. Dangerous close calls prompted many survivors to discover religion, for they otherwise could not explain how they endured calamity.

Others may have desired guidance on romantic issues when the "Friendly Invasion" of Americans grew a bit *too* friendly. (Over 70,000 British women married U.S. personnel and 24,000 Anglo-American babies were born out of wedlock during the war.) On these matters and more, Wakefield had his hands full. He estimated that, in best case scenarios, each chaplain in the Air Forces on average served 1,200 men. Even those who lacked faith respected the Holy Joes. Clergymen acted as counselors, stretcher bearers, letter writers, and advisors on every conceivable moral issue. Imagine how many private sessions Chaplain Charlie held in his nine months overseas. Every Sunday, he transformed our base gymnasium into a house of worship.[27]

A prevailing sense of unanimity was found in so many places and exhibited by so many people. One of our older ground chiefs was previously a school principal. Given his administrative background and abilities to instill discipline, the brass wanted him in a bureaucratic position within the Training Corps. His response was, "No way! This is my one chance in life to do something different!" His attention to detail and a profound sense of stewardship (both commendable traits in any good principal) made him one of the finest crew chiefs on our base. Like so many of us, the demands of war compelled him to accept new and exacting responsibilities. He never once failed us.

To this day, I have nothing but absolute respect for ground crewmen. Flyboys receive all the glory and laurels, but those mechanics were the guys who made our missions possible. Working out of ramshackle huts constructed with spare parts, the men labored through deplorable English weather—fixing aircraft initially thought to be unsalvageable. They carried out their unsung deeds while munching on cold sandwiches and gulping endless streams of black coffee. They mastered the art of technical ingenuity. "When there are no tools suitable for doing a job, the ground crewmen improvise them, or work mechanical miracles with hammer and wrench," one journalist lauded. "When there are no parts, they salvage them from wrecked aircraft, including the enemy's, and when there is no sheet metal, they patch flak-riddled airships with C ration cans." The level of creativity was contagious.[28]

Yet energy did not prevail in all things. Whether on the ground or in the air, we all lived an existence of sleep deprivation. Mechanics worked when we slept, and we worked when they slept. The routine moved in robotic, assembly line fashion to the point that we ourselves sometimes felt like robots. Sleep. Eat. Fly. Repeat. This was our fatiguing ritual.

Another one of our crew chiefs was a tough and knowledgeable master sergeant. He ran a tight ship. Paved hardstands were located all around the base. Planes were parked in a scattered formation. If the Germans felt daring and decided to attack our field, they couldn't strafe our planes in a neat single line as the Japanese had done at Pearl Harbor. The chief oversaw three ships, and I came to know him well. After each mission, we conducted a walkthrough of the aircraft so he could repair any damage. Naturally, he and his men had to work like hell all through many nights on our behalf. In nearly all circumstances, a ready plane awaited our crew each morning.

Beyond the base gates, life in East Anglia appeared as serene as it does today. Ipswich and Norwich were the only fair-sized cities in the region. The rest were quiet farms and villages that were Shakespearean in appearance. Halesworth was postcard worthy but little more than an old market town.

That community and nearby Holton had a combined population of some 2,000 civilians in 1944. The airfield could accommodate nearly 3,000 servicemen. The townsfolk thereby contended with more people than they had ever seen before in their districts.

Second Division airman Jacob Elias complained about a lack of social activities. "Girls were very scarce in Norfolk," he grumbled. "That was hard on young, red-blooded Yanks who would leave an airbase full of thousands of men, go into Dereham or Norwich and find hundreds of men in uniform walking the streets hoping for the sight of a pretty girl." As he aged, Elias's views on dating grew more restrained. "Now that we are parents of young women, we can understand," he attested in 1980.[29]

I hardly ever left base. There was simply little to do nearby. Despite boredom, I am often glad I was not stationed near a sizable city vulnerable to enemy attack. Norwich had endured some grueling bombings earlier in the war. An account of a British schoolboy named David J. Hastings was once shared in our division newsletter. Neighbors thought the Hastings family mad for building a bomb shelter in 1939. The construction project turned out to be a sound decision when Nazi ordnance rained on the community. "The noise was indescribable, with each explosion seeming to be louder than the previous one; the ground shook and the lights went out," David recalled. "If you have never been bombed, then you can never understand the noise, the smell, the shaking, and the fear."[30]

Given the unusual balance of tedium and terror, we did our utmost to maintain warm relations with British neighbors. Empathy was instrumental in discourse and diplomacy. As one bit of propaganda literature professed to Americans, "The British don't know how to make a good cup of coffee. You don't know how to make a good cup of tea. It's an even swap." This sense of mutual understanding went a long way in ensuring local friendliness.

The only social opportunity was the occasional, sparsely attended church dance. The ladies of the area were glad to see us because so many of their men had been in the service for so long. We were relative newcomers to the war. The British people knew little else but shortages and hardship for five years. Now, we had arrived to help settle the score. To show their appreciation for the company and much-needed military support, the women hosted a Sadie Hawkins dance, in which females from surrounding villages invited GIs as companions.

Contrasting tastes in music exposed additional cultural differences. While young British ladies adored our sprightly American swing music, the same could not always be said of their parents. Some thought the Yanks corrupted civilian youth. One elder complained to the newspaper, "Let us hope that after the war there will be a return to a saner type of lowbrow music: even jazz played straight can be tuneful." A more compromising resident supposed that English hosts had failed to offer Americans "any other enjoyment than what can be derived from the mournful, monotonous drone" of British tunes. As one might expect, such conversations failed to weaken vitality on the dance floor.[31]

My encounters at these gatherings resulted in some very cordial dates, dinners, and teas, but little more than neighborly socializing. Over the following months, I had so little time for healthy distraction. Deadly work awaited me.

CHAPTER 4

Hell After Breakfast

We faced three enemies: poor weather, mechanical problems, and the Germans. Combat posed only a fraction of the numerous dangers we confronted daily. Before I impart the particulars of specific bomber missions, the reader must gain a fuller understanding of what launching a mission entailed. Both in logistical scale and human strength, that vast process has never failed to impress me. The scope is unparalleled in history.

Mental preparation for a mission settled in as night fell. If our crew was alerted on the squadron area bulletin board, the message was clear to hit the sack early. Nerves could be a bit frayed for some when lights were doused. Uncertainty always lingered on the eve of a mission. On a personal level, emotional anxiety was no match for my constant state of exhaustion. I slept heavily but never long enough. The distant clatter of ground personnel and mechanics going about their nocturnal chores never deprived me of shut-eye either. Occasionally, airmen were awakened by the dull hum of the Royal Air Force embarking on a night raid. The sound portended our own impending tasks. Come daylight, we Americans often resumed the destructive handiwork of our British brethren. In official military communiques, this strategy was referred to as "round-the-clock bombing."

For some airmen plagued by insomnia, every mild sound was accentuated as they attempted to sleep: pattering rain, rumbling trucks, laughing comrades returning from pubs, the bark of a dog. "The sounds that always got my attention, though, were when the trucks at the motor pool would start up," wrote Jim Davis of the 489th. "By the sheer number of trucks, you knew it would be only a few minutes until you would hear those footsteps outside your door. The door would open, and you would soon be told it was time to go. To some degree I could relate to how it must be for a person on death row to hear the footsteps of the warden coming down the hall."[1]

Sure enough, in the predawn, a clerk crept in our Nissen hut and shined a flashlight in our eyes. He shook us to life, one by one. These unpleasant wakeup calls normally occurred between 1 a.m. and 4 a.m. We quietly dressed in the dark so as not to disturb others who flew long missions the day before. Strict blackout rules were observed. The literal darkness of these mornings cast an ominous tone for long and demanding days.

Next was a drowsy but prompt trip to the ablution building to splash cold water on our faces and stir awake. A common complaint from a man in our group went, "There are two faucets, why the hell can't we get hot water out of one?"[2]

Hot water or not, shaving was essential to prevent chafing from extended oxygen mask use at 20,000 feet. On a different note, writer John Steinbeck analyzed the psychology of shaving when he embedded with a bomb group the year prior. "You go out clean-shaven because you are coming back, and you make dates for that night because then you must come back to keep your date," he observed. "You project your mind into the future and the things you are going to do." Some men didn't make their beds. Others left small personal items and letters under their pillows, to be reclaimed when they returned.[3]

After washing and dressing, we were transported by truck to our respective mess halls for an early breakfast. Menu items included powdered eggs and milk, cereal, SPAM, dried fruit, "shit on a shingle" (cream chipped beef on toast), and tea or coffee. I never drank the tea, and the food was awfully bland. A caffeine boost offered a dose of vigor. "A soldier doesn't regard army coffee as a beverage," one reporter accurately confirmed. "To him it's just another vaccination."[4]

Cooks filled garbage cans halfway with powdered eggs and then poured in a healthy dose of baking soda. The ingredients rose inside the receptacles and possessed a spongy texture. We jokingly accused the mess hands of adding ping pong balls for further consistency. Lt. John Moir, also in the 489th, often declared we should have received Distinguished Flying Crosses for regularly consuming the eggs. Men thereafter bitched about the foamy food during flight debriefings, claiming "powdered eggs don't mix with combat."[5]

In fact, several food items did not settle well in our stomachs during missions. We were purposely spared gas-producing chow such as cabbage or beans for fear of intense abdominal distress. Gas could expand in our bodies and cause painful cramps with the power to incapacitate. In at least one instance, a pilot turned over his controls to the second in command until his plane dipped to a lower altitude and the agony eased.

Minus gassy grub, we devoured any camp cuisine placed before us until we were thoroughly stuffed. That meal had to sustain us nine to twelve hours, depending on a mission's length. Men likewise ate heartily when considering that any of these breakfasts could very well be their last. In flight, we had no substantive food or drink. Liquids froze at the extreme heights. Again, we lost two degrees for every 1,000 feet in altitude. Do the math. At 20,000 feet, the air was forty degrees cooler than at ground level. No insulated containers were durable enough to maintain the liquid state of coffee or soup.

Following a plentiful breakfast, trucks hauled us to the flight line for briefing. The orientation area was within a large Nissen hut. After everyone entered, an armed military policeman bolted the door behind us. Nobody else was permitted to enter due to security measures. Up to that point, we had no inkling of the target, duration, or opposition. Mystery lingered until the dramatic moment when the briefing room's black draw curtains were pulled, revealing a ceiling-high map of Europe. Red lines highlighted routes in and out from the target. The intensity of groans from the audience indicated expected problems based on location, previous experiences, or knowledge of our destination as a "hot" target.

All crew members were prepared with a mission overview. Eventually, the navigator, bombardier, and radio operator split off for special instructions. Pilots remained for further briefing on the target, weather, secondary target, taxi and takeoff sequence, assembly, formation position, bomb load, fighter coverage, flare colors, and the latest intelligence on German defenses. Officers delivered these presentations from a stage in front of the large map at the end of the hut.

Base intelligence officers briefed us on expected fighter opposition and known flak gun locations. Enemy emplacement was often left to speculation because the Germans mounted guns on train cars relocated by night. The CO normally offered a few tough words about target importance and the necessity of maintaining strong aerial formations. Additionally, we were instructed never to reference our altitude over the radio. We were provided a reference position guarded with the utmost secrecy. Briefing sessions were whirlwinds of information. The demand to absorb and retain these details was absolute.

For each mission, we were issued a cockpit "poop sheet" containing crucial details such as times, enemy artillery positions, flight paths, checkpoints, division lineup with tail colors, fighter support, recall information, altitudes, etc. We were furnished a checklist of sorts—a document indicating the route to a target, the path from that destination, codenames, and the initial point (the location of the actual bomb run). My map outlining the October 15, 1944, mission to Cologne, Germany, can be found in the archival collections of the National Museum of the Mighty Eighth Air Force in Savannah, Georgia.

Specifics were sometimes provided on where to drop tinfoil chaff—strips of confetti we threw out of planes to muddle German radar. Some flyers had reservations about the effectiveness of such a tactic. I believe the ruse occasionally worked. Any deception providing even the faintest degree of empowerment or additional safety was a worthwhile trick.

When briefing concluded, we adjourned to the equipment station to don our many layers of gear. There, we were issued heated flying suits including boots and gloves—coveted apparel we lacked in the States. An electrical wiring system stretched throughout the layers of fabric, allowing us to plug into the plane for warmth. All we had to do was set an individual thermostat to remain comfortable in the cockpit. The waist gunner, manning .50 caliber machine guns at open windows in an unpressurized plane, was exposed to the elements in a way I was not. On a later mission, our tail gunner's heating system was shot out and he damn near froze to death.

Also distributed were parachutes, oxygen masks, and head-gear to protect us from flying debris. We acquired M1 helmets typically used by infantrymen, carted them to the blacksmith shop, and had them banged out so our earphones could fit within the steel pots. Pilots were provided chest chutes, which were stored behind our seats and snapped on a harness if worse came to worst. Oxygen masks were typically hooked into the plane itself. If a crew member was to move throughout the fuselage, he had to plug into a walk-around oxygen bottle, which lasted about twelve minutes.

Flak vests—composed of hundreds of steel discs inter-locked beneath a canvas cover—were designed to safeguard us from enemy projectiles. Many an airman lost his life from whistling bits of shrapnel before these vests were introduced. While we were pleased to have these shields, the armored aprons were an additional twenty-five pounds. This weight was especially arduous on our waist gunner, who stood for the entirety of missions. But the lined fabric had the capacity to halt a hunk of metal dead in its course. One lieutenant expressed thanks to the former dressmakers at Fashion Frocks of Cincinnati, who produced 40,000 vests per month in the summer of 1944. A piece of flak "ripped the fabric and bent the steel plate but did not so much as bruise me," he wrote, "for which I thank God." My own crew confronted similar perils more times than I can recall.[6]

We sported another practical style of vest as well: the Mae West. This yellow rubber vest was slung over our heads and draped over our chests. The preserver inflated by pulling two cords at the base, allowing compressed CO_2 cannisters to expand double-breasted chambers. The vests took only three seconds to bulk up. A mouth valve maintained inflation in case of slow leaks. Younger readers might wonder who Mae West was and why a flotation device was named in her honor. One columnist predicted this conundrum that August. "The Mae West tradition is amazing and will even find its place in World War II history with mention made of Mae West life preservers," she speculated. "And possibly in the far future some research worker will come upon the term and hunt to discover how it got its name." If you fall within that category, I encourage you to commence searching. The amusing answer is easily found.[7]

Equipment inventory continued with an escape kit containing high-energy food bars, morphine syringes, gauze bandages, a compass, fishing line with hooks, and a silk map of France. If we crashed into a body of water, the fabric map would not bleed or wither under the adverse conditions.

Among the "pep pills" included in our emergency packages was Benzedrine, a central nervous stimulant now known as amphetamine. This performance-enhancing drug was accessible to servicemen on both sides years before its addictive qualities were widely understood by physicians. At least one of my crewmen abused the substance to combat post-traumatic stress, then known as battle fatigue. Many more self-medicated with hard liquor because men were conditioned not to express their troubled feelings to others.

Once equipment was distributed, transports shuttled crews to assigned aircraft. In many cases, the sun had not yet risen by that hour. Radio silence was strictly observed. Crews found their planes positioned on hardstands—well-spaced concrete pads connected by a paved road circling the field. Envision these slabs as circular parking spaces. Each bay held one bomber and was connected to the taxiway. Upon entering our plane via the bomb bay, we stored chutes and mission information. Crew members meanwhile reported the status of their stations. We pilots also conversed with the ground crew chief to discuss repairs undertaken since the previous flight.

The chief may have offered cautionary words such as, "Watch the left brake, it pulls a little." We conducted a visual inspection of the exterior for damage, tires, control surfaces, leaks, filler caps, and a host of other potential problems. We were always on the lookout for abnormalities. He walked us through engine temperature gauge checks, ignition checks, engine checks—the works.[8]

Down the field, officers in the control tower shot a flare skyward when we were to board the plane. Additional colored flares from the tower signaled to start engines, taxi, mission delayed or aborted. After the first flare, Lt. Predgen and I headed to the cockpit to scrutinize extensive checklists prior to takeoff. Flight engineer Lou Wagner drained fuel from each tank to eliminate any condensate. He also evaluated fuel levels, our oxygen, the generator, and much more. Meanwhile, gunners examined their turrets and ammunition. When the bombardier arrived, he checked the bomb load and safety pins. The process moved like clockwork.

All the while, ground crews were engaged in their own myriad responsibilities. If a plane had flown the day before, there might be battle damage to patch, engines to replace, or other maintenance to complete. Teams had to refuel, fill oxygen tanks, load bombs, clean windows, insert ammunition, inspect systems, and check engines. To shelter themselves against damp English weather, the versatile technicians had constructed sheds made from ammo boxes beside hardstands. They were always under pressure to have as many planes as possible ready for the latest operation. Sometimes mission plans were altered during the night. Consequently, crews rushed to redo bomb types, their quantity, and fuel load since weight was adjusted according to mission length. Mechanics sometimes went days without any worthwhile sleep. Their daily trials forged a brotherhood mirroring our own.

I was very close with my crewmates. An anecdote representative of our camaraderie occurred when our wily sergeants joined us in a bar intended exclusively for officers. We were separated only when a baton-wielding MP chased them off. As time permitted, we played softball and hit the towns to blow off steam. Removed from my real brothers, I found that the fellas filled a void in my personal life. I didn't make them salute me and I always felt at ease in their presence. When we were together, there was no acknowledgment of military hierarchy. Although our sergeants lived in different barracks, a sense of inseparability nonetheless prevailed. Both in and out of the plane, our tight-knit support system was a means to live, laugh, and survive.

Further description of our aircraft, the Consolidated B-24 Liberator, might be helpful. The plane had a wingspan of 110 feet, weighed 64,000 pounds when fully loaded, and was powered by four 1,200 horsepower radial engines. There were ten .50 caliber machine guns—two in each of the four turrets and two in the waist. Living arrangements within the Liberator were crude. There were no personal luxuries. The plane was meant to carry a heavy bombload and little else. Ten men climbed into the thin aluminum shell containing 8,000 pounds of bombs, up to 3,000 gallons of 100-octane fuel, thousands of heavy machine gun rounds, plus numerous oxygen tanks. Amenities were nonexistent. No pressurized cabin, no heat other than our suits, and no provisions for food or drink. Just men in a machine.

Before boarding, all were wise to take a leak since they might have to man a position for four to eight hours. Beer consumed the night before could be quite problematic. High altitude caused gases to expand, creating a "must" situation on the matter of relieving oneself. The lavatory was a funnel with a hose to the outside—which froze solid after the first tinkle. We generally dared not wet ourselves because of the small electrical systems wired throughout our flight suits. Airmen were supposed to use the latrines before missions. On one fateful occasion, I was so consumed with preparatory tasks that I forgot to make use of the men's room. I paid the price. Nature took its course on that very long flight. I suspect the reader will not think less of me for the offense.

Dilemmas of the bladder and bowels were universal. Pilot Will Plate of my bomb group explained the complicated relief process when the urge grew acute. "As we worked our way through the many layers of clothing, the frigid air reached the sought-after area before we did, and the object of the search went into hiding behind our hearts," he remembered. After considerable coaxing, the natural stream began, only to be halted by an inundated, frozen tube. Plate had no other option but to stop mid-flow and await his return to base. From then on, he and his co-pilot placed reused bomb fuse cans beside their cockpit seats as makeshift urinals.

On a separate mission, Plate's ball turret gunner, Ray Alnor, performed similar gymnastics while undressing in the subfreezing temperatures. The gunner successfully located a small box on board to drop a deposit. As the plane returned to base and descended to a lower altitude, the contents began to thaw and stink. Alnor peered out a window, spotted no aircraft nearby, and heaved the box into the sky. After debrief, he heard an enraged pilot exclaim, "If I ever find that son of a bitch who threw that box out the window, I'll kill him!" Unfortunately for that pilot, our B-24s lacked windshield wipers.[9]

Turret gunners like Alnor and our own Dick Bunch squeezed into their cramped nooks and generally remained in place the entire journey. Waist gunners had .50 cals jutting out open windows and were always on their toes. All flight controls were manual, with no power assist. The only way to move from the waist to the flight deck was via a narrow catwalk through the bomb bays. The singular route of going from the flight deck to the nose area was through a crawlspace next to a retracted nose wheel. Tail, waist, and ball gunners remained in the waist. The nose gunner, bombardier, and radio operator were stationed on the flight deck. The engineer and radioman assumed positions behind the pilots.

On the tarmac, we completed the mandatory takeoff checklist while watching for the designated flare color signifying "start engines." This list was in a pocket on my side of the plane. We would have been in trouble without that list. The many check procedures had to be confirmed verbally.

"Fuel," I said.

"Check," Predgen replied.

"Prop governors."

"Check."

"Key switches."

"Check."

"Flaps."

"Check."

"Booster pumps."

"Check."

At the signal, engines started in a prescribed sequence with a ground crew member standing by. As engine temperatures reached proper levels, each was tested at full takeoff power and then placed at an idle setting. Radio contact remained prohibited at this late stage of preparation. There was a constant fear of Germans eavesdropping on our chatter and trying to determine the day's mission.

As another mode of precaution, a member of the intelligence staff entered each plane to safety wire an IFF radio signaling device on the frequency for the day. IFF (Identification, Friend or Foe) transmitted a special signal to Allied radar screens. This was a crucial piece of technology because, prior to my arrival in Europe, German planes sometimes pursued American bomb groups back to England. I'm sure the Germans must have recovered hundreds of radio sets from downed aircraft and could consequently monitor American frequencies. Before IFF units were installed, GI radar technicians had no way of differentiating good guys from bad guys. Enemy pilots therefore squeezed between our bombers and picked them off, knowing our anti-aircraft guns could not engage without heavy risk of friendly fire.

One fateful evening, German fighters tracked the group back to the airfield at dusk. They strafed several planes in the landing pattern. Civilian residents referred to this episode as "Night of the Intruders." I once spoke with a local who was a teenager at the time. He was walking his date home that night when the action erupted. The couple was so alarmed by the commotion that they jumped into a roadside ditch for cover. Eventually, the girlfriend beckoned her companion to return to the path, for she felt little safety in the ditch. IFF sets were fitted to lessen the possibility of such surprises occurring again.

After those radios were wired up, ground crew personnel manually turned over the props. They then stood vigilantly with fire extinguishers as engines started. Lou Wagner walked to the waist, observed, listened to the engines, then reported to the cockpit. On three occasions, he expressed concern regarding the sound of an engine. In all three cases, the engine failed during the mission. Lou had a good ear for machinery. Yet the demand for us to fly was great. We flew unless technical problems were fully evident. Had crews been able to back out of missions due to slight inconsistencies, we would never have been near full strength.

We increased engine rotations per minute, checked the magneto drop on each engine, examined all instruments, and then set the engines at fast idle until the taxi signal was observed. When that signal was observed, we fell into the designated sequence. At a precise time, another colored flare signaled us to enter assigned takeoff positions. Excitement intensified. The task now was to send as many as thirty-six planes into the air in the shortest time possible. To accomplish this, two planes were always in takeoff position. The sea of rumbling aircraft made for an impressive sight at sunrise.

Takeoff was a continuous motion, with one plane in takeoff position and another on standby. As soon as a plane was little more than halfway down the runway (the point of no return), a green light flashed for the next one to go. For these purposes, a biscuit gun light was operated at the tower and aimed at a plane, flashing either red or green. Before receiving the green signal, engine controls were switched to full power. Both pilots had to stand on the brakes to hold their position and keep the plane reined in. The noise was overpowering.

With a green light, the brakes were released, and the plane leapt forward. We jolted in the cockpit seats. Our longest runway was 5,000 feet, which is not long at all. With a heavy B-24, we tended to use three-fourths of the runway before we pulled a takeoff at 100 or 120 miles per hour. These were tense moments with little room for technical hiccups. The flight engineer stood between the pilots on both landing and takeoff, continuously yelling out the air speed. If the plane wasn't up to the desired speed, we had to pull back. Takeoffs could be either exhilarating or horrifying.

After liftoff, power was reduced to maintain a steady climb to assembly altitude. The combined sound of 144 Pratt & Whitney engines renders an astounding roar for those listening and watching on the ground. Due to my headset, I couldn't hear any of them except the thrum of my own engines.

Each group had a special, stripped-down, brightly painted B-24 as an assembly plane for pilots to rally on. That bomber flew in a wide circle while firing designated flare colors. Our group's assembly plane was called *Lil' Cookie* and was adorned with large yellow polka dots. She needed to be highly visible. Now the task was to climb to assembly altitude in our assigned airspace while avoiding three dozen aircraft clustered in the same area. All pilots homed in on their assembly plane, forming up in three squadrons. Many men within the outfit flew *Lil' Cookie* over the months. Her rotating crew "measured the temperature, determined the wind direction and velocity, and passed that information to the base operations officer," remembered Will Plate. The lead plane sought out *Lil' Cookie* and relieved her. That lead ship then fired more flares so fellow ships could follow. When this formation was complete, the assembly plane returned home. We flew *Cookie* a couple of times. It was great. The poor bastards in other planes headed out but we landed and headed back to bed. Naturally, this duty did not count toward our quota of required combat missions.[10]

Our first plane was simply named *Jo*. The title was inherited from her previous crew. We never renamed any of our planes because we were replacements. I suppose changing the name of an aircraft was begging for bad luck. I never discovered who "Jo" was, but she must have meant a great deal to a man who previously piloted the ship. The signature was painted in bright cursive on the nose. Unlike many aircraft displaying saucy artwork of scantily clad women, Jo was quite chaste and lacked that style of sexual flair.

Some of the more theatrical names bestowed upon planes in our group were *Ace of Spades, Blackie's Bastards, Buckshot Annie, Consolidated Mess, Ike & Monty, Lethal Linda, Lonesome Polecat, Malfunction Junction, Myasis Draggin, Piccadilly Commando* (the nickname of any London prostitute), *Pregnant Peggy, Rum Runner, The Shaft,* and *Urgin Virgin*. Sensational names or imagery on some planes were purified to conform to public relations standards. "GI artists were ordered to put undies and bras on the hussies gracing the bombers," observed one newspaper that June. "They just won't let boys be boys," the periodical complained.[11]

But *Jo* also had a dark legacy. The skipper heard that the engineer from the plane's previous crew had been killed onboard. "A grim reminder of what happened was always evident when Wagner flew and could see the patched-up holes in the top turret dome," wrote Predgen. These were the small but troubling reminders that stood out to airmen before takeoff.[12]

For our many missions, a lead plane maneuvered to leave the English coast at a precise, pre-planned place and time to assume a position within the Second Air Division line. Ten to twelve airfields often composed a division. Each of those fields might have four squadrons. A squadron had fourteen crews. For a maximum effort mission, each group was supposed to send up three dozen planes, but this was rarely accomplished.

As soon as we were airborne, wheels were retracted to diminish drag, power was reduced, props were reset, mixture was adjusted, cowl flaps were closed, and flaps were raised. The pilot was prudent to take off while the co-pilot monitored all engine instruments with his hand on the throttles, ready to cut in case of trouble. All engine instruments were located on my side of the cockpit.

Scary moments occurred when we encountered faulty prop governors. A governor regulates the angle of the propeller blades, allowing a larger or smaller "bite" of the air. Sometimes these would go flat, and we'd lose all power. This forced us to jump on a feather button to reduce drag. When the engine produces power, the blades slice perpendicular to the horizon, allowing the propeller to "pull" the plane through the air. Whenever we had to reduce drag, the blades were feathered by adjusting them to be parallel with the horizon, acting as small "wings" to render minimal resistance through the air. This action diminished the dangers of props windmilling and breaking. Luckily, we never lost an engine on takeoff. Nevertheless, surging off the runway with a full load of gas, bombs, and ammunition could be a dicey proposition. We always remained alert.[13]

I've never been an excitable man. I have the tendency to keep my calm and not become flustered. I suspect that instinct is linked to the war years because I had to stay focused and bypass so many emotional triggers. I had to be calm for my men. (In all the years since, I've tried to do the same for my family.)

At about 5,000 feet, the waist gunner armed our bombs by pulling safety pins and saving them for possible reuse. Gunners armed their weapons while we set the autopilot. If control cables were ever shot out, there was a chance we could flip a switch and let the autopilot hold the plane level until we bailed out. As we approached 10,000 feet, everyone went on oxygen. Some may have already masked up if they were feeling groggy from the lack of heavy air. Predgen or I called for another crew check to ensure all oxygen systems were functional.

A group formation looked like this:

(17)

By that time, we gained a sense of the larger situation forming around us. Examine my hand-drawn sketch above to visualize the vista. The right squadron flew high, and the left squadron flew low whenever the lead plane made a turn. Low squadron slid underneath, and the right squadron slid above. This way, all three squadrons could maintain the same speeds, and nobody would stall out.

This configuration eased the planes' abilities to maintain consistent air speeds and avoid collisions. During one operation, we were in the extreme left position of the low squadron (known as "coffin corner"). The lead plane made a left turn. Our squadron leader did not slip under. This forced us to lose airspeed, stall out, and plummet a mile before recovering. Luckily, we were still over England.

The lead plane typically jockeyed for a precise time and altitude to cross a coastal departure point. There may have been as many as fifteen B-24 groups comprising a division line, which stretched out many miles. In addition, there could be as many, if not more, B-17 groups in the air at the same moment. The result could be an air armada of more than 1,000 planes.

We steadily ascended to 18,000 feet, and then 20,000 feet as we neared the continent. We still had a long way to go. During the climb, gunners test-fired their weapons. The administrative officer remained on an outside frequency while the engineer officer stayed on the intercom. On the radio, I regularly announced, "Crew check, please." Then each man, from nose to tail, answered one-by-one to indicate his preparedness or lack thereof.

"Bombardier, okay."

"Navigator, okay."

"Radioman, okay."

And so on. If a station did not report, another crew member was assigned to investigate. These checks were more frequent when we were under fire. Predgen and I took turns flying the bomber during long missions. Since there was no power-assist, sharing responsibilities on an eight-hour mission was essential. We punched each other in our arms when we were ready to shift duties. Whenever we swapped roles, we likewise flipped switches so we could communicate with the proper parties inside or outside the plane.

Reaching the continent, we maintained a wary watch for the enemy. There was often a sense that they lurked in the distant haze, ready to spring their trap. Germans placed four-gun 88mm batteries along the coast to welcome us. Their job was to destroy lead planes but, of course, they would obliterate anything they could strike. One of the batteries at Abbeville, France, was especially lethal. The occupiers received their share of devastation as well. When the little town of Abbeville was finally liberated, its citizenry claimed to have been bombed 150 times throughout the war.[14]

Our concerns extended well beyond the coast. Flak could be encountered at any time due to a lack of intelligence or lead planes flying off course. A good formation was always sensible because fighter attacks were likewise possible all the way in and out.

Escort coverage was a welcome sight across the division line. On prolonged trips, fighters worked in relays. Some were assigned to escort us from points A to B and return to England. Second-wave aircraft then escorted from points C to D, repeating the procedure on the return. Shorter missions were completed in as little as four hours. Longer missions—like those to Munich or Berlin—might have taken six or eight hours. Those hours tallied only for actual flying time. We sometimes sat in our plane for twelve hours total when accounting for preparation and return protocols.

Flying in proximity on high alert of enemy attacks kept everyone on edge. On a few occasions, the unexpected occurred when a lead plane took a position too close to the group ahead. Prop wash caused severe turbulence, making formation flying a white-knuckle job. A prop wash is when heavy winds form behind a spinning propeller. If a pilot lands too close to a plane in front of him, he catches turbulence from those props. A friend of mine who flew a smaller aircraft was once caught in such a whirlwind and his plane flipped. He did not survive.

Our next major threshold was the initial point of the bomb run. Distance to the target could be fifty miles or more. While on a run, a tight formation was necessary to deliver an effective bombing pattern. A change in altitude at the start of a run was sometimes used to avoid radar-controlled flak. We lucked out more than once. During one mission, we descended 1,000 feet and then observed a terrific barrage 1,000 feet above us moments later.

Stomachs churned when we saw dark flak clouds dead ahead. The German 88mm was considered the finest artillery piece of World War II. We experienced the gun's effectiveness firsthand while dodging its wrath.

"As long as you just see black, the flak won't hit you," was a common explanation to rookie crews. "When you see red, look out!"[15]

Spotting the red core was always an unnerving sight because the closeness of the blast guaranteed damage. A single hit could cripple a ship, drop the plane out of formation, and render it vulnerable bait for the Luftwaffe. But there was little we could do other than keep our heads straight and disregard the worst possible outcomes. "That detached feeling that it can't happen to you probably is the key to the mental quirk which keeps most crewmen from going 'flak happy,'" observed air correspondent Walter Cronkite.[16]

Unfortunately, our close-knit patterns made running the gauntlet even more hazardous. The intensity of destructive bursts was normally in proportion to the importance of a target. If we headed to a hot spot like Berlin, Magdeburg, Brunswick, or the Ruhr Valley, we were guaranteed to run through showers of hot metal. In fact, the Ruhr Valley was known as "Flak Alley" by our men. During my group's tour of duty, flak accounted for over 82 percent of American bomber crew casualties.

The best-defended targets were generally fuel depots, tank factories, railroad yards, and aircraft assembly plants. Interestingly, the group encountered the least resistance from the Luftwaffe when we attacked its air bases. The reasoning? German pilots remained grounded because they feared having nowhere to land if they took flight during our attacks. In any case, the enemy had a thorough ability to bloody our noses regardless of whether they dispatched planes to intercept us.[17]

At some point on the bomb run, a code word signaled all planes to drop chaff. As soon as the target appeared, the lead bombardier took charge of the aircraft. He engaged the Norden bombsight. This high-tech gadget used an analog computer to recalculate the impact point as our flight path shifted. Every adjustment the bombardier made was transferred to the controls via the autopilot. When the crosshairs of the device centered, the bombs were released, thereby signaling all other bombardiers to salvo their payloads. As soon as the formation cleared the target area, the lead plane made a gradual, prearranged turn for home—and hopefully away from exploding shells.

Mid-air collisions were less frequent than flak but no less dangerous. The likelihood of these accidents multiplied when a plane was struck by the enemy and veered into the path of a sister aircraft. But most of these crashes were caused by poor visibility, airmen not following orders, thick plane concentration, or pure bad luck. Considering how dense the air traffic of East Anglia was in 1944, many airmen were surprised there were not more mid-air collisions.[18]

Some lead planes had crews specifically trained for radar-controlled bombing (also known as Pathfinder bombing). Electronic countermeasure planes were scattered along the line to monitor, intercept, and jam German radio transmissions. Sections normally split off from the division line to strike different targets. After bombing, they fell back into line for the return trip. Even after we dropped payloads, we maintained a state of alertness for both fighters and flak.

After departing the continent, the formation initiated a slow descent. When we dipped below 10,000 feet, oxygen masks came off. This act moderately eased our tensions as it usually signified the worst was behind us.

At that moment, I sometimes treated myself to a candy bar or cigar. At our post exchange, we were permitted to purchase five packs of cigarettes per week. Eight out of our ten-man crew smoked cigarettes, but I did not. One cigar was worth one pack of cigarettes. Early on in our missions, I purchased one cigar per week and gifted four packs of cigarettes to my men. As our mission tally grew, however, I started buying five cigars a week and the crew received nothing extra. I suspect tobacco was used as a calming method for some. I always found relief in lighting up on the way home from a mission. The smoke usually drifted back through the plane to the point where I'd pick up a lot of static on the radio. Tobacco habits formed during the war led to my children growing up in cigar and pipe smoke.

Service members develop unusual traditions in battle. Some guys pocketed rabbit's feet or religious medallions as good luck charms. "Closely related by the motive to influence the future mystically are wartime military superstitions," veteran Paul Fussell noted of these rituals. "Rigorous attention to such usages will guarantee for the believer a lucky, seamless personal narrative, enabling him to come out of the war as undamaged as he went in." I never subscribed to such fantasy. I did, however, wear one of Irene's rings on my left pinky finger. Looking down at the small piece of jewelry always afforded a degree of comfort and reminded me what I was fighting for.[19]

A portrait of Irene taken while I was away.
John Homan collection. (18)

After recrossing the English coast on such missions, we neared our field and braced for landing. Often, we descended through a thick blanket of clouds. When there was a low ceiling, the lead plane circled above the overcast while subsequent planes peeled off at intervals of so many seconds. They headed out over the North Sea at a given air speed and a rate of descent until water was visible. On a dull, cloudy day, we had difficulty distinguishing gray sky from gray water. To overcome Mother Nature's hurdles, each base had a "buncher," a radio compass homing signal. When tuned in, the buncher automatically pointed to the station. During the descent, there was a plane about thirty seconds ahead of us and another thirty seconds behind.

Our plane returns to Halesworth on a gray English day.
John Homan collection. (19)

Aircraft with mechanical problems or wounded aboard shot red flares to request landing priority. There were two emergency fields in England for crippled planes. These had extra wide, 10,000-foot runways with 5,000-foot grass over-shoots at each end. Before landing, gunners cleared and safe-tied their .50 calibers.

If a mission had to be aborted while in flight, pilots landed with a heavy fuel load plus bombs that had to be deactivated by replacing pins prior to landing. Individual planes aborted for various reasons. Ultimately, the decision was left to the pilot whether to drop his bombs in the North Sea. I once saw a plane return with a full bomb load and level off too high. It dropped hard on the runway, blowing the tires. The ordnance shattered its shackles, smashed through the bomb bay doors, skidded down the runway, and rolled under another plane. Ground crewmen rightfully disdained removing bombs that could have been discarded elsewhere. In most instances though, touching down on the runway offered mental relief. One more mission accomplished meant one step closer to home.

Following landing, we taxied to our assigned hardstand, filled out a mechanical status form, conversed with the crew chief about any problems, reassembled our gear, exited by way of the bomb bay, and inspected outside for battle damage. Predgen and I always strategized with flight engineer Lou Wagner after each mission to devise new ways to better our chances of survival. Along these lines, we also afforded Lou some stick time so he could fly in case the pilot and co-pilot were both incapacitated.

During long waits on the flight line, I implemented a personal drill method on my own initiative. I often closed my eyes in the cockpit and memorized the location of all instrument controls in case I was blinded in flight or didn't have time to think. Every part of my job needed to be second nature. Running my hand up the right wall were the four Ignition Switches, then the Emergency Ignition Switch Bar, then the Main Storage Battery Switches, then the Heater and Defroster Switches, and onward. The various throttles were in the middle between the two seats. I committed all these and more to memory with constant repetition.

We returned all our equipment and were then transported to debriefing for interrogation about flak locations, lost

aircraft, plane bailouts, fighter activity, and bombing observations. (Records of downed aircraft and parachute sightings
were used by the Red Cross to check on German reports
regarding prisoners of war.)

Outside, we hopped into a truck and were transported to
the mess hall. Our stomachs growled upon entry. At last, our
weary, hungry men queued in line for chow. After eating, we
stumbled back to the squadron area to check the bulletin
board. If the crew was alerted for the next day, the routine
started all over again in a few hours. We hastily washed and
collapsed into our cots. We survived the day, but who knew
what tomorrow might bring?

CHAPTER 5

The Nut House

An unpleasant, bright light shined in my face. "Sir," a voice whispered.

I rolled over in my wool blanket. "Sir," the sergeant tugged on my shoulder. "Mission this morning, sir," he reminded.

I grumbled, wearily dragged myself out of the sack, and dressed in the dark. The date was July 6, 1944. That early summer morning stands out in my memories. It marked my maiden mission into battle.

Only the day before, we learned that the ship of Lt. Harold Turpin, a fellow officer from our days at Casper, was shot down on its first mission. Men on our crew had good friends among the fatalities. This news set an ominous tone for our own initial operation.[1]

We were certainly not alone in our struggles. Over one quarter of the 1.5 million American service members in England belonged to the Army Air Forces. In the first half of 1944, over 10,000 of these airmen and 3,000 of their planes were lost over Fortress Europe. The war's escalation in France marked new chapters of conflict threatening air and ground combatants alike. On these hardships, Lt. Bert Stiles reflected, "Blood is the same whether it spills on aluminum or Normandy mud. It takes guts whether you fly a million-dollar airplane or wade in slow with a fifty-dollar rifle." All that mattered was to win, he argued, win now so there would never be another war. This sentiment reflected a binding resolve among men and women of the various branches.[2]

I do not consider myself a hero, but I certainly lived among many heroic individuals. No figure in the 489th Bomb Group loomed larger in this regard than deputy commander Lt. Col. Leon Vance. The officer was a no-nonsense, twenty-seven-year-old West Pointer whose plane was *The Sharon D*, so named after his baby daughter. His coolness in action earned him immeasurable respect. Given that Vance was to become the most honored and commemorated man in our entire unit, his tale is worth sharing here. This inspiring episode highlights the caliber of men in our ranks.

Three weeks before I joined the bomb group, it was ordered to strike V-1 flying bomb sites near Wimereaux, France, as a pre-D-Day diversion on June 5. Lt. Louis Mazure was in the lead Liberator. Vance joined Mazure's crew as overall mission

Lt. Col. Leon Vance.
Air Force photo. (20)

commander. Once over the target, red-hot enemy bursts commenced. The wicked black puffs of shrapnel had the capacity to convert a bomber into a thirty-ton colander. At this precarious point, Mazure's bomb bay doors jammed. Because his was the lead aircraft, no other planes in formation dropped their payloads. The bomber circled around, and the German gunners soon had it zeroed. The air itself seemed aflame when flak erupted in the head plane's open bottom. Mazure was struck in the temple and killed instantly. The co-pilot was grievously wounded. Vance was likewise hit when flak mutilated his right foot, leaving it dangling only by a few bloody strands of flayed muscle.

Meanwhile, a shell sliced the fuel lines, spurting gasoline out the bomb bay. "Shortly all other motors cut out and there we were over the Channel but with virtually no airplane," crewman John Kilgore recalled. Three of the four engines were lost, and the right rudder was gone. Engineer Earl Huppie stood precariously on the open catwalk attempting to plug the gushes of gasoline with his field jacket. His drenched trousers and shirttails flapped fiercely in the high winds. The crew was bathed in fuel. "We were soaked with it. The plane was like a sieve. One spark and we would have all been charcoal," Kilgore admitted. "To take a swim was one thing but to catch fire was more than we could stomach."

Vance pried his mutilated foot from the jagged metal and hobbled to the pilot's seat. The colonel promptly cut off the switches, feathered the prop, and headed into the wind. Navigator Pete Henry tightened a belt around Vance's thigh when the colonel went into shock from blood loss. As the returning, crippled aircraft sputtered over England, Vance ordered all to bail out. Believing a seriously wounded radioman was still aboard, the colonel opted to turn the plane and ditch the "flying boxcar" into the sea. Upon impact, the plane exploded into bits and hurled Vance from the cockpit. Remaining afloat with his Mae West, the injured officer rested on a battered plane wing until it sank. Unable to locate the wounded radio operator who was not there in the first place, Vance feebly paddled toward shore until an RAF seaplane fished him from the choppy waters.

Bailed-out crewmen were scattered all over. "Although I broke my leg after landing on the hard ground, I was lucky," Kilgore confessed. "I landed just twenty feet from a British minefield." Although he survived, the battered and bruised Vance was in far worse shape. His shredded foot was amputated. But his selflessness saved several lives.[3]

This incident was the talk of the base when I arrived at Halesworth weeks later. Vance's deeds set a very high bar for replacements like me.

Slated to receive a prosthetic foot, Vance started rehabilitation in England and was scheduled to return home. Fellow survivor Pete Henry visited him in the hospital. "The colonel told me that he was eager to get back into combat and that once he was well, he would," Henry recalled. "He then expressed his gratitude to me for having saved his life, promising to put me in for a very high decoration." The two men shook hands and expressed hopes of meeting once more.[4]

They never crossed paths again. After Vance received medical treatment, his transport plane en route to America disappeared on a flight between Iceland and Newfoundland on July 26, 1944. All hands were lost and never recovered. For the beloved colonel to survive all that he did and then perish during his return home was a twist of exceedingly tragic irony.

I had passing interactions with Vance before he went missing and greatly admired his gallantry. He became something of a role model for all of us recently arrived pilots. Decades later, Vance's daughter, Sharon, attended many of our group reunions. I became well acquainted with her over games of golf. Sharon was presented her dad's posthumous Medal of Honor when she was only three years old. I suspect her participation in our reunions was a means to connect with the father she never really knew.

At those same reunions, my wife often asked my fellow veterans how many missions they completed. She never did meet anyone who flew more strategic missions than I did in such a short amount of time. In 1943, the B-17 *Memphis Belle* gained national acclaim when she became one of the first American bombers to fulfill a twenty-five-mission quota. Her crew became the subject of an iconic documentary and returned to America with great fanfare, hoisted as poster boys for war bond sales. Unlike the fortunate members of *Belle*, I could not head home after twenty-five missions. Much had changed in the year since. Generals realized they could no longer forfeit our skills after two dozen missions. Attrition rates were too high for experienced crews to be released. The mandatory number for a full tour of duty thereby rose to thirty. The odds seemed increasingly pitted against us.

Two days before my first mission, men on base celebrated the 168th birthday of the United States with a wild Independence Day volley. Neal Sorensen, another new man to the outfit, claimed he was initially hesitant to participate in the festivities due to his "greenness." Seasoned crews were unrestrained in their patriotic revelry. The American Revolution was partially renewed when British Home Guard arrived on scene. Oblivious to our national holiday, they were alarmed by the fusillade of flare and pistol shots and rushed to the rescue. Their angst was remedied with a few complimentary pints and some friendly ribbing from the former colonists. The celebration was not without repercussion. On July 5, as

Sorensen recalled, some "sniffers came through our Quonset huts to check firearms. The penalty was five pounds for the group fund, plus a modest chewing out!"[5]

The next day, that of my inaugural mission, was more restrained. A sergeant awoke us at 1:30 in the morning. All was grim and quiet. We carried out what would become pre-dawn routines. At briefing, we learned that our crew's first target was Germany's Kiel shipyards on the southeastern stretch of the city's canal. The site was considered by some as the most heavily defended waterway in the world. The canal was a significant military landmark because it connected the Baltic and North Seas. In the days prior, RAF Mosquito bomb-ers dropped mines and blocked traffic in the canal for well over one week. The feat reportedly logjammed the flow of Swedish iron ore and coal. Any bit of infrastructural damage inflicted on the enemy's home turf was good news to us.[6]

Our job now was to perpetuate that destruction. Lt. Harry Wagnon of my group was thrilled by the prospect. "At last," he recalled of July 6, "we were sent to attack the submarine pens and port facilities at Kiel. That was just what I wanted: an important target on German soil, and one that would require only a shallow penetration of enemy territory. [This] was my idea of a dream come true." Twenty-two aircraft from our outfit set forth on the task that morning.[7]

I'll never forget how beautiful and bright the day was. In fact, the initial serenity of the crystal blue skies was rather disarming. Our route took us all the way across the North Sea to Denmark. This course was chosen to remain beyond the reach of enemy fighters for as long as possible. The smoothness of the flight made me think this mission stuff wasn't going to be too hazardous to my health. We reached the initial point without a single shot fired at us. *This isn't so bad,* I naively thought.

That gullible delusion changed in a hurry as we approached the city. The Germans anticipated our arrival. They ignited a thick smokescreen to conceal the target. Their guns unleashed a piercing barrage. With those opening shots I endured my first taste of battle.

Exploding enemy shells grew larger and more numerous with each passing mile. The sensation made for quite the psychological experience. Our plane encountered heavy, accurate flak over Kiel, and sustained no less than eleven holes in the ship. Shards of metal ripped through our aluminum fuselage like knives through tinfoil. One twisted chunk severed the waist gunner's microphone cord. Another precariously bounced off the belly turret. By the end of our tour of duty, ball turret gunner Dick Bunch was a nervous wreck. He saw every bit of swirling combat from his retractable sphere beneath us. All he could do was shoot and imagine the most gruesome outcome. Continuous thoughts about potential dismemberment could scrape at a man's soul. I considered myself comparatively lucky. I generally focused on my instruments and had less opportunity to immediately ponder the likelihood of death.

Yet there certainly were terrifying moments that widened my eyes. As we neared the target, I gazed up and saw a B-17 group drop its ordnance right through our formation. Their bombs were only yards away from plowing into us. A hit would have meant certain death. My first mission nearly ended by being obliterated by my own fellow airmen.

I had the sudden realization, "Damn, this *can* be hazardous after all!" Still, our crew took the incident in stride. For whatever reason, I was not afraid in that moment. Perhaps my adrenaline and concentration were too intense for me to be consumed by dread.

Harry Wagnon's team was similarly galvanized by the wave of violence. Wagnon expressed his ardent desire to pulverize the submarine pens. His ambition was handicapped by the mass of smoke still cloaking the area. Short on time, the officer rendered a judgment call: "I didn't want to drop our bombs in the water, and I didn't want to take them back to Halesworth either," he later explained. The pilot therefore ordered his salvo to be released. "No crew ever made more of a blind drop than we did that day at Kiel," he acknowledged. Wagnon had no clue where his bombs landed. The sub docks? A neighboring residential area? In his opinion, it did not matter. "Anything in Germany was fair game at that time of the war," he confessed. Wagnon spotted black billows rising above the smokescreen. He concluded, "I know we hit the place because water doesn't burn."[8]

Taking subsequent battles into account, this seven-hour mission was an easy one. The Associated Press thereafter described how our July 6 assault on Kiel was part of a much broader thrust into Germany, France, and Italy that consisted of 3,000 heavy bombers. The scale of this undertaking still boggles the imagination.[9]

Back at Halesworth, we were greeted with cheerful pats on our backs. Not a single plane from our group was lost. At most debriefings, there was a bottle of whiskey on each table as reward. I took a heavy gulp after this first mission but was so keyed up that the beverage did not sit well in my stomach. That day marked the first and only time I consumed alcohol at debriefing.

Looking back, I cannot comprehend how I returned to base and simply fell asleep that night. The experience should have rattled me to the core. Perhaps renowned wartime reporter Ernie Pyle best analyzed my condition. He wrote, "Moral: always be too sleepy to give a damn." No matter how fatigued some men were, though, sleep often evaded them. They relived missions in their minds. They dreaded the next journey into fire-filled skies. "I lay down on the cot and wished I could go to sleep, but that was impossible for me, although some probably could," 489th veteran Jim Davis recorded. "So many thoughts are rushing through your mind." First and foremost, he was "always aware that tomorrow might end up in a disaster."[10]

Regrettably, disaster did await several of our men the next day—July 7. We were beckoned from bed at 2 a.m. As Davis acknowledged, our existence was an exercise of perennial sleep deprivation. We were initially informed that our unwelcome awakening would come at 12:30 that night, so the additional ninety minutes of slumber was an unexpected indulgence. The bit of extra rest was highly warranted when considering what was to come.

For all the worst reasons, the mission to Aschersleben was unforgettable. The flak was furious. The Luftwaffe engaged our plane for the first time. German aircraft charged our division line head-on as if in a jousting duel. Dogfights cut in and out of our formation with astonishing speed. Men fell from planes with their chutes on fire. The group on our right lost over 100 airmen. And then there was Lt. Frank Fulks's chewed up bomber—its top turret eviscerated and the gunner within beheaded. His bright red blood smeared toward the plane's tail and presented a ghoulish contrast against the bright sky. I could hardly absorb the gory sight outside my window. The scene was otherworldly, both grotesque and compelling.

On subsequent flights, occasional reminders of the slain gunner drifted into my busy thoughts. I shook myself and tried to think of something else. I could not allow such images to haunt me. I had a job to do. There was no choice but to move on and repress the bad dream.

"A day I'll never forget," similarly admitted our flight engineer, Lou Wagner. "We escaped by a miracle," he recorded in his logbook. The death of the turret operator was imprinted in Lou's memories as well. "The rush of air caused all of his body's blood to be flung out on the fuselage. It was an awful sight to see," he wrote. "I hope that if I have to go, that it is quick. This mission was rough, I'll never forget it."[11]

In preparing this book, I at last learned the backstory of that ill-fated turret operator whose grisly end I witnessed. The dead gunner in Fulks's plane was a once-robust sergeant named Paul W. Redden. A blond-haired preacher's son and star athlete, he had enrolled at Oregon State College prior to joining the Air Forces. One week prior to his death, Redden observed his first wedding anniversary. His wife, Dorothy, was his high school sweetheart. Following their marriage in May 1943, she followed him to all his stateside military postings to delay separation. She dutifully remained with him until he departed for Europe in the spring of 1944. Dorothy received notice of her husband's demise thirteen days after he was killed. Redden was only twenty-one, never to celebrate another anniversary alongside his bride. His tragedy, in so many ways, is the story of the Second World War. Fulks did not make it home either. He died in a plane collision that September.[12]

There was so little time to mourn. We were up at 1 a.m. the following morning and were instructed to bomb a three-span masonry bridge and two railroad bridges at Nanteuil-sur-Marne, a picturesque French commune on the Marne River, located approximately forty-five miles northeast of Paris. The day was a dreary one. Soupy weather beleaguered us across the entire country, and we could not see the targets. Visibility was practically non-existent. To our dismay, there was no option but to abort the mission and return to base.

After our experiences the day before, we were all hyper-alert, peering for enemy fighters in the haze. I increasingly evaluated the Germans with a "dog eat dog" mentality. If we didn't shoot them, they were going to shoot us. Kill or be killed. The harsh arithmetic was brutally simple. This newfound disdain and trepidation of the Luftwaffe may have contributed to an act of misidentification on my part. During our July 8 mission, I called the top and nose gunners, alerting them of two "bogeys" at ten o'clock high. They called back reporting they couldn't see anything. After rudely accusing the crewmen of poor eyesight, I noticed the bogeys were not moving. On closer inspection, I was looking at two specks on the windshield. I radioed the gunners back and confidently declared, "It's okay, fellas, they went away."

We were not yet out of the woods. Just after turning the plane around, propellers one and three ran away. When a prop runs away, its RPM exceeds normal range and can become uncontrollable and violently detach. In simpler terms, imagine a bicycle moving down a steep hill in low gear. The pedals will spin wildly and the cyclist can lose control. We had to bring the props back in with feather buttons and sweated them all the way home. To make a precarious situation even more so, some light but accurate flak was encountered along the French coast. Elsewhere, five of our aircraft suffered minor damage. We landed with an 8,000-pound bomb load, which always posed additional hazards.

What factors dictated whether we retained or disposed of our bombs when a mission was scrubbed in-flight? We never

returned to base with a full bomb load if an engine was out or
if fuel was leaking. Bombs were dumped into the North Sea
when necessary. Luckily, we suffered no leaks or engine failures this round. Not all were as fortunate during our first week
of combat.

On July 9, camp water restrictions imposed several days
earlier were lifted and we could shower again. The water was
ice cold and we heated it with 100-octane fuel via a copper
coil. The next morning, our mission for Calais was scrubbed
shortly after briefing. Poor weather persisted. The short break
allowed Predgen and me to attend a tea dance at the officers'
club. Later, we swiped a vehicle and sneaked into town. We
compensated for the free-spirited R&R with a trifecta of strikes
into southern and western Germany over the following days.[13]

We were blessed with a 4 a.m. wakeup on the 11th of July.
This was sleeping in when compared to previous missions. The
target was Germany's third-largest city: Munich. In addition
to being a highly populous metropolitan area, Munich was a
major rail center in southern Germany, a junction connected
to the Brenner Pass through the Alps. Symbolically speaking,
Munich was also the birthplace of the Nazi Party. We took the
war straight to the enemy's doorstep.

Our flight was chock full of drama and frustration. After
we took off and reached oxygen altitude, one of our crewmen
announced over the intercom that he was unable to locate his
oxygen mask. No one could find the mask or a spare. If we
continued to rise, the man would have died.

What were the skipper and I to do? For better or worse, we opted to turn back and land. We retrieved a new mask and hurriedly took off on a wild goose chase to relocate the group—now far ahead of us. Our efforts were futile, and we eventually returned to Halesworth. Even if we had discovered the group, we probably would have depleted our fuel before we reached England. We were in trouble either way.

As was to be expected in such circumstances, we were promptly summoned to the commanding officer's shack for the most intense chewing out I witnessed during the war.

"I should have you all court-martialed!" he yelled as we stood at nervous attention. He informed us in very clear and colorful language the repercussions of a repeat transgression. "If this ever happens again," he warned, "you better just throw the son of a bitch out of the plane!" Although I suspect there was a hint of hostile exaggeration in this demand, I cannot say for certain. In any case, the CO's point was clear: Don't turn back unless you're told to turn back. We never pulled such a stunt again.

Not until many years later at a reunion did I learn that the offender who "misplaced" his mask did so deliberately. He was guided by the correct assumption that "losing" his oxygen kit would spare him a trek into the flak zone. Upon learning of this misbehavior, I grew even more agitated by the fact that the guilty crewman was present at our reunion. I had to restrain my anger and quietly keep my distance from the man so as not to assail him before our fellow veterans. The decades separating us from the incident did not lessen the sense of betrayal. Then again, we were a rookie crew. Foolish nervousness had the capacity to grip anyone.

That July 11 flight was perhaps the first 1,000-plane mission to Munich. Our group suffered thirteen battle-damaged ships. A missing oxygen mask spared our plane from being among them. At the same time, the troubled journey did not count toward our required number of missions. The crewman's misdeed only prolonged our time away from home.

A comeuppance arrived the following day when we were again instructed to strike Munich. This was to be a nine-hour mission conducted by radar bombing. The radar was used to navigate features on the terrain to provide our bearing. This was the longest combat flight we had yet flown, and we came within thirty-five miles of Switzerland. Flak was heavy over the target at the city center, but we were spared any damage and thankfully encountered no enemy fighters. Some of the German explosives were quite unusual in appearance and application. A group after-action report stated, "Balls of fire were seen suspended from a parachute." These small bombs, about the size of hand grenades, burst after floating in the air for a brief period. Some airmen wondered what other death-dealing devices the Germans had up their sleeves.[14]

While returning to England, I heard a B-17 from a different outfit radio in. The plane had its oxygen shot out and was forced to descend to a lower altitude. Her crew required fighter coverage. The Fortress was flying just slightly above some cloud cover when she was picked up by very accurate radar-controlled anti-aircraft guns. Then, like bats out of hell, two American P-38 Lightnings flew in to rescue the imperiled bomber. The fighters took turns flying beneath the B-17 to misdirect the flak on a vigorous pursuit until the Fortress cleared the area. This is the essence of teamwork.

When we took off that morning, our meteorologists predicted that a stalled weather front over Ireland would remain stationary. Unfortunately, inclement conditions regained momentum during the mission and hovered over eastern England. The clouds were low and heavy. Nearing base, our planes peeled off at thirty-second intervals, letting down through a solid haze over the North Sea. A radio compass allowed us to home in on the base. In the middle of each base was a transmitter that emitted a signal. Our Loop Antenna above the waist gunner helped us find home.

We cautiously set the rate of descent at a given airspeed until we finally saw the North Sea from a mere 200 feet altitude. At that moment, our crew spotted a downed B-24 in the drink. Perhaps her rate of descent was too great, and the pilots could not pull up in time. Coordinates of the crashed plane were immediately dispatched to air-sea rescue. Our ambition now was to avoid a similar fate. None of us wished to test the effectiveness of the Mae West life preserver.

Matters grew tense. Dusk settled and visibility further deteriorated. As we neared the field, a dark hulk flashed by at a distance too close for comfort. The shadowy aircraft dashing through the mist must have been another B-24. Soon, the mystery plane was no longer detectable. We crossed over the landing runway at ninety degrees, made a standard 270-degree turn, and took the runway heading. Red flares shot upward to expose the shrouded strip for wandering pilots. This infrequent act undertaken by the control tower underscored the precariousness of the situation. The ceiling was no more than 300 feet. We cautiously dipped from the gray murk with white knuckles on the controls. We landed without further delay and breathed a collective sigh of relief. That evening was as scary as any episode of combat.

Only one week into our missions, the psychological fatigue of rough landings and battle was already apparent. Some men in our crew were unsettled by the destruction they both sustained and delivered. The "Germans say we hit orphanages, hospitals, and an old maids' home," Lou Wagner penned on July 12. "I wonder today about how many persons I have been indirectly responsible for killing. We really never think about it." Indeed, these were harmful thoughts I tried to avoid.[15]

Miserable weather hounded the 489th throughout that week. My crew was briefed for an afternoon mission to bomb a bridge south of Paris, but the flight was scrubbed. We were always thankful when an operation was cancelled. We returned to bed.

Other squadrons in the group, however, ventured to Saarbrücken, Germany, on July 13. Once more, planes relied on radar bombing due to thick overcast. The 489th sent thirty-five planes into battle that day and one-third of them failed to release their bombs due to mechanical problems. One crew confronting multiple technical failures bailed out over England. Another Liberator in our squadron, *Lethal Linda*, suffered a direct enemy hit to the nose. The plane lost its oxygen, and the windshields were blown to bits. Sgt. John Nilsson served as nose gunner on that flight and was terribly wounded. His lower leg was practically severed by an explosion. Somehow, Nilsson continued to man his gun until danger subsided. Crewmates were simultaneously busted up and covered in broken glass. The gunner was left exposed to the elements in the shattered nose.

Nilsson remained calm. He slowly disconnected his heated boot and removed it. The cold thereby coagulated the spurts of blood. The freezing temperatures saved his life. Astonishingly, Nilsson's comrades didn't learn of his wounding until fifteen minutes after the fact. Not until letdown did the gunner announce, "Will someone help me out of the nose, cause they blew off my foot." The man somehow resisted any urge to cry out in pain or yelp for aid until then. "He didn't whimper once," his captain recalled, "just took it like a man." Nilsson rightfully received the Silver Star for his quiet yet determined heroism.[16]

Not all airmen were graced with such durability that day. One of the most tragic episodes involved a ship called *Phony Express*. Piloted by Lt. Philip Sherwood, the plane had engine trouble, lost power, and backtracked to England. A second engine sputtered off and on. Tail gunner Ted Harris, a friend of mine, recalled what happened next. "We were over the North Sea approaching base," said Harris, "when Lt. Sherwood called the crew to discuss whether or not we should dump the bombs in the sea before landing." The lieutenant claimed the plane was handling well under adverse conditions and convinced the crew to keep four 2,000-pound bombs onboard. This was a major mistake. As previously mentioned, landing with a full payload during engine trouble posed immense risk. Sadly, the crew of *Phony Express* paid dearly for the error.

The men assumed landing positions as they circled the base. Moments later, their aircraft ran short of the runway and plowed headlong into a farmer's field. The rear bulkhead "flew open, and green vegetation started flying in, just like cut grass leaving a rotary lawn mower," Harris remembered. The gunner was thrown clear of the fiery wreckage. His broken body was thereafter rushed to the hospital and placed in a full body cast. None of his crewmates survived. Thankfully, Ted overcame his injuries, and I had the chance to lunch with him at his winter home in Naples, Florida, after the war. He was damn lucky.[17]

That same week, Keith Turnham of the 489th was asked to serve on the cleanup team for another ship that had crashed in the vicinity. No matter the plane or the circumstances of its demise, wreck sites were deeply disturbing places. Each man on the team was handed a bag and gloves before they set out to locate dismembered body parts. The field "smelled like Death Row one week old," Turnham remembered. "The odor turned my stomach. When I came upon a hand, I didn't want to pick it up, nonetheless, I did what I was told." The combined stench of burned flesh and gasoline was nearly too much for him to bear.[18]

There was no mission scheduled for July 15 due to poor weather, but we still endured a close call. Following a good night's rest and a gentle morning, I decided to catch a movie at the post theater for some healthy distraction that evening. I enjoyed a black and white feature until the windows blew in and the whole building shook from the concussion of a massive detonation. A domino of distant booms echoed across the field for several minutes. Above a tree line, a mushroom cloud rose in the near distance.

Our hearts raced. We had no idea what happened. Did the Germans drop a bomb on our base? Had saboteurs infiltrated the post? Was somebody carelessly smoking in a restricted area?

In actuality, the bomb dump at nearby Metfield—home of the 491st Group—had gone up in an accidental blast. The eruption spewed bits of metal all over the grounds, perforating some two dozen B-24s parked nearby. Hangars and sheds became blackened shells. A crater marking the former location of the dump must have been twenty feet deep. Locals were in a panic.

Impact craters underscore the level of destruction our planes inflicted on and around railroad yards like the one shown. *John Homan collection.* (21)

But what caused this small-scale disaster? I have my suspicions. German bombs had about 30 percent more power than ours because aluminum powder was incorporated. When our Air Forces tried to catch up with the ingredient mixing, the process was one of serious trial and error. My guess has long been that this accident resulted from increased bomb volatility. Having grown up in a town that produced gunpowder, this is pure speculation on my part. Little official word was said on the matter. Top brass usually did a fine job of covering up such blunders. Certainly, nobody back home learned of this incident in newspapers.

Another rumor spread around camp that the Irish Republican Army was responsible for the explosion, and the paramilitary organization planned to strike our bomb dump next. Additional guards were stationed on the grounds for several days thereafter.

In any case, bomb accidents could occur seemingly anywhere at any time. On one occasion, Charlie Freudenthal stood alongside Lt. Col. Byron Webb on the field when a one-tonner from an adjacent plane thumped onto the concrete. "We heard the noise, we saw the bomb, and we saw the red smoke pouring out of the grenade fixed in the tail fin," Freudenthal remembered. "We all took off. I mean, we lit out for somewhere—anywhere!" Webb quickly outran his subordinate, turning his head over his shoulder and shouting, "Move out! That's a two-thousand-pound SOB!" Droves followed him. The bomb never went off, though some men ran so fast and far that it took them thirty minutes to walk back to the field.[19]

These incidents of peril seldom slowed our pace in waging the war. After a two-day standdown, we were slated to return to the marshalling yards of Saarbrücken with three squadrons. *Jo* suffered no damage on this run since flak was thankfully minimal. We inflicted a fair bit of damage on railroading and steel plants in the vicinity. This was my fifth mission. Only twenty-five more to go—or so I hoped.

Next up was an afternoon mission against a "NOBALL" target on July 17. NOBALL, according to one historian, "was the Allied codename for operational use of any German Vengeance Weapon," or a V-Weapon. This categorization usually referred to the V-1 flying bomb or the V-2 long-range rocket. The enemy position in question was located at La Houssoye in the Nord-Pas-de-Calais region of France. Our rocky trip to the site presented more irritations. Regrettably, the lead bombardier missed his target, forcing us to circle back and make a second run. This rare scenario always triggered curses and grumblings. But circling was sometimes a better option than locating the secondary target, even if flak intensified as we looped.[20]

Unlike the previous day, this flight was anything but smooth. First, we fell behind in the formation due to the element's lead plane losing an engine. Then flak zeroed in, making our ride quite turbulent. We sustained a hit in the right waist window. Navigator Chuck Reevs was impressed by German accuracy. "These fellas are the best squirrel shooters to date!" he declared.

There were formidable anti-aircraft artillery stations in these sectors of northern France and Belgium. Each position consisted of a full battery of guns. Their goal was to pick off lead planes, wreak havoc on formations, and dismantle the chain of command. When the guns had us in their sights, flak from four-gun units straddled our wings and rattled our teeth. The gunners were like long-range sharpshooters. We somehow avoided serious damage.

Upon return to base, I was elated to learn that I was granted my first coveted pass to London. I had certainly earned a brief escape from the hostilities. While other squadrons in the group embarked on missions to Grentheville and Erfurt from July 18 to 20, I absorbed the wonders and terrors of the United Kingdom's capital. I hurried to catch a train departing from the humble Halesworth Station. The summertime excursion through the English countryside was pleasant enough. However, as soon as I exited the bustling London train station, I was greeted with multiple air raid sirens. There were so many "buzz bomb" alerts, outsiders like me couldn't discern the difference between an alarm and an all-clear signal. London's additional safety measures included mandatory blackouts, imposed from 10:51 p.m. to 5:22 a.m. during my first visit.

A "buzz bomb," or a V-1, was an 1,800-pound flying bomb, powered by a ramjet engine and launched from pads on the continent. Aimed in the general direction of London, it was a "to whom it may concern" weapon. This early cruise missile fell at random when it ran out of juice and often struck highly populated areas. The unmanned weapon was not accurate and did not discriminate in its varied destinations. I read much later that Germany launched 9,500 buzz bombs at England throughout the conflict. During the summer of '44,

Germans sometimes attached these "doodlebugs" under their bombers flying north of our field and launched them south toward London. We stood atop our bomb shelters and watched the show as English radar-controlled anti-aircraft guns targeted them. The blazing spectacle made for quite an evening's entertainment.

Lt. Robert E. Crotty of the 489th visits ravaged London. Crotty became a POW soon after this photo was taken. *John Homan collection.* (22)

Up to that time, I was under the impression the bombs were an occasional nuisance. When I arrived in London though, I witnessed unbelievable damage wrought by the killer machines. Some Londoners who endured the Blitz of 1940 still sought nightly refuge in the city's Underground. They held toiletries in one hand and their children in the other. I saw scores of worried residents prepare bedding on the tiled platforms. To endure such fear for four years is nearly unimaginable. To come of age amid that terror must have been even worse. One fellow GI accurately summed up the situation when he observed, "Any night of the week you will find an American soldier handing a piece of candy or some gum to the little tykes who don't know what the war is about but have experienced more than most of us." The levelheaded stance of Brits both young and old impressed me.[21]

Despite the bombings, London seemed as busy as ever.
John Homan collection. (23)

I found buzz bombs intimidating, but they never deterred me from what I wanted to see or do in London. Life was potentially short, and I opted to live it to the fullest when opportunities arose. I attempted to carry myself with the same aplomb I saw in the daily lives of civilians. They were generally unflappable and downright stoic. They just carried on, and I tried to do the same. Peer pressure played a role in a flyboy's bearing as well. Airmen accused fellow pilots of cowardice if they didn't take leaves in London. Nonetheless perturbed by disruptive bombings, one of my fellow 489th officers lamented in a letter, "We wonder why we came to London anyway."[22]

The day I arrived in "The Big Smoke," the Army newspaper *Stars and Stripes* mocked the Nazis when a buzz bomb boomeranged to occupied France. "If the Germans can't be certain of hitting the 700 square miles that comprise Greater London," the paper teased, "then their threat to the people and to the 640,000 buildings in just the dense portion of the city is not as frightful as they would have us believe." Rest assured that carnage was still abundant.[23]

Despite the city's devastated landscapes, the place was alive with motion and merriment. London was incredibly cosmopolitan. Australians, New Zealanders, South Africans, Canadians, Free French, Dutch, Polish, and Americans roamed in uniformed herds. I gained further appreciation of the vast Allied coalition. Many people from many nations waged the war with me. For the first time, Yanks sensed they were part of an international enterprise.

"Here was literature personified," teenager Earl Sutherland of the 489th remembered of his first trip to the city. He fondly recalled all the classic tales read during childhood that were set in London. "It seemed like a city that had lived forever and never slept."[24]

Nowhere was this swath of humanity more dynamic than Piccadilly Circus, a major transportation hub and popular watering hole. The bristling public space was also a prime venue for prostitutes advertising the world's oldest profession. At night, streetwalkers sometimes lit a flashlight over their legs and inquired, "Yank, do you want to have some fun?"[25]

"I was propositioned twenty-eight times in forty minutes," buddy Jim Davis declared with a degree of satisfaction. "That will really build a man's ego."[26]

Some men in the 489th formed the unlikely pastime of watching "Piccadilly Commandos" solicit customers. This spectator sport apparently provided many hours of drama and carnal comedy. Reminiscent of gamblers at a horse track, these onlookers placed bets on which distant soldier would acquire which woman and when. GIs could gamble over anything.[27]

I shuffled through the Circus and noticed a sizable crowd of service members hovering over each other's shoulders. The focus of this anxious congregation was a knockout gal wearing a tight blouse and short skirt. Resembling actress Lana Turner, the seductive streetwalker posed against a wall and auctioned herself off to the highest bidder. The officers encircling her ranked captain or higher. These "gentlemen" were apparently soldiers of means demonstrating the privileges of rank. I wasn't about to play with this fire and pushed through the masses. At one pub, a lady of the night descended the steps and said to Predgen, "For a few American dollars we can go upstairs."

Without missing a beat, he replied, "I didn't come here to buy your ass, I came here to save it!"

As previously mentioned, the wartime influx of Americans is still referred to as the "Friendly Invasion." That friendliness was reciprocated, even if mischievously. Moments of levity constantly played out between soldiers and civilians, regardless of circumstance. The oft-repeated phrase Brits used to describe Yanks was that we were "Overpaid, oversexed, and over here." This jab was frequently countered by the equally pithy rebuttal that the Tommys were "Underpaid, undersexed, and under Eisenhower."

My favorite of these humorous exchanges is a joke that involves two GIs standing atop a train platform beside an English woman. A freight train of small boxcars rolls through the station. One of the Americans turns to the woman and asks, "Do you know what we do with those in our country?"

Preempting a sassy punchline, the matron answers, "If my observations are correct, you smoke them, drink them, or kiss them." Yarns like these are what I remember best about our patient and often witty British hosts.

I checked into the grand Imperial Hotel on Russell Square, a swank establishment with tall spires, terra-cotta roofs, gargoyles, and a deluxe sitting lounge. Upon my inquiry, the desk clerk recommended a place removed from the Central London bomb zone for a quiet lunch and pint. I hailed a cab and entered one side when a paratrooper sergeant, uninvited, hopped in the other. In a serious manner, he immediately asked what I flew. I demanded to know what this sudden inquisition was all about. In a firm, no-nonsense manner he again insisted, "What do you fly?"

I told him I flew B-24s, and he responded, "Oh, you're okay then."

He then inquired about my destination. When I replied, he proclaimed, without invitation or hesitation, "I'm going with you!" Not until we concluded lunch did my mysterious companion explain his bizarre introduction.

The hotel clerk's recommendation was on the mark. The humble English pub was quaint and tranquil, offering fine food and ale. I enjoyed an easygoing meal with the sergeant, during which we discussed our recent battlefield travails. He had jumped into Normandy and his division recently returned from France for rest and reconditioning. Before we parted, I asked him why he chose to spend his afternoon with a stranger.

He explained that when C-47s dropped paratroopers behind the lines on D-Day, airborne soldiers were widely scattered to the point they were unable to fight as units and consequently suffered high casualties. Therefore, when surviving paratroopers obtained leave, they prowled London and beat the shit out of any C-47 pilot they could get their hands on.

"I was worried one of my buddies might get geared up and not ask questions first," the sergeant informed me.

Evidently, I had a dedicated and capable personal bodyguard for the day. I only wish I could recall the man's name. He was topnotch.

I did not interact with too many paratroopers, but my impression was that they were rough characters. They endured brutal training and were solid soldiers. I'm glad they were on our side. In more recent years, I befriended a distinguished paratrooper veteran who resided in my retirement village. His name was Edward Buss. Ed served in the Third Battalion of the 506th Parachute Infantry Regiment in the 101st Airborne Division and attained the rank of captain. His regiment was depicted in the famous miniseries *Band of Brothers*. After the war, Ed earned a PhD and became a Professor of Agriculture at Penn State. During the COVID-19 lockdown, he and I secretly mingled for bull sessions and beer on Sunday afternoons, often reminiscing about military exploits. I suppose we still retained a smidge of youthful, rebellious spirit. Nobody gave us trouble for socializing. After all, I had a paratrooper in my corner!

I once posed to Ed, "What was the farthest you ever walked in a day?"

"With full packs, I'd say twenty-four miles," he replied. I cared not to live such a harsh existence, hence my enlistment in the Air Forces. But I respect any soldier who withstood trials matching or surpassing those of Buss. Ed passed away just two months shy of his 100th birthday in 2021. I miss my chats with him very much.

Back to London: My airborne compatriot and I finally went our separate ways. We shook hands while I told him I had to leave and meet three crew members for dinner. This was exactly two months before the ill-fated Operation Market Garden, which claimed many a paratrooper. I hope my impromptu drinking buddy returned home safely.

I summoned a cab and sped to our crew's designated meeting place at Trafalgar Square with time to spare. Since this leave was my introduction to London, I decided to explore some sites of interest within walking distance. I strolled only a few paces when the air raid alert sounded again. Before I had time to decide on a course of action, I heard the distinctive, rhythmic, backfire-type pulse of a ramjet engine. The bomb seemed dangerously close.

I ducked into the nearest storefront for cover. In prompt fashion, an English gent—complete with a homburg hat and umbrella—pursued me and announced, "Lad, I don't think you are in a good shelter," while pointing to all the glass windows. He directed me to a safer location. By the time I scurried a very short distance, the throbbing noise of a buzz bomb quickly approached and passed directly overhead. I soon learned that the moment for genuine concern was when the bomb's engine stopped. That was when the projectile began its deathly plummet to the streets.

After the all-clear sounded, I continued my limited tour until I reunited with officers of our crew. Chuck Reevs and I attended a performance of the stage comedy *Something in the*

Air. Later, we discovered a class-A restaurant called the Ivy, where we had a surprisingly luxurious meal. Apparently, this establishment was somehow exempt from stringent food ration rules. Popular attractions for men in my bomb group included Whitehall, Westminster, and Big Ben. Some enjoyed a few stiff drinks at the Lyons House before watching Noel Coward performances. Men in our crew enjoyed Madame Tussaud's Wax Museum. On Bond Street, 489th boys purchased radios for barracks, souvenir trinkets to mail home, or snazzy new Ike Jackets. But mischief often prevailed. One comrade succinctly described his London leave as "more fun, more fights."[28]

My own evening ended in similar style. The time neared nine o'clock and the pubs closed at ten. We delegated tasks for our important mission of the night. Two of us hunted for a bottle of Scotch and the other two searched for a club with late hours. On Regent Street, we approached an entryway of a popular jazz lounge. The door had a speakeasy-style eye slit for a security guard to peek through. A gruff bouncer with a thick accent greeted us and demanded the password. Amazingly, one of my chums knew it and we gained entry. Out of the corner of my eye I noticed a massive paratrooper approaching with a blonde in one hand and a bottle in the other.

Once again, the bouncer requested, "Password?"

The paratrooper spun his head with boozy indignation and asserted, "I don't have the password, but you damn well better keep that door open!" The guard wisely assented.

We sat at a table in front of the stage while a male singer performed. As we made ourselves comfortable in the dark den, a bottle flew over our heads and struck the performer. He confidently finished his number but concluded, "The person who threw that bottle ought to be man enough to stand up!"

A drunken Dutch paratrooper who didn't speak English had the misfortunate of arising at that same moment to use the lavatory. The club emcee, mistaking the Dutchman as the offender, coldcocked the soldier to the floor. Agitated by the unwarranted attack on his ally, the brawny American paratrooper who muscled his way into the club lunged at the host. The club staff, coming to the aid of their manager, joined the fray. Within seconds, the entire venue erupted into a melee of punches and kicks. Tables were overturned, bottles were smashed over heads, and many a nose was bloodied. All we desired was a quiet sanctuary to enjoy a bottle of Scotch. Instead, we were suddenly consumed by an impromptu Allied offensive within the crowded nightclub.

Wielding batons, Military Police in white helmets soon intervened. When the fracas subsided, the manager pointed over the shoulder of an MP at the airborne sergeant.

"That's the bloke! He's the one who started all this!"

Without uttering a word, the burly trooper sauntered around the MP and barreled his fist into the Englishman's face. The host collapsed like a marionette with its strings slashed. Teetering over his latest victim, the sergeant displayed a satisfied grin at his handiwork.

The MP turned and silently curled his finger, beckoning the sergeant to step forward. The trooper knew better than to confront a policeman, so he sheepishly followed the MP out the exit. I suspect the cop shrugged off the sarge and simply warned, "Go someplace else."

Appropriately enough, the name of the club was The Nut House. The establishment more than earned its title that zany evening. Al Burnett, a notable British impresario and nightclub celebrity, acted as emcee at The Nut House during the war years. Perhaps he was the victim of the sergeant's ire. Unlike many staff and guests, we escaped the club without injury or censure.

When I at last returned to the Imperial Hotel, I unsuccessfully attempted to enter my room. I heard a woman's voice behind the door. She informed me to check with the front desk. Baffled by the presence of an unknown woman in my room, I followed her instructions. The lobby clerk said the woman desired to check in but was afraid to stay in a room on an inside wall. (She requested a room along an exterior wall to quickly escape should the hotel fall victim to a buzz bomb attack. The woman was therefore booked in my room, and I was relocated.) Her cautious instincts were more than warranted. Later that night, I was awoken by a bomb that landed in a park only one block away. The concussion rocked the hotel and shook my bed. I remained awake all night listening to the racket of explosions and sirens.

That was my memorable first trip to London. Bombs, bars, and brawls. At the end of it all, I was back at my job.

Bad news awaited me. On July 20, superiors announced that our number of required missions was raised from thirty to thirty-five. There was plenty of moaning and groaning over this update. Morale dampened a bit. Older crews speculated if they would ever be released from military service.

In earlier phases of Eighth Air Force campaigns, the prospect of surviving twenty-five missions was only 30 percent. Those odds improved to 50 percent with the arrival of more consistent fighter support. None of us should have been surprised when the minimum requirement was eventually altered to thirty-five missions. When Eisenhower was appointed Supreme Allied Commander, I sensed he didn't want to ship any of us flyboys back prematurely lest the Normandy invasion fall flat on its ass. He needed the planes. He needed the crews. Therefore, the mission count was again raised. We felt ever more expendable. I recalculated my mission tally. Twenty-nine to go until I could pack for home.

I questioned whether my luck could persist that long.

CHAPTER 6

SNAFU

The glow of morning slowly brightened the English countryside as I manned our unit's colorful assembly ship, *Lil' Cookie*. The stripped-down plane soon circled over the field, cutting through silvery overcast. Once airborne on July 21, 1944, our crew fired flares out the waist to serve as visual beacons for crews bound for Kempten, Germany. When everyone was up in formation and on their way, our temporary plane returned to base and was put to bed. Landing her was then followed by putting ourselves to bed. The 489th Bomb Group was to strike a Bavarian aircraft components factory. Although helming *Lil' Cookie* for a morning assembly did not count toward our mission requirements, I was quite glad to have avoided that day's venture into enemy territory.

Bad weather caused formations to scatter, making the operation an uncoordinated effort. The group ended up hitting Munich yet again. On the way home via Frankfurt, heavy enemy fire was encountered. The outfit initiated evasive action to sidestep incoming rounds. One plane fell to earth as a swirling inferno, with one man killed and six wounded. Back at the Halesworth control tower, ground crew and officers awaited the group's return. When they heard engines in the distance, they perked up, raised binoculars, and nervously counted incoming ships. Losses that day could have been worse, but twenty-nine bombers sustained damage amid the messy assault. Bungled missions like this one typically meant a return to the same target on a future trip. We kicked ourselves with frustration whenever these mishaps occurred. Such episodes prompted repetitive usage of the phrase "SNAFU," meaning "Situation normal: all f----- up." This was not merely a military mantra. It seemed a way of life.

My next combat destination was the airfield at Juvincourt in northern France on July 23. Constructed by the French Air Force prior to the war, the site had been occupied by the Luftwaffe since 1940 and was greatly expanded as a staging area. Our aim was to curtail the facility's capacity to dispatch Germany fighters from that installation. If we could annihilate the field, such a feat would hopefully limit the Luftwaffe's lethal range.

Low cloud levels beleaguered us during the entire trip. Semi-blindness was not the sole challenge. Our number-two propeller ran away as we crossed the French coast. We held it in by using the feather button with only moderate success. Predgen and I increased power on the other three engines, enabling us to stay in formation to complete the bomb run. Persistent cloud cover ultimately necessitated instrument bombing. The group couldn't even determine results after we released our payloads. In any case, American forces seized Juvincourt about a month later and the site was utilized as an advanced landing ground by the Ninth Air Force for the duration of hostilities.

We feathered the troublesome engine again right after we passed the target. Our plane limped back at a dreadful 135 miles per hour, making an instrument letdown and landing at 10 p.m. Exhausted from my prolonged travels, I finally hit the sack at midnight. To my horror, we were alerted for the next mission only an hour later. I felt like the walking dead. I often wonder how I was able to function. We took off at 7 a.m. on July 24. The next thirty-six hours were rife with shock and scandal.

Despite a briefing that made the upcoming mission sound like an easy "milk run," our assignment was nonetheless vital. The group was scheduled to support Operation Cobra, the Allied thrust to break out of Normandy's dense hedgerows by penetrating German defenses west of Saint-Lô and capturing Coutances. Over preceding days, the AAF leveled perhaps 95 percent of Saint-Lô. The community became a martyred symbol of French liberation and earned the nickname of "The Capital of Ruins."

Friend Charlie Freudenthal best encapsulated the many dilemmas of our problematic July 24 flight. The overarching mission "was disappointing from several standpoints," he opined. "There were weather problems, target identification problems, the tragic shortfalls that killed a number of ground forces personnel, and controversy over the value and effectiveness of the air contribution."[1]

Over 1,500 Allied aircraft participated in the objective to eliminate German defenses. Inadequate visibility sadly led to inaccurate bombings. At least two dozen American ground troops were killed before our planes were recalled. Squads of surviving infantrymen were so enraged that they fired back at U.S. planes with small arms. Damage inflicted by the tragic bombardment could be considered slight in contrast to what awaited some GIs the following day.

Thankfully, our plane did not release any bombs. We approached the target at 13,500 feet. This was much lower than the typical 20,000 feet. The area was obscured to the extent that we could not safely drop ordnance. We feared hitting American foot soldiers. The same was true for many planes in our group. When a small break in the clouds did open, however, we caught plenty of hell from camouflaged Germany artillery. I saw the plane of Lt. Edwin Florcyk suffer a direct hit in its open bomb bay and explode before my very eyes. The Liberator was flying to our right, there was a bright orange burst, the wings folded, six bodies flew out, and the props spun as the tail collapsed inward. Then the ship was gone. The whole episode seemed to play out in slow motion. An airman positioned behind Florcyk's bomber, named *Fearless*, recalled the sight with terror. "We flew through remains and thought we had caught fire," he admitted. "Flak hitting the belly of the ship sounded like someone throwing gravel at us."[2]

Radio operator Frank Trowbridge was the only member of Florcyk's crew to survive. He was in the bomb bay when the blast struck, was blown clear from falling wreckage, and successfully deployed his parachute. The radioman landed in enemy territory and sought shelter in a church basement. Trowbridge endured his brief entrapment in France by sneaking out of the church at night to pluck carrots from an adjacent vegetable garden. He miraculously evaded capture for four days until American tanks secured the sector. Afterward, he was held in London for two additional days by Army Intelligence until his identity could be verified by our officers.[3]

I devoted substantial thought to fears of bailing or being captured. We didn't wear parachutes in the cockpit. They were behind our seats. Would I have had the ability to affix my chute if my aircraft was plunging to the ground at 250 miles per hour? Probably not. I saw planes burst into balls of fire and tailspin in a matter of seconds. There was no time.

Anxiety heightened due to my counterintuitive dread of heights. Nightmare scenarios played out in my mind. I envisioned myself standing apprehensively in the bomb bay, frozen by fear, and unable to jump. I wondered if I had the guts to bail out of a smoking plane careening from 15,000 feet. I hoped never to test my mettle in such a frightful way. As a coping mechanism, we could do little more than express gallows humor about such perils. I once ribbed Predgen on the matter, kidding, "If we have to bail, I'm going to beat you out of here."

One day, the crew played on my fear of heights. A microphone cord came loose in the bomb bay area. I told the skipper, "I'll take care of it." As soon as I inched onto the narrow catwalk, the bomb doors flung open beneath me, and I flinched with terror. They got me good.

We returned from Normandy with fifty-two 100-pound bombs still in our plane. I am relieved we did not drop any. But we were not yet done with Saint-Lô. We were slated to return on July 25. I suspected the flight was not going to be a "milk run" at all.

Roused at three in the morning, we were up and off by 7 a.m. The energy at briefing suggested something momentous was afoot. The high priority of the operation was underscored by a moderately painful injury endured by pilot Jim Davis. During his pre-flight inspection, Davis gashed his skull on a bomb fin and instantly felt blood trickling down his forehead. Hurried to the hospital, he was under the impression he wouldn't have to return to Saint-Lô. Doc Levine had other plans. "Son, you did a good job of cutting it open—and it will need sewing up," confirmed the physician. "But for now, I will try and tape it together and I'll sew it up after you get back. You will come back, won't you?" he winked.

Davis insisted he couldn't even wear his helmet let alone fly. He was in pain and lost a decent amount of blood. The doctor couldn't oblige. "Son, the colonel has told me there'll be no medical excuses for this mission, and you don't need a helmet—you'll only be at 12,000 feet." The pilot was shaved and taped up to the point that he resembled a mummy. "Let's say you'll be a cut above the rest today," Levine joked. An unamused Davis was sent back to his plane.[4]

Weather had improved since our previous mission. Three squadrons from our group departed with a potent mix of fragmentation bombs. Our plane alone carried 8,300 pounds of these "frags." We flew at 10,000 feet, half our normal altitude. By the time we reached the target, a south wind and earlier bombings had partially obscured the area. Also, our artillery was to mark the target with red smoke shells, but the billows blew north over our own troops. The same thing happened the day before. Most ships neared the target by heading perpendicular to nearby American lines. The goal was to clear a way for the bottlenecked Allied advance. Miscommunication and miscalculation wrought devastating consequences.

There is no easy way to tell this tale. The payloads of our group and others dropped short amidst the saturation bombing. They hit Allied troops instead, including Americans. Over 100 of our ground troops were killed and nearly 500 more were wounded in the calamity. Among the fatalities was Lt. Gen. Leslie McNair, who that day became the highest-ranking American to perish in the European Theater of the war. (Interestingly, my co-author's grandfather, Thomas Nycum, was among the men of the 4th Infantry Division positioned in the vicinity when this incident occurred.) When the smoke cleared, the ground resembled a moonscape. Hundreds of craters filled with the body parts of GIs littered the terrain. Thankfully, our crew again opted not to release the bombs. We couldn't distinguish any landmarks and the whole area was blanketed with smoke. We were too nervous to roll the dice.

Naturally, not all crews were as cautious. The plane on our right, commanded by Lt. Jack "Blackjack" Slein, dropped its ordnance and was then hit squarely by an 88mm. His aircraft splintered like a paper piñata. We roared right through the flying debris. Somehow, we sustained only minor hits in our bomb bay and rudder.

Slein's co-pilot, Harold Morse, left disturbing testimony as to what happened next. "I heard a sharp crack," he remembered. He looked back and saw the bomb bay consumed with fire and dense smoke. The heat was unbearable. Slein unbuckled himself to extinguish the flames. Morse never saw his captain again. The co-pilot pressed the alarm bell several times and flew straight as long as possible to permit crew evacuation. "I then got up and saw there was no way of my getting out of the bomb bay," he continued. Morse knocked open the top hatch and lifted himself out. As he did so, the plane began a slight descent. "The last I remember I was being pulled out by the slipstream." He then lost consciousness.

The tattered and bewildered airman awoke in a pasture surrounded by trees. He had no memory of parachuting onto the battlefront. A sharp pain ran up his back. His boots, socks, and helmet had been ripped off his body when he was swept from the plane. Then, for the next fifteen minutes, artillery and bombs raked the area around him. He clung to the ground for dear life. When the barrage subsided, Morse spotted four nearby combatants and begged their assistance. "I soon noticed they were German soldiers," he remembered weeks later. The enemy carried him to a foxhole and a vague line of communication opened. "I wanted a doctor," the airman affirmed. "They told me that they would take me later when it got dark. They asked me a few questions and did their best to make me comfortable." The Germans evacuated their position and abandoned Morse three hours later when a column of American tanks advanced across the pasture. Morse's short time in captivity thus ended.

The co-pilot was very anxious to learn the fate of his crewmembers. He did not see them bail, nor did he see any sign of them after he regained consciousness. "Several officers at the Aid Station told me they had seen an aircraft burning in the middle and said they saw five chutes come from it," Morse recalled. Another witness claimed all ten crewmen parachuted out of the fiery Liberator. Sadly, Morse was the sole survivor. Any of the others who safely reached the ground were shortly thereafter killed by the ongoing U.S. bombardment. Infantrymen were not the only Yanks claimed by friendly fire that day. The July 25 affair was a tragedy on many levels. Several air groups wouldn't admit to having dropped their bombs because they realized the blood of fellow Americans was on their hands.

However, the action was not a complete failure either. Several years later, I was having a drink in a bar and struck up a conversation with a former tank captain who was outside Saint-Lô at the outset of Operation Cobra. When I informed the veteran I flew that mission, he insisted on buying me a full bottle of liquor.

"When we pushed on through the next day," he declared, "there was nothing left. It was completely clear for us."

This bit of anecdotal evidence is supplemented by the words of Fritz Bayerlein, commander of the Panzer-Lehr Division, which we were sent to destroy during that operation. "The shock effect was nearly as strong as the physical effect upon the dead and wounded," the general said of the bombing. "Some of the men got crazy and were unable to carry out anything. I was personally in the center of the bombardment and could experience the tremendous effect. . . . [T]his was the worst thing I ever saw." Our mission, though terribly flawed, ultimately succeeded in its aims.[5]

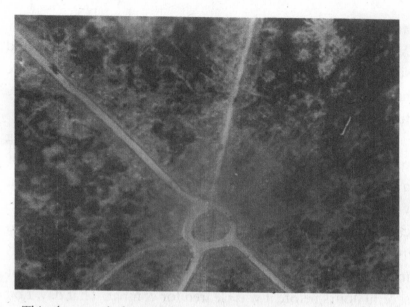

This photograph shows the devastation at a Normandy crossroads.
John Homan collection. (24)

We returned to base and decided some stiff drinks were in order. Better yet, we broke away from post for a few hours of reprieve. The urge to blow off steam was immense. A couple of us borrowed bicycles and rode into the market town of Beccles to quench our thirst. A bike was the typical mode of local travel. Some innovative GI on base even welded two frames together to craft a tandem for sightseeing airmen. Such a display presented great amusement to villagers.[6]

We dumped a fair amount of change in the pub and remained there until it closed at 10 p.m. The night was very dark when we began our trek to Halesworth. Wobbling around during a blackout, we literally ran into a bobby. Moderately riled, the police officer confiscated our bikes and summoned a truck for our transportation. The bicycles were never returned to us. This minor incident added insult to a day full of injury.

The remainder of the week afforded us some breathing room. On July 26, we ate breakfast at 1 a.m. and prepped for a mission bound for an airfield southwest of Paris. The flight was scrubbed at takeoff due to an unfavorable weather forecast. In lieu of a mission, we "slow timed" a ship from 7:30 to 10:30 that morning. Whenever a new or rebuilt engine was installed, it had to be tested and run at reduced power for several hours before it was cleared for combat. That day, Lou Wagner jokingly called Predgen and I "just a couple of chauffeurs." For that, he was ordered to the co-pilot's controls to have a taste of chauffeur life. This payback provided worthwhile entertainment. Over the next two days, we conducted several of these slow time checks plus practice missions in which we firmed up formation flying.[7]

Our mechanics completed necessary engine work in the field over long nights. They kept quite busy. New props frequently ran away on takeoff and indicators were all over the dials. Once we were airborne, however, the machinery tended to settle down. Engine runs were essentially joy rides for pleasure. We relaxed, savored the weather, switched on the autopilot, and cruised over the bucolic English countryside. We did have to remain mindful of our flight path. All pilots had maps of England indicating no-fly zones clearly marked in red. If an aircraft entered any of the restricted zones, it would be shot down by British anti-aircraft gunners. That week, we carelessly roamed into one of these forbidden areas. A burst of flak off our right wing surely caught our attention. We executed a fast-turning dive to get the hell out of there. I don't know whether the gunners sought to hit us or simply scare us. I think the English were trying to tell us something!

From July 29 to 30, I enjoyed my second leave to London. Our crew log succinctly noted of this trip, "A great day was spent with wine, women, and song, and occasionally a buzz bomb." I visited the elegant Covent Garden, the beautifully manicured Regent's Park, and the London Zoo—which was quite the attraction in wartime. During previous Nazi raids, some exotic animals escaped and roamed the ruined streets.

Buzz bombs were indeed a nuisance. In the Sunday pictorial, articles chronicled how these infernal machines continued to hinder daily life. One story explained how a band of heroic nurses ran into a partially demolished building to rescue babies and elderly residents. In that same issue was an article heralding the success of Operation Cobra. "Eighty minutes before zero hour, 60,000 bombs of all types were rained down on the Germans by 2,323 bombers," proclaimed the piece. "It worked out at ten bombs to the acre!" An unnamed American officer was quoted, "It was beginning to demoralize even me." The article failed to mention the AAF had killed scores of our own men in the process.[8]

With the Allied advance pushing ever closer to Paris, many of the boys were eager to experience the liberated "City of Light." I was never particularly eager to explore the French capital. Home always seemed more important to me. Sideline adventures became less and less significant as missions tallied up. Completing my job and returning safely to New Jersey were my paramount aims. I had little time to relish London's many luxuries to begin with.

Our superiors couldn't grant too many leaves at any one moment. "Hundreds of American soldiers arriving in London on pass and furlough are failing to get beds almost every night at American Red Cross clubs and are being forced to sleep on chairs, floors, and in a large air raid shelter because many units are overstepping their London quotas," explained *Stars and Stripes*. The city remained a bustling getaway brimming with spirited Yanks full of zeal and liquor.[9]

The next morning, I was back to the real world. Our destination for July 31 was an IG Farben chemical complex outside Ludwigshafen. Farben was one of the world's largest chemical and pharmaceutical corporations and gained infamy for using slave labor during the Holocaust. Our group launched thirty-nine aircraft on this Pathfinder mission. The day was a classic SNAFU. During takeoff, the number-two prop ran away but we controlled it with the feather button. The situation improved by the time we reached 6,000 feet, so we continued in formation. Unfortunately, our lead later strayed off course and veered into airspace over Saarbrücken and

Mannheim, both of which were heavily defended. Flak barrages over these cities were intense and close. Lou Wagner said he saw a piece of incoming metal miss his turret dome by a mere foot. "Mission was rough," he wrote.[10]

Keith Turnham agreed. "[We] were in some of the heaviest flak we had ever encountered," he admitted. "Most of our planes were dropping chaff as fast as possible, but the Germans were doing a remarkable job of finding our altitude with their anti-aircraft guns." Turnham's day was soon to become even worse.[11]

Lead planes were not meant to make any radical turns once the group was on the bomb run. Our lead pilot screwed up something awful and proceeded on the wrong heading. The result was a top-bottom collision that led to seven deaths. Mistakes happen in war, and men die. By this tenth mission, I was ready to go home. Yet I was not even one-third of the way there.

The fight intensified once we reached the target. I saw the red centers of exploding shells rupture just yards from our plane. We had numerous holes in our ship. Swallowed up by the storm of shrapnel was *Lethal Linda*, piloted by Lt. Frank Palmer. After Palmer's plane was struck on the bomb run, it collided with Lt. Wallace Bishop's wounded Liberator. Both ships plummeted following the mid-air pileup. Once more, all we could do was watch.

Turnham was a member of Palmer's crew and never forgot what happened that day. "Frank announced that we should get out of the ship before it exploded or before another shell made its entry. There was no way he could fly our plane any-more," he recalled. Turnham was one of the last men to bail, as he suffered a horrible leg wound. When he finally leapt, he discovered that his parachute was in tatters. He careened toward earth and blacked out when he landed on his damaged limb.

Turnham awoke to a German soldier hovering over him. In sharp English, the armed enemy asked if the American was hurt.

"Yes, very much so," was Turnham's reply. He was certain he was about to be put out of his misery and mentally prepared for the end.

Instead, the German announced, "Let me carry you to my duty station."

"I couldn't believe what I was hearing," confessed Turnham. "This soldier was going to help me, not kill me here." Turnham survived the war and wrote his own memoir sixty years later.[12]

Palmer and all his men remained prisoners for the war's duration. Their capture made us the last functioning crew from our cadre formed at Casper, Wyoming, only months earlier.

Germany had two prisoner of war systems. One was over-seen by the Army and the other was managed by the Luftwaffe. A friend of mine, Robert Buckley, who flew Spitfires during the war, was shot down over Holland. He ended up in Stalag Luft III, the camp made famous by *The Great Escape*. Buckley insisted Germans treated airmen fairly, perhaps due to a code of chivalry among flyers. Prisoners were not fed well, but neither were their guards.

I could not mentally prepare myself for the possibility of capture. We were provided little instruction on how to interact with would-be captors. Naturally, we were informed to provide nothing more than our names, ranks, and serial numbers if apprehended. Additionally, we were ordered to escape by any means necessary if an opportunity presented itself. While many airmen sported sidearms during missions, I purposefully left mine in my footlocker. If I was shot down and Germans were hunting me, I might have been tempted to use the weapon. Such an act surely would have been a death sentence for me. I therefore removed my pistol from the equation.

Captivity was most dangerous of all for flyboys of the Jewish faith. Ira Weinstein was shot down later in 1944 and survived two weeks on the run, attempting to reach neutral Switzerland before he was ultimately seized. The lieutenant was hurled into a holding cell with a dozen other Americans, including two badly wounded airmen. Weinstein requested an audience with the commandant and demanded proper medical treatment for the ailing captives.

"You Jews and Americans are bombing our churches, our schools, and hospitals," the well-dressed German major declared. "I'll show you what I think about the Geneva Convention." The commandant then smashed a riding crop across Weinstein's face, splitting his lip, and knocking him to the floor. The lieutenant survived this initial beating but was bound for equally daunting trials. He was relocated to a camp later toured by Heinrich Himmler, the brutal leader of the Gestapo and Waffen-SS. "Himmler came to the camp and left word that all Jewish officers were to be separated and shot," the captive recalled. Weinstein's brave American superior intervened, warning the Germans, "You march one Jewish guy off this camp, and we'll riot." The Nazis never carried out their threats. Weinstein and his fellow prisoners were liberated May 11, 1945. Not all "GI Jews" were as fortunate.[13]

We were briefed for an afternoon route to Rouen in northwestern France on August 1. A field order summarized wide-ranging military considerations. "The purpose of the entire mission is to clean up the immediate tactical target picture," our leaders explained. "The oil dumps have increased in importance with each successful attack on oil refineries." However, our plane lost two turbos before we left Halesworth, forcing us to abort takeoff. Determined not to be left behind, we returned to the field, acquired a replacement ship, and soared off again. We flew nearly to the French coast but couldn't locate the group. Annoyed by our misfortune, we had no option but to turn around and go home. This was yet another instance in which we didn't receive mission credit for a flight. Irritation worsened when English gunners shot at us as we returned. (We were a lone bogie in their sector after all.)[14]

Operations the following two days ushered us to NOBALL targets in the vicinities of Amiens and Calais. We again passed over the feared enemy batteries at Abbeville, manned by some of the sharpest flak gunners in the business. If an American plane flew straight and level there, the Germans were sure to clobber it. Despite our best efforts, we suffered a solid strike in the waist, a jarring near-miss for Bo Cochran. The shrapnel went "through the right waist window, out the left side of the ship above the left windows, and shattered the right window," Wagner recalled. Our number-four engine was likewise hit during the melee.[15]

Adversity followed us into August 3. Number-two engine developed a serious oil leak and a prop ran away, forcing us to feather that engine. Realizing we likely wouldn't last the whole journey, we dumped our bombload in the North Sea and returned to Halesworth. No mission credit for the second time in one week. This was an annoying, demoralizing pattern. Whether confronting flak or engine failure, our routines could eat away at men's spirits. "So far we've had three missions in four days, and about twenty-one hours in the air," one of our comrades declared. "My back is awfully sore from wearing all that armor-plated vest and helmet." Many an airman in the outfit could empathize with these sentiments.[16]

Three group squadrons departed for Wismar on the Baltic Sea the following morning. Our crew was on alert but ultimately scratched from the mission list. I slept all day and could have slept several more. I now suspect Lou Wagner might not have dozed as well as I did that day. "I'm beginning to notice that I'm getting kind of nervous," he wrote in his diary on August 4. "When we fly, I'm scared and when we don't, I'm scared too. What a life! I believe it's getting me down. While flying I'm okay until I see the first burst of flak. Then I nearly drop through the turret," he confessed. "I only pray for one thing: that if I have to go, that it's quick or else I have a chance to bail out. Going down in flames is too much for me. Oh well, I'll forget about such things. If they come, let them." All combatants cope with fear in their own way. Lou wrote about his anxieties as an emotional release. I just tried to sleep it all off whenever I could.[17]

Even so, I hardly felt refreshed at 4 a.m. on August 5 when I was summoned to help attack a Messerschmitt assembly plant near Brunswick. The journey was made a bit easier thanks to stellar support by P-51 escorts. Before we left the target area, we saw five large fires burning below—sure indicators of success. Flak on the way was inaccurate as far as we were concerned, but gunfire damage did force one crew to bail out just off the Suffolk coast. Thankfully, all the men were scooped from the waves by RAF rescue boats and a fishing vessel. Shortly thereafter, I experienced a dose of excitement myself with a shaky prop wash landing.

More difficulties ensued during our August 6 takeoff to oil refineries at Hamburg when the number-one prop ran away. Thankfully, we were able to control the engine. No oil leaks this time either. Even better was the fact we had perfect weather with unlimited visibility. Then again, clear skies also made us clearer targets. We came in at 22,000 feet. The waist took another heavy hit, and a shrapnel fragment cracked my window. Lt. Mark Osborne's plane, *Cover Girl*, to our front took a direct hit to the number-three engine and caught fire. I watched with stunned amazement as the aircraft doggedly surged on to the bomb run with a whole wing ablaze.

"Get the hell out of there!" I uselessly yelled at the nearby crew. "Get out!" Somehow, the overwhelmed Liberator pushed onward.

Airmen on the imperiled plane then dropped their bombs, pulled out of formation, and speedily bailed. That was gutsy. Just seconds after the tenth and final crewman parachuted, the burning wing snapped off and the plane tumbled to the city. Osborne and his entire team became prisoners of war. Years later at a 489th reunion, I spoke with a fellow veteran who said he bailed out over Hamburg. His recounting triggered my memory.

"Was your number-three engine on fire?" I inquired.

"Yes, it was," he replied.

"I was yelling at you guys to get the hell out!"

He appreciated my concern. The man's name was Fred Meyer, a sergeant from Osborne's crew. He also explained additional threats he encountered after parachuting to the ground. "We suffered some severe and rough treatment at the hands of the German populace until we reached the military," he recalled in a postwar article. "I was shot through the left side by a uniformed civilian and pitchforked by the others as I was required to run through a gauntlet of town folk from the area of Stade where I had landed." Meyer ended up in Stalag Luft IV. His ability to overcome those countless hurdles amazes me still.[18]

All of us were quite drained by the time we were debriefed. Many in the group had flown five of the last six days. Several of our buddies were missing in action. Some survivors had lifeless, thousand-yard stares on their faces. Imagine our disbelief then when we were told to report to the hangar for a special surprise—the Glenn Miller Army Air Force Band! This transition was a steep and sudden emotional rollercoaster. Hours earlier we had been engaged in a fierce death struggle. Then in a twist of irony we were tapping our toes to some of the most joyful and celebrated tunes of the age.

The band was a self-contained unit of sixty-five men—including an announcer, instrument repairmen, and stage technicians to place the music stands. A combat crew favorite was "The GI Jive." For an hour or two, the hangar echoed with Big Band classics. Spectators sat on plane wings and perched themselves on scaffolding stretching up to the rafters. Glenn Miller's lead drummer Ray McKinley ran much of the show. The performance was a wonderful means of distraction. The entertainment momentarily took my mind from the violence I had just witnessed. Dwight Eisenhower said of such concerts, "Next to a letter from home they were the greatest morale booster in the ETO."[19]

Little did we then know that Miller's band wasn't originally slated to perform for us. "The story behind Miller's appearance, incidentally, is that he was scheduled for a concert at a fighter base that evening," Charlie Freudenthal revealed years later. "The 489th was asked to provide the airlift. Col. Ezekiel Napier [a West Pointer who was our first and only commander] agreed on the condition that they play at Halesworth first. No play, no airlift. It sure was a great concert." I'm glad our commanders engaged in some quid pro quo for our benefit. We all needed our spirits lifted.[20]

I'm particularly fond of Miller's rendition of "Take The 'A' Train." I still listen to the songs on discs. They revive many bittersweet memories. Miller's plane famously went missing over the English Channel the same week the Battle of the Bulge began. He was bound for Paris to lead a holiday concert. His disappearance was announced to the world on Christmas Eve 1944. Miller was yet another fine American lost amidst the countless calamities of the air war.

Miller's band performed in a hangar rather than outdoors due to poor weather. Sure enough, skies the following day were drenched with rain and fog. Our target was an oil storage dump near Brussels, but we couldn't see a damn thing. Back we went with a full bombload. We fared better on August 8 with an assault on a German single-engine aircraft replacement pool east of Laon.

Left: Col. "Zeke" Napier after the war. Right: Glenn Miller's band
performs at Halesworth. *Air Force photos.* (25 and 26)

Boys in the bomb group had another treat in store after
this solid mission performance. Billy Conn, a Light
Heavyweight Champion who memorably squared off with Joe
Louis, visited the base only two days after Glenn Miller. The
"autograph hounds had a field day," Freudenthal remembered.
Halesworth was mighty busy hosting celebrities that first week
of August 1944.[21]

An August 9 exercise in a Link Trainer was followed by
another pass to London. Our crew always seemed to end up
at the Lion's Head Tavern off Piccadilly Circus. This popular
venue became our unofficial headquarters when we hit the
town. During our visit, the front page of the *Daily Telegraph*
portended the liberation of Paris within a week. "Tanks in

Chartres, 45 Miles to Go," one headline proclaimed on August 11. Many airmen in my outfit remained anxious to explore an emancipated Paris. There was also the hope that the city's capture would domino toward a rapid victory in the European Theater. Would the whole show be over by Christmas? Then again, every war is supposed to be over by Christmas.[22]

While I enjoyed diversions in London, a tragedy with far-reaching consequences transpired a few miles east of my Halesworth base. I learned much later that Lt. Joseph Kennedy, Jr. and his co-pilot flew their Liberator on a secret training mission to test the potentials of robot-controlled aircraft. Both men were killed when experimental explosives on board prematurely detonated. The incident demonstrated the constant dangers of trial and error endured by airmen. More significantly, the calamity passed the family ambitions for the fallen pilot to his younger brother, John F. Kennedy.

When I returned from the big city, my ship joined twenty-five planes headed for Wittmundhafen Air Base in Lower Saxony on August 15. The site was a training field for Germany's new and rather mysterious jet aircraft. I never spotted one of these ultra-fast modern marvels in the sky, and I am grateful. The following day, however, these jets purportedly swooped down on American bombers that were smashing industrial sites in the Reich. "Many of the targets which have been bombed in German territory and enemy-occupied countries have been factories contributing to the manufacture of jet propulsion engines," one reporter commented that week. All the while, given the high rate of fuel these aircraft consumed, German scientists tried to devise alternative fuels for jet propulsion. As was the case with many logistical dimensions of the war, this undertaking was a race against time.[23]

Par for the course, our target the next day was an oil refinery at Magdeburg, Germany. The mission turned out to be a royal mess. The head plane with our commander had to abort due to a mechanical problem. The baton was passed to the deputy lead. Temporarily loaned to another crew, our navigator Chuck Reevs anxiously imparted instruction to the new lead, trying to offer proper direction. In the effort to compensate, the leader committed careless, corrective turns. Our group stayed off course and crossed over thickly defended flak areas not on the planned route. Screwups multiplied when we realized the squadrons had approached the target on the wrong heading. Meanwhile, Magdeburg was concealed by a heavy smokescreen. Crews grew jittery when enemy fighters were reported all along the division line.

A chain reaction of misfortune persisted when the lead plane experienced a bomb rack malfunction and dropped its load four miles short. Of course, successive planes in formation released their bombs at the same ill-timed moment. Our mission results were naturally poor. These blunders resulted in a premature turn beneath another squadron during the bomb run. Consequently, explosives dropped on my pal Walter Springer's plane, sending it down in flames. Only two of his crew members survived. Everyone who witnessed the accident

was jolted by the spectacle. The day thus far was an unmiti-
gated disaster.

At first, those of us aboard *Jo* thought ourselves relatively
blessed. We had survived the worst of the flak, were spared major
damage, and were now homeward bound. Any self-congratulat-
ing on our part proved rash. About fifty miles after the target, the
oil temperature of the number-three engine slowly rose. Believing
there was a gauge problem, Predgen and I kept sharp eyes on the
panel. The plane then began to violently vibrate. We immediately
started to feather the props. Since we were deep in Germany, we
certainly didn't want to fall too far behind formation. We con-
served fuel and opened the cowl flaps to keep the cylinder head
temperature down. Additional power was then added to the three
remaining engines. This was only a short-term solution.

Our plane kept pace with the group for only a while. Over
time, fellow Liberators grew smaller and smaller on the horizon. Soon, we were all alone, vulnerable in the middle of our
enemy's land. Our only option was to call for fighter protection
and return the engines to normal operation. I summoned
escorts using specific codes assigned for the day. We referred
to our guardian fighters as "little brothers." In impressively
short order, a flyboy duo announced their arrival with, "We
have you covered, big brother."

Craning my head, I responded, "I can't see you."

The immediate reply was, "Look up."

And there they were—two beautiful, shiny P-51s gliding
5,000 feet above. The pilots remained with us all the way to

England. (Maybe they unsuccessfully used us as bait. No matter!) When we started our letdown over the North Sea, they descended with us, putting a propeller under each wing. As we crossed the English coast, they peeled off and said "so long" with wing wags. Those Mustangs were our defenders when we were most exposed.

I have long wished I could have located the two airmen who shepherded us home. I owed them the best booze in the house. Since such a quest proved a difficult task, I did the next best thing: Whenever I met a P-51 pilot, I bought him a drink and expressed my thanks—big brother to little brother. We loved to see P-51s. I think just about everybody in my class applied to be a fighter pilot when they graduated from flight school. But somebody had to fly the heavies.

Steve Birdsall, a fellow veteran of the Second Air Division, shared equally endearing thoughts on our fighter brethren. "If you were unfortunate enough to be caught in a lame bomber somewhere over enemy country there was no sight quite as heartwarming as one or two small, fast and friendly fighters singling you out to take you back home," he claimed. Many of our yellow-nosed little brothers hailed from the 361st Fighter Group out of Bottisham Airfield. The group flew 441 missions throughout the war. The outfit destroyed 331 enemy planes and lost eighty-one aircraft in the process—all in the name of protecting American grunts and bombers. These men have my eternal appreciation.[24]

Back at Halesworth, we discovered the root cause of our mechanical malfunction. A chunk of flak severed an oil cooler. That engine turned out to be all right, but the other three overworked engines had to be replaced. Sometimes I felt as if I had nine lives. I undoubtedly spent several of them over Europe. Many aviators increasingly contemplated their odds.

Along these lines, men were fazed by the loss of Walter Springer's aircraft to our own bombs. Walking through half-empty barracks lacking its familiar faces haunted some. Footlockers and duffle bags of dead men were solemnly processed for shipment to next of kin. At times, life seemed cheap.[25]

Wilmer Plate felt equally despondent after one of our flights when he noticed that some of his bunkmates had vanished. "The three biscuit mattresses were folded at the head of the beds. The clothes racks were empty, and the footlockers were gone. I was at a loss," he reflected. "My friend and his crew were gone." Buddies of the fallen might have hung over glasses of beer for days, drowning out their sorrows. But the war went on.[26]

Some grew despondent with pessimistic outlooks. "I began to realize that we were only a number," pilot Jim Davis of our outfit complained. "It did not take me long to realize that at this level, each of us was expendable. If you could not accept that, you really had a problem. That was the cold, cruel reality, and many of us could not accept or adjust to it."[27]

Readers might be familiar with the iconic "Willie and Joe" cartoon series by GI artist Bill Mauldin. One piece depicts a ragged soldier speaking to another in a foxhole at night. He exclaims, "I feel like a fugitive from the law of averages." I did not share such a fatalistic view. But as I now absorb the casualty figures, I realize how damn lucky I was. The war was a big game of chance. There was no sound way to rationalize who lived or died. For all the good fortune I had, however, I never found religion or prayed for deliverance.

Mother Nature afforded our bomb group a brief respite from new missions, though the sullen weather hardly cheered our spirits. Heavy rains grounded most of the Eighth Air Force from August 17 to 23. During that same week, Paris was finally liberated. *Stars and Stripes* marked the occasion by declaring, "Paris is a mad, crazy place—a city gone wild. Trying to describe Paris is like trying to take a moving picture of a dream, the sort of dream a dope fiend has. The story is a jumbled picture of laughing people, crying people." Watching from afar, we airmen perceived the unshackling of Paris as another indicator of the war's outcome swaying in our favor. This was certainly welcome news after a particularly hellish week. At that moment, I was halfway done with my missions.[28]

After several days of being grounded by meteorological conditions, our outfit went operational again. Weather was still poor when I was awoken at 3 a.m. on August 24. The fog was dense, and the mud was thick. Many crews entered the briefing room soaking wet. Guys thought the Operations team was nuts for organizing a mission on a morning like this.[29]

The group took off anyway around 7 a.m. to attack an aircraft assembly plant and field at Waggum near Brunswick, Germany. The low squadron slid under the middle squadron on the bomb run. Mirroring events of our prior mission, a plane in the lower squadron took an American bomb straight through its left wing. Despite extensive damage, this crippled bird was fortunately able to reach home. Navigator Chuck Reevs watched flak guns on a racetrack firing at us from below. He used his stopwatch to time the rate of ascent at 1,000 feet per second. Chuck recorded the time between the gun flash and the explosion as twenty long seconds.

There was intense flak over the target and our nose was hit. Gunner George Puska had many close calls in that position. Throughout our missions, the nose turret was struck no less than three times. George was mighty cold with all that air blowing through bits of broken turret plastic. On this particular journey, a piece of shrapnel bounced off Puska's flak jacket. This layer of armor generally worked well in shielding us, and we were glad to have it. Such near-misses often left small burn marks in the heavy fabric.

Luck ran thin for some of our crew. In one instance, small bits of plexiglass spewed into Puska's eye. Radio operator Dean Leonard was nicked by a red-hot tracer round. In addition, when Cochran's gun jammed, he anxiously swiveled the .50 caliber piece inside the plane to clear the obstruction. When finished, he slid the weapon back into position and commenced firing. However, he failed to engage the locking pin. The recoil hurled him and the gun back inside—all while the .50 was still firing. The interior of our plane was sprayed with our own rounds.

Discovery of this damage came as a great surprise to Predgen and me when we conducted our walk-around inspection with the ground crew chief upon return. We noticed all the slug holes coming out the left side of the plane, but no entry holes in the right side.

We looked at each other with puzzled expressions. "What in the hell caused *this?*" we wondered.

I then turned to Cochran and noticed his signature shit-eating grin. When he explained what transpired, the crew chief was far less amused. Years later at a reunion, tail gunner Vernon Long pointed at the old waist gunner and asked, "Do you remember the day that son of a bitch almost killed me?" It's easy to chuckle over such memories now, but the incident underscores the many ways we could be hurt in flight.

On August 25, newspapers reported on the wider endeavor in which we had just participated. Vast formations of bombers and fighters out of the United Kingdom and Italy smashed at Germany's shrinking oil supplies, communication centers, and aircraft production facilities. One correspondent called the mission "the most extensive single day's strategic bombing operation of the war" up to that point. Out of Britain, a 300-mile-wide phalanx ravaged targets stretching from Kiel to Brux, to our objective outside Brunswick.[30]

We returned to Germany the same day these accomplishments were touted in the headlines. Some 1,100 bombers and 750 fighters from Britain pushed across the Channel to pummel enemy plants at Rechlin, Schwerin, Wismar, and Lubeck. The 489th set its sights on a Heinkel aircraft factory at Rostock on the Baltic Sea. Flak was severe. Vic Cochran, a pilot in our group who had barracked with me in Ireland, lost an engine during the clash. He and his crew initially started back to England but couldn't risk flying that distance in such a precarious state. My war diary indicates he was shot down, but that was not the case. In fact, Cochran flew across the Baltic with hopes of reaching neutral Sweden. "There were a few anxious moments as we approached Sweden when two fighters suddenly appeared and we made a move for our turrets and waist gun, only to realize that we had dumped the ammo," Cochran recalled. "But the fighters were flying parallel to us and didn't seem hostile. They came close enough so that we could see that they didn't have German markings." Rather than being shot down, the Americans were guided to a Swedish landing strip.[31]

If a damaged plane was closer to Switzerland or Sweden than England, its pilot could risk a long flight home or opt to reach one of these neutral nations and be incarcerated. Over 1,400 U.S. aviators who fled to Sweden were consequently placed under house arrest. In conversations after the war, I learned the Swiss were severe sticklers regarding rules of neutrality. There, our men were jailed and presented few luxuries.

The Swedes, on the other hand, were very lenient and granted internees generous flexibility. Yanks gained employment and married Swedish girls. Cochran's men even skied at a resort where they were confined. This scenario was drastically better than imprisonment at a dreary stalag.

With Cochran's disappearance, the officers from our plane were the last men standing from our days in both Wyoming and Ireland. All the rest had been killed, wounded, captured, rotated out, or went missing in action. This was a startling statistic for us.

But not all were lost. Several men I presumed had perished were very much alive. When I eventually completed all my missions, I was cycled to a repple depple for rotation to the States. To my astonishment, I spotted Cochran and several previously MIA airmen suddenly around me.

"Where the hell did you fellas come from?" I asked with amazement. "I thought you were dead!"

Cochran turned to me with a grim expression and warned, "You haven't seen me. You don't know me."

Initially befuddled by his cryptic response, I later learned he and many stranded Americans were smuggled out of Sweden via a "secret airline." The Swedish government privately collaborated with our Air Forces to make clandestine recovery operations a reality. Some of our B-24s were painted black, covertly flown into Sweden, picked up Yank airmen, and cautiously ferried flyboys to freedom over Nazi-occupied Norway or Denmark. When Cochran returned, he was still technically classified as a POW and could not be sent to the combat zone again. He was therefore granted the option of choosing a stateside post until discharged. A native of Cincinnati, he wisely picked Ohio's Wright-Patterson Air Base. All things considered, this was an ideal outcome for the lieutenant.[32]

For the rest of us, the work went on. Effective smoke-screens and thick haze made for a bewildering mission to Ludwigshafen on August 26. Due to poor visibility, we turned to our secondary objective—marshalling yards at Ehrang, some forty miles away. Skies cleared and we pulverized the target. Changes in weather were always consequential. "It must have been easy to shoot at us as there were telltale vapor trails following for miles behind us," airman Bill Campbell recalled. Such vistas were marvelous but also murderous. Close-up flak sounded like staccato booms of thunder. When explosions shattered in front of us, smoke then swirled through our slipstreams. I saw multiple planes from other groups go down. One of them was in a flat spin—a gut-wrenching sight to behold. Six chutes emerged from the Liberator. Unlike several others, we endured this flight without any serious hits or mechanical failures.[33]

The journey to Ludwigshafen was especially memorable for John P. Zima, a co-pilot who embarked on his first mission that eventful day. "I grew more horrified as we approached our target, and my Hail Marys were coming fast and furious," he admitted. "I wondered how anything, especially a four-engine bomber, could get through. Our nose gunner, who had the best view, said he couldn't stand it and cradled his head in his arms. As the formation in front of us went through, there was a sudden ball of fire, a puff of smoke, and chunks of airplane fell downward to earth." Following a brief lull, the speed of combat accelerated.

The sky was completely engulfed in flame. As they whizzed through the flak, Zima's crewmates watched helplessly as other planes met their ends.

"He's hit!" one of the crew called.

"He's on fire!"

"He's spinning down!"

Intercom chatter grew more frantic.

"He's on fire!" another repeated. "My God, this is terrible!" Battle proved more harrowing than the crew expected.

The fiery crash of the 490th Bomb Group's *Little Warrior* over Germany remains a nightmarish example of horrors in battle. No crew survived. *Air Force photo.* (27)

"All things, good or bad, come to an end, and finally the unsinkable aircraft carrier that was England came into view," Zima concluded of the trip. "We landed, and our first mission, tough as it was, was completed."[34]

Prior to missions, P-38s often ventured over primary and secondary target areas as weather ships to measure mission viability. Meteorologists briefed us accordingly. Weather still bested some. Once again, the visibility ceiling caused by "thick soup" was dangerously low. Very close to the water's edge, we identified a ditched B-24 and called in the position to recovery teams. A sister outfit within the Second Air Division deserving of praise was the Air Sea Rescue Squadron. This unit retrieved hundreds of airmen from the frigid waters of the Channel. The squadron's crews made ample use of releasable airborne rafts and eventually procured PBY Catalina amphibious aircraft from the Navy to conduct lifesaving operations.[35]

P-38s also snapped aerial photography to evaluate the success of strikes. To our continual amazement, those planes often returned and had developed the film by the time we came back to base. They were much lighter and less cumbersome than our transportation.

We slept in late to 6 a.m. on August 27. The 489th was to lead a wing of bombers against an airfield at Oranienburg, only sixteen miles north of Berlin. Our trip became a bit sketchy when oil pressure in the number-two engine acted up. At the Danish coast, we met slight flak resistance. Shortly after, we were ordered to turn back due to a 40,000-foot

weather front on the far horizon. The mission was scrubbed
but we were nonetheless granted sortie credit.[36]

After four deep aerial penetrations in as many days, I
enjoyed some catchup time on sleep at the end of August.
Although we carried out mild training exercises, there were
also many recreational opportunities. Reevs and I competed
in a division tennis tournament and earned second place.
Notwithstanding the physical fatigue of war, I was glad to dust
off my athleticism. We thereafter hailed our victory during a
three-day pass to London.

Other airmen had reason for celebration as well. By month's
end, sixteen crews had completed their operational tours.
Among them was the crew of *Pregnant Peggy*. Crew chief Paul
Thomas recalled, "It was customary for a crew returning from
its final mission to buzz the field." However, the colonel threatened to fine any perpetrators $500. "Not one to pass up a
challenge," Thomas continued, "*Pregnant Peggy*'s crew collected the money in advance. Then they gave Halesworth a
demonstration of buzzing that was long talked about, after
which they reported to Colonel Napier as directed and paid
the fine." Half a grand seemed a fair exchange to commit a
defiant act of euphoria. *Peggy*'s new crew died in a mid-air
collision with *Bomber's Moon* less than two months later.[37]

The day after our crew returned from London, a new type
of mission awaited us. We participated in a string of flights
coined "Operation Truckin,'" September 1 to 9. During the
rapid advance of Allied armies across France, the Eighth Air

Force destroyed bridges and enemy assembly areas to stall German retreats and thwart potential reinforcements. All this logistical hustle strained American supply lines. Our B-24s were called forth to help relieve pressure on Gen. Patton's troops by lugging fuel, medical supplies, ammunition, rations, and some fresh foods. On average, we packed three tons of this cargo on a given flight and departed from Beaulieu near Southampton.

We flew in at low altitude and were offered a stark perspective of damage on the ground level. In fact, it felt strange not being shot at. This was near Orléans, south of Paris. We had bombed this same airfield not long before. The runway was pocked with massive craters, forcing us to veer around them as we landed. Several planes did not dodge the blast holes and completely washed out. A quarter of the field was unusable. We later found out that peripheries of the runway were still mined when we had arrived.

The front lines were only ten miles away. Dead livestock and an abandoned German Messerschmitt were amidst the rubble. I playfully sat in the cockpit of the forsaken enemy plane. The space was so comparatively small but ultimately better designed. Its controls were hardwired and therefore essentially interchangeable. All the instrument and control panels had been easily ripped out before the Germans abandoned the rest of the aircraft.

Meanwhile, Free French civilians emerged and unloaded our plane. They conveyed warm wishes and bartered with battlefield souvenirs. Lugar pistols were particularly popular. One of the GIs who helped unpack the plane presented me a captured German wooden bullet, which I still have on display in my home office today. Apparently, these nasty rounds—sometimes used by enemy snipers—splintered and spread upon impact.

The wooden German bullet gifted to me by a GI in France.
John Homan collection. (28)

Easing pressure on Army supply chains was a very rewarding undertaking. "The roughest thing we have done yet, and above all the most gratifying to me, was the help we were able to give our frontline boys on several occasions," Chuck Reevs informed family. Even so, there were no missions credited for these runs. Chuck also acknowledged his appreciation of receiving a free subscription to his local newspaper while overseas. "I'd like to tell you how much we appreciate hearing about the other fellows in the service and about events around the hometown," he wrote. "It proves to us we are being thought of by the folks back there, and I guess that is worth more to us than all the medals that one could get."[38]

Lou Wagner was equally satisfied by charitable deeds. "Believe I did today the best thing we could ever do," he reflected. "Instead of bombs we carried flour for the French. We landed at Orléans about 15 miles from the front lines. It was a thrill to land in France. The people really were glad to see us. The people in Orléans and Paris are starving. Maybe this mission will ease the situation."[39]

Airman George A. Reynolds shared similarly fond memories of these truckin' runs. Across from the landing strip, "village night spots became alive at dusk with the sound of music, fun, and games," he wrote. "Being freedom loving GIs, of course, we decided to help the friendly natives celebrate their recent liberation." However, one crewman had to stay behind and safeguard the plane. A coin toss was the democratic method to determine who remained. "Tossing was fast and furious," Reynolds remembered. "The loser sighed, strapped on his trusty .45, and settled down to guard duty. Gesturing to his grinning, departing airmen, the pilot realized he was the only one of the crew who spoke any French." C'est la vie.[40]

Arriving behind our lines in France allowed me to contrast the conditions of airmen and foot soldiers. On the matter of creature comforts, my life was so much better. I had a shower, warm food, movies, and a roof over my head. As to actual time in combat, though, I dodged as much hot steel as any ground pounder. Despite this, I always used to joke with infantrymen about my living quarters—especially how hard my mattress was. Their reactions were always priceless.

These comparatively tame tasks of mercy did not suggest we were out of harm's way. Despite everything I endured over previous weeks, I had yet to experience my most dangerous mission.

CHAPTER 7

Out of Darkness

"I'm hit!"

A combat airman rarely hears words more terrifying over the intercom.

Severe flak over Magdeburg, Germany, inflicted heavy tolls on September 11, 1944. Amidst the brawl, our waist gunner, Bo Cochran, cried for help.

"Somebody go check on him," I instructed. My hands were quite full as we commenced the bomb run. Imagine my surprise when I then heard chuckles over our two-way radio.

"Hey, what's going on back there?"

"He's fine," another gunner assured. "He's just clowning around!"

Not until after the mission did the details behind this confusion become clear. A jagged lump of shrapnel had ricocheted off Cochran's helmet. The waist gunner was stunned by the blow. Sizzling metal pierced his headgear, cracked the leather liner, and flung Bo to the cabin floor.

Initially, Cochran thought Dick Bunch was horsing around and had bashed him over the head with a box of chaff.

"Cut it out!" Bo hollered. "You're giving me a headache!" He then turned to look out his window.

"Oh my God, Bo," Bunch declared. "Look at that hole in your helmet!" Bo then panicked. "I'm hit!" he announced.

The huge gash was ripped across his helmet's rough surface. Cochran was lucky his skull did not resemble the blistered steel pot. Bo was spared a bloody wound, but I doubt he appreciated the dismissive heckles that soon arose from crewmates. The gunner endured perhaps the closest near-miss I saw among our crew during the war. Cochran shook off his bewilderment and resumed his position. We still had a full flight ahead.

The day's targets at Magdeburg were yet more oil refineries. Thick clouds concealed our primary destination. The lead plane, helmed by Capt. Harry Wagnon, experienced a poorly timed bomb rack malfunction. Consequently, bombs within Wagnon's Liberator were prematurely dropped. Subsequent ships in formation naturally followed suit and released loads in imprecise, pell-mell fashion—dropping high explosives all over the city. Many of these salvos undoubtedly fell upon dense residential districts.[1]

On this point, I must draw a line of distinction: I was never ordered to bomb households, schools, hospitals, or churches. Every single mission in my logbook indicates a strategic location that superiors deemed had to be eliminated. Without fail, these were sites of transportation, military, or industrial significance.

Yet this cannot be said of all Allied air commands, and collateral damage was all but certain in many circumstances. Whether the victims of incidental or purposeful bombings, German citizens of numerous metropolitan areas suffered terrible tolls. City dwellers departed communities in droves, often shellshocked and unable to comprehend recent hardships. One Bavarian diarist who conversed with refugees from Hamburg reported that conditions were "beyond the grasp of imagination." Some German civilians likened constant air raids to the Four Horsemen of the Apocalypse. By September 1944, 5.6 million Germans had abandoned their city homes.[2]

Many of those who remained would perish by the tens of thousands—especially when American planners shifted away from pinpoint bombing to more indiscriminate warfare on urban centers in early 1945. Gen. Jimmy Doolittle vehemently protested the change, claiming such a move would "violate the basic American principle of precision bombing of targets of strictly military significance." He was overruled.[3]

Germans naturally sought to inflict steep retribution on us as we flew over their Fatherland. Hazards intensified after our muddled dash over Magdeburg. Enemy fighters swept in something fierce after we cleared the city. One was shot down right in front of us. The plane was flung through the frigid air like a shattered toy model. Four B-24s likewise swirled downward in flames.

"Come on fellas, bail!" was the common reaction to such traumatic scenes. These incidents always made our hearts sink.

An aura of confusion and desperation pervaded throughout the action. All groups in formation reported enemy jets, although I personally did not spot any. Jerries were particularly mischievous during this operation. Some enemy 109 pilots painted white stripes on their aircraft to replicate the appearance of American P-51s. Elsewhere, a German aviator crept toward us in a British Spitfire painted black with a Maltese cross on his fuselage. Far off, the plane naturally resembled a friendly. These wolves in sheepskin were meant to lure bomber crews into a false sense of serenity before mauling us. The double-dealing intruders surely kept us on our toes.[4]

Tales of potential bushwhacks made our crew especially apprehensive. We were fully alert when a mysterious B-17 approached, established radio contact, and announced she was going to fly alongside us. Unsure if the American plane was in fact piloted by Americans, the skipper told her to point her guns away from us or we would blow the bogie out of the sky. Our concern was that Germans could have repaired a captured B-17 to operating condition and then infiltrated our formation. We took no risks during this uncertain encounter. We made damn sure that plane wasn't going to deceive us. Our own gunners kept a clear eye on the Fortress for the duration of the flight. "We were set to fire if he did not drop bombs," Predgen cited in his mission report. When the Fortress released its load, we noticed that the explosives were painted orange. The rendezvous is still a mystery to me.[5]

Bogies appeared at several instances during September missions. When in doubt, some crews instinctively went on the defensive. Dick Wagner of the 489th recalled one such uneasy exchange:

"Three bogies at seven o'clock low," his tail gunner announced.

Most of the crew could not make out the inbound planes.

"Can you see them through the side bubble?" the pilot asked the navigator.

"Look like twin-engine fighters, 217s maybe."

The tail gunner jumped back in. "They're flying a pursuit curve on us, closing from seven o'clock low!" This was a hostile indicator since our fighters were instructed not to point their noses at bombers.

"The aircraft recognition exercise became academic at this point," Wagner recalled, "especially since the Germans were reportedly flying some captured P-51s."

The planes continued their approach and the navigator yelled, "Shoot!" A volley was unleashed.

"When the P-51 pilot saw all the hardware coming his way he flipped his wing and peeled off," Wagner concluded. "All three got out of there in a hurry. I often wonder what he had in mind when he flew that curve on us." Were the incoming pilots friends or foes? The crew was never quite certain. The September 11 journey to Magdeburg and back was an arduous one. We had many flak holes to be patched afterward.[6]

Our ship was loaned to Lt. John P. Burns for the next day's mission to Kiel. During his flight, the number-three engine quit, and the feathering system failed entirely. Vibrations were so severe that the propeller and reduction gear fell off. Upon return, the plane was a strange sight since the front of that engine was absent. I was glad to have missed that trip.

The next four days I did little else but eat, sleep, and play volleyball and tennis. A humorous note from our September 14 crew log notes, "Crew changed huts today. Other one too dirty. Other crews wouldn't help clean it up. New hut has a radio." Meanwhile, tail gunner Vernon Long tinkered on his motorcycle, only to have parts fall off when he started its engine. Predgen enjoyed Ping-Pong, though the balls were rationed and difficult to obtain. On the afternoon of the fifteenth, our crew lost a softball game 20-16. Creature comforts were well-deserved considering hardships ahead. Unfortunately for Predgen, he spent our brief reprieve recovering from a dental operation resulting in a yanked wisdom tooth.[7]

The group was pulled from its late summer respite for a low-level practice mission on September 17. At briefing, we were ordered to fly at low altitude to the initial point, then climb to 500 feet, drop our payloads, and thereafter descend to our original elevation. During the maneuver, we flew formation "on the deck," practically scraping the ground and skimming tree-tops—something we had never dared before. We were so low that British cows, sheep, and horses scattered across pastures and jumped into ponds. From the cockpit, we could even identify a little girl with a red coat that had white buttons. Elsewhere along the way, a man sitting in front of his house dove for cover as we roared overhead. We must have also crossed through an RAF bomb range, because a Stirling bomber released a practice bomb through our formation. When the squadron returned to base, speculation ran rampant. The only way we could attack at the practiced altitude without blowing ourselves up was the use of delayed action bombs. The rumor mill spun madly that evening. What was high command scheming now?[8]

By this point of the war, Allied forces had advanced well beyond the Normandy hedgerows and Paris. Just days prior to our precarious training mission, the first U.S. troops entered western sectors of Germany. "Allies are battering the Siegfried Line and I hope they can wade through Germany like they did France," Predgen wrote to family on September 16. "The German people should be a bit tired of our bombing." Also sensing Nazi vulnerability, multiple Army Groups—including those of Sir Bernard Montgomery and Gen. George Patton—feverishly pushed east. But with this strategic sprint to the enemy's borderlands also came bottlenecks, persistent supply problems, and stiffened resistance.[9]

These circumstances prompted Montgomery to propose a mammoth operation code-named Market Garden. Eisenhower acquiesced to the British general's pleas and halted plans to invade the Reich via a broad front. The ensuing operation consisted of nearly 35,000 British, American, and Polish paratroopers and glider troops dropped behind enemy lines in Nazi-occupied Holland. The big show took place on September 17 as we conducted our preparation run. At that moment, we had no concept of the concurrent undertaking unfolding nearly 200 miles away. Our job was to deliver much-needed supplies by airdrop the next day.

The overarching objective of the airborne divisions was to secure a series of bridges and clear the way for British forces to dash across the Rhine River into northern Germany. If successful, the feat of Market Garden had the potential to bring the war in Europe to a dramatic close by Christmas. But fate and folly intervened.

Decades later, I learned many operational details from the fantastic book *A Bridge Too Far* by Cornelius Ryan. Firstly, Germans obtained the total Allied battle plan on the first day from a crashed glider. I also realized that English intelligence photos showed German Panzer divisions being rested and refitted in the area prior to the engagement. This intelligence was ignored, and the officer who made the discovery was transferred. Furthermore, Germans had overrun our drop zone and the paratroopers had to clear them out in vicious hand-to-hand combat if they were to receive our supplies. None of these factors boded well for us.

Troops under Gen. James Gavin of the U.S. 82nd Airborne Division waged furious assaults to clear the drop zones, sometimes at bayonet point and outnumbered five to one. Our planes in this sector provided a vital supply lifeline for the division. Without the delivered goods, the paratroopers would be forsaken in the face of counterassaults. "The woods remained infested with a hodgepodge of German infantry, and it was obvious that these enemy forays heralded more concentrated and determined attacks," wrote Ryan. "By juggling his troops from one area to another, Gavin was confident of holding, but he was only too well aware that for the moment the 82nd's situation was precarious."[10]

Most of these impediments transpired before I even departed for Holland. Further logistical and timing challenges led to additional operational breakdowns. The deck was already stacked.

Over 250 B-24s of the Eighth Air Force's Second Air Division took part in the operation, with a parachute supply drop scheduled for the second day. We joined over 2,000 other aircraft consisting of C-47s, Stirlings, Horsas, Wacos, Hamilcars, and various fighters in a convoy stretching more than 100 miles. My logbook lists sortie number twenty-four to Groesbeek, Holland, near the German border on September 18 to drop supplies for the 82nd Airborne. This was to be my most dangerous day of the entire war.[11]

A Service of Supply sergeant was assigned to each plane to oversee the loading and dropping of deliveries. He meticulously tied off a big bundle of crates so their chute would automatically open upon release from our plane. Supplies hung in the bomb bay and were piled in the waist to be kicked out of the lower hatch. Each 200-pound load was generally full of ammunition, fuel cans, rations, or medical supplies. Plans had changed and now called for us to fly at from 500 to 1,000 feet. Even in ideal conditions, this would have been a daunting proposition.

Matters worsened immediately before takeoff to Groesbeek. Due to a wild clerical error, individual crew briefing maps and documents were accidentally swapped with those of another unit. Our officers had no option but to thoroughly examine these new materials while in flight.

As I recall, the journey was conducted in poor weather; ceilings were from 1,500 to 2,000 feet with limited visibility. There were large formations of C-47s towing gliders on the same heading and altitude, requiring our faster formation to maneuver continuously to avoid collisions. The sky was completely blanketed with aircraft. Many of the gliders eventually snapped like pencils upon landing. Constant course corrections, dodging cargo planes, and steering clear of engineless craft across the sea and beyond made for a hectic beginning. I knew right then that this was not going to be a typical mission. We were in the third wave—and the Germans had plenty of time to prepare for us.

When we entered Holland, an unidentified object struck the top of the number-three engine, tearing a gaping hole in the cowling and causing loss of power. There was no known explanation because we didn't observe any enemy activity. Perhaps a loose piece of machinery or cargo from another aircraft barreled into us.

The next scene I gazed upon will never leave my memories. Due to our low altitude, we could easily discern features on the ground level. In the middle of all the chaos, I spotted a young girl in a yellow dress standing solitarily near a house. She looked upward, undoubtedly entranced by the massive formation thundering overhead. One could speculate she had lived much of her life under Nazi occupation. Was she inspired or frightened by our arrival? I will never know. I just hope she lived to experience liberation and beyond.

The Jerries then opened on us. Gunfire spurted out of woods on our lower right. These rounds shot down two planes to our front. This hairy situation was further complicated due to the very small size of the drop zone. We had limited time and flexibility to deliver supplies because we dropped by squadron rather than by group.

Squadron leader Lt. Ed Wall could not identify the drop zone on the first pass due to restrictive visibility. He therefore initiated a second pass. The lieutenant was determined to deliver the supplies directly on target. But on the return, another squadron was in the drop zone, forcing us into a third run. There was a collective groan from our ranks as patience and nerves frayed. We ran through a wicked gauntlet of enemy ground fire with every spin. Red and yellow incendiary and tracer rounds spurted from fixed enemy positions below—an up-close threat we were unaccustomed to.

On each pass, we must have crossed into Germany because I spotted a farmer, with a woman standing next to him, firing a shotgun at us. Other crews in formation noticed this bold gesture as well. The absurd act of defiance both astounded and angered me. I nearly instructed our tail gunner to reciprocate the favor and spray some hot lead with Uncle Sam's compliments. Discipline prevailed over my temptation. Our gunners were under strict orders to withhold fire anywhere near the drop zones for fear of inflicting casualties on American troops. (Our self-restraint was the only factor sparing those fascist farmers. Twin .50 caliber machine guns would have mowed them down into bloody bits. We were otherwise of the mind to let them have both barrels.)

We had bigger fish to fry anyway. On the third and final run, the enemy had us zeroed with utmost precision. Our plane was riddled by heavy machine gun rounds. A rapid succession of staccato thumps and thuds ripped into our fuselage.

Zip, zip, zip!

But we kept going. Despite the dangers, we dropped our supplies right in the zone—and then did our best to get the hell out of there.

Right after we released supplies from 400 to 500 feet, we suffered a string of devastating hits. I cannot recall the exact sequence or timing of what occurred next. Everything fell apart so quickly over the course of a few tense seconds. The following seemed to occur simultaneously: The hydraulic system was struck, filling the cockpit with atomized hydraulic fluid, which resembled smoke. This had never happened before, and we thought for certain we were aflame. We could hardly see through the hydraulic fuel fog. Number-four engine was soon after knocked out.

Then we heard those dreaded words again.

"I'm hit!"

Dean Leonard, our radio operator, stood between Predgen and me when he cried out. He fell forward on our console controls. We hurriedly yanked him off so as not to interfere with the plane's functions. I summoned Lou Wagner out of his top turret to pull Dean aside and render whatever aid he could. The skipper and I were overwhelmed in the cockpit. The moment was one of absolute chaos. Our hearts pounded as we assessed tremendous levels of damage.

These responses were all crucial and executed in a matter of seconds: We pushed the stick forward into a dive to maintain air speed. This allowed us to prevent stalling and dodge further ground fire. The number-four prop was immediately feathered, which was imperative to avert crashing. This act required instant precision. If we placed too much power on one side of the aircraft, maintaining balance would have been tricky. The bomber leveled off at a mere fifty feet! Power was cautiously added to the number-one and -two engines. The plane was at treetop level, speeding at 200 miles per hour, when we were finally able to pull the stick back. Our recovery from this critical descent was something of a miracle.

We struggled up to approximately 800 feet and navigated a course to a British emergency field for cripples at Woodbridge. The airstrip had a 10,000-foot extra-wide runway with 5,000-foot grass extensions for gear-up landings. Our speed gradually slowed as we limped back to East Anglia. The flight with two-and-a-half engines lasted a nail-biting two-and-a-half hours.

Lou Wagner's diary indicates that part of our left tail was shot off. When we dove to maintain airspeed and evade fire, planes in our squadron lost sight of us and reported us shot down when they returned to base. Many of our comrades thought us dead or captured.

Without hydraulics, our brakes were out of commission. Wheels and flaps therefore had to be manually cranked down since we lost power. The engineer took on this time-sensitive task. We all hoped the cranks wouldn't become stuck, or our goose was cooked. I also suspected our gas tanks were full of holes. Fortuitously, these tubs were sealed with neoprene, a flame-resistant synthetic rubber. This material possibly spared us from absolute disaster. In any case, arrival at Woodbridge was perhaps the most high-pressure moment of my life.

The situation spiraled out of control. When we finally neared the field, we noticed a B-24 in flames halfway down on the right side of the runway. The blazing crash left us no option but to use the left side. Lacking hydraulic pressure, we knew we had no brakes. What we didn't know was that our left tire was completely shot out. It shredded into scorched chunks upon landing, strewing burned rubber in all directions. When we hit the runway, the plane pulled left with no means of stopping and little engine control. The ship violently and abruptly weighed down on its carriage. This was one massive jolt, like sitting at the epicenter of an earthquake.

With little power available on the right side, it seemed inadvisable to add power on the left engines. This move would have propelled us toward the burning bomber. There was nothing else to do but let the plane veer off the left side of the runway. Some of the fog-dispersal piping system was obliterated in the process. We skidded uncontrollably off the airstrip. I don't think I ever held the controls tighter. I gritted my teeth. There was a feeling of helplessness in our efforts to halt the aircraft. The sensation was like being hurled from a massive slingshot with little power to control direction. The experience was utterly terrifying.

The plane grated against the earth, trembling something fierce.

"Come on! Come on," we collectively hollered. All were worried that leaking fuel might turn us into a blackened pile of ash at any second. Everything was out of our hands.

When the plane at last came to a halt, we shut down the engines fast and killed the switches. My immediate instinct was to jump out of the ship as quickly as possible and get the hell away. We did not waste any time putting plenty of distance between us and that plane! The last time we saw the Service of Supply sergeant, he was running full speed ahead of us. We were not far behind. The entire crew hightailed it, figuring our bomber was about to blow sky high. The landing was the scariest of my career—if you could even call that a landing.

This was the end of *Jo*. She served us well, but her time was up. Thankfully, ours was not. For as disastrous as Operation Market Garden was, we survived. *Jo*'s steel and aluminum corpse, however, was hauled off the runway and ultimately scrapped.

When Wagner removed Leonard's pants to inspect for wounds, he found that a tracer bullet had gone through his trousers and skivvies. The round thoroughly singed Dean's rear end, but not enough to merit a Purple Heart. The radio-man retained the trousers as a grim memento until his passing in 2013. I wonder if his family still owns this relic of a close brush with death.

"Quite an exciting day. I'll admit it was too much!" Wagner recorded. "Everyone got out safe," he wrote with thanks. Still, his one-word conclusion in caps best summed up our experience: "ROUGH!!!"[12]

Our jaded crew remained at Woodbridge for the night and was treated to a dinner of mutton and boiled potatoes in the officers' mess. The next day, the 489th dispatched a plane to retrieve us. We learned fifteen of our group's planes were reported with minor damage and five with major damage. I assume *Jo* was among the latter.

Two planes right in front of us had been shot from the sky. They were *Rum Runner* and the ironically named *Heaven*

Can Wait. These scenes left us traumatized. *Heaven Can Wait* was piloted by Lt. Claude Lovelace and Lt. Evan E. Allan. During the drop, the skipper suffered a ghastly blow to the head and died instantly. His lifeless remains slumped onto the controls. Allan was likewise struck in the skull. Bleeding heavily, he struggled to keep the craft airborne. With his engines shot out and on fire, he determined a crash landing was the best chance for survival. The twenty-two-year-old officer belly-landed his ship near the River Kendel. The battered bomber darted across a swampy pasture, slid into a pond, and finally lurched into a dike. *Heaven Can Wait* split in two. Allan did not survive the impact. Five of his men, though taken prisoner, owed their lives to the lieutenant's skill. On the sixtieth anniversary of the bomber's crash, Dutch and German residents dedicated a plaque to the crew near Hommersun, Germany. Lovelace remains missing in action to this day.[13]

I cannot recall ever suffering from survivor's guilt but hearing about Lovelace's fate was an emotional punch in the gut. I had lost friends and acquaintances before, but perhaps the particularly tense nature of this mission made the losses sting more than usual.

I don't wish to sound heartless, but my first reaction to the reported deaths of buddies was, "Thank goodness it wasn't me, because it *could* have been me." If your time was up, your time was up.

The losses of September 18 were not entirely in vain I suppose. Back across the border, U.S. paratroopers collected

80 percent of the supplies our group and others dropped. Gen. Louis Brereton of the First Allied Airborne Army commended our deeds. "I should like to express my appreciation of splendid support given by your Air Force," he announced, "responsible for successful completion of troop carrier missions. Bomber resupply beautifully executed. Many thanks to all ranks for outstanding aid."[14]

The sentiments were sincere and appreciated but rang a bit hollow in our ears. Of the 252 B-24s assigned to the task, 130 were hit by enemy guns. Thankfully, we avoided friendly fire because Gavin's officers recognized our tail colors. Despite our own operational success, Market Garden was a colossal flop. While some Dutch communities were liberated, the ensuing campaign bogged down airborne divisions for weeks of stalemate in Holland's marshy pastures. Various military engagements also revealed the Germans had more fight left in them than originally thought possible. Many veterans within my group referred to the encompassing calamity as "Monty's Folly." From the fiasco, one fact became certain: the war was not going to end by Christmas.

Predgen was promoted to first lieutenant for his actions in Holland. For my own efforts in the enterprise, I was later awarded the Distinguished Flying Cross. The medal hangs in my office as a vivid reminder of my most terrifying day.[15]

Regular operations resumed September 21 with a mission to Koblenz. Because *Jo* had met her demise, we were issued a new aircraft with a more colorful title. She was called *Rebel*

Rebel Gal and her new crew. Front row, left to right: John Predgen, John Dalgleish, John Homan, and Chuck Reevs. Back row, left to right: Lou Wagner, Marion Cochran, Vernon Long, Richard Bunch, Dean Leonard, and George Puska. *John Predgen collection.* (29)

Gal. Once more, we had little concept of who the plane was named after, but we presumed it was christened in honor of a previous crew member's southern sweetheart. The mascot showed a blonde in a white bathing suit taking a dive. *Jo* had lacked any distinctive artwork and featured only a cursive signature, so having racy nose art was an entirely new trait of our crewmen culture. The plane was named and previously commanded by Lt. Hugh Bernard Carroll, while my co-pilot's seat was once manned by Wendell Buck, who had been promoted to captain.

We didn't fly very far on our inaugural run with *Rebel Gal*. The plane developed a severe gas leak in the number-four engine. The leak fogged the right waist window. The prop was feathered, the fuel valve was shut, and we dropped our bombs in the North Sea during the return to base. All these bombs had safeties on them but, dear God, there must be thousands of tons of unexploded ordnance at the bottom of the English Channel. Even in London or Berlin today, excavations for new buildings are regularly halted when construction crews discover eighty-year-old explosives buried deep in the dirt. In 2021, the BBC reported that the British Ministry of Defence disposes of approximately sixty German bombs per year. At least a dozen German bomb technicians have been killed over the last two decades. In 2011, according to the Smithsonian, "45,000 people—the largest evacuation in Germany since World War II—were forced to leave their homes when a drought revealed a similar device lying on the bed of the Rhine in the middle of Koblenz." All these years later, the war still inflicts its dark toll on civilian populations.[16]

The bomb discovered in Koblenz very well could have been released by my group on September 21, 1944. Although our crew turned back, the rest of the outfit proceeded to the city's marshalling yards. Airman Ed Johnson confronted dangers like those we faced on our previous mission. "On the run from the IP to the target we took a very close flak burst that knocked the electric hydraulic pump off the bomb bay wall," he recalled. "This sent red fluid spraying into the rear of the plane, and the waist gunners thought it was gasoline." When the ship reached Halesworth, Johnson had to "manually crank down the main gear, kick out the nose wheel, and crank down the flaps." Mercifully, his ship landed safely and was towed to a hardstand. Ours, meanwhile, had been hauled off to the scrap dump. Such was the luck of the draw.[17]

Our crew averted catastrophe again on September 27 when we were assigned to fly *Lil' Cookie* with a Col. Webb, in lieu of traveling to Germany. Lacking guns, bombs, and equipment, the assembly plane was so light in weight that morning that we couldn't set her down on our initial landing attempt. She just kept floating down the runway. We coasted across the field and ultimately had to do another loop to at last land. This was a mild inconvenience compared to what our pals would endure 400 miles to the east.

A disastrous example of leadership error was committed later that day when the 445th Group of our division took off with thirty-six planes to bomb Kassel. The lead ship mistakenly turned on the bomb run fifty miles short of plan. Only seven planes returned to base. Additionally, two aircraft from the 489th tangled in a mid-air collision near Halesworth. None of their crews survived. Reflecting on these situations prompts one of my beliefs about warfare: the side that screws up the least wins. Amazingly, we were still able to attain victory despite *many* monumental screwups.

For whatever reason, I could not fall asleep that night. Come morning, our crew arose at 3 a.m. to attack Kassel's Henschel Locomotive Works, which had been transformed into a tank manufacturing plant. We sailed through some very close flak on this journey. A navigator from another crew defined the mission as "A really rough one. We saw the flak about forty miles away from the target. It was like a big black cloud over Kassel." True to form, our nose gunner—George Puska—caught several bits of plexiglass in his eyes a second time. John Dalgleish tried thawing out medicine to assist George, but the materials were too frozen. We sustained multiple blast holes in the fuselage. Enemy fighter jets were reported in the vicinity but our luck in avoiding these high-speed aircraft stood firm. "German reliance on Focke Wulfs and Messerschmitts was reported by the bomber crews, who often tell of seeing jet planes but add that they usually flew along in the distance and gave little trouble," reported the United Press.[18]

Luck was not as solid with our propellers, three of which ran away until we brought them back with feather buttons. We sweated them all the way home, encountering some coastal flak along the way for good measure. A spice of danger was added to the mix since we were unable to drop our 8,000-pound bomb load due to a concealed target. This lifestyle grew increasingly tedious. Nothing suggested the coming month would be any easier.

Coincidentally, my girlfriend, Irene, had a brother who flew over Kassel the previous summer as a bombardier. He barely survived. Lt. Edward Piech was an officer on a Fortress named *Poisonality*. His plane was sent to Kassel on June 30, 1943, to help smash Fiesler Aircraft plants. During the journey, half the crew became casualties, a shell burst into an oxygen tank, triggered a fire, and the B-17 somehow returned to England on a single engine. My future brother-in-law tried to conceal the story from his folks, but his heroics were eventually touted in *Stars and Stripes* and additional newspapers. "Anytime you want to hear a description of Hell, ask us," he thereafter wrote home. "In the heat of battle, I recall thoughts going through my mind such as, *This can't be happening to me, things like this only happen to guys in books.*" I experienced a similar level of disbelief during my own flight to Kassel.[19]

Our mission to Stuttgart for October 2 was scrubbed and we instead ventured to Hamm, home to some of Germany's largest freight yards. From the city, extensive rail lines radiated in all directions to key landmarks of industry and transportation. All told, over 1,000 U.S. heavy bombers and fighters scorched three major railroad centers along a 270-mile front.[20]

Throughout it all, we experienced mechanical problems with all four engines, but none serious enough to warrant return to England. Flak at the target was heavy and accurate. In addition to witnessing four B-24s from other groups go down, I spotted the feared red centers bursting between us and the adjacent plane. Unsurprisingly, we sustained numerous punctures in the forward section. A damaged ship from our group could not reach base in time and crash-landed a few miles from Halesworth with one fatality.

The Hamm mission also introduced us to the obstinate leadership style of our group's new deputy commander. He was a gung-ho West Pointer who desired his share of glory in a hurry. While over enemy territory, he uttered demands like, "If you can't drop on target, hit any town you can. There might be a Luftwaffe pilot home on leave." We rolled our eyes and generally ignored these orders. This rookie officer led the

The B-24 *Bomber's Moon* of our outfit helped attack Manheim on October 3 as our crew sought some needed respite. This plane crashed two weeks later. *Air Force photo.* (30)

group on October 2, acting like we were as new to the war as
he was. Every fifteen minutes he barked over the radio,
"Tighten up that formation!" We were all aware that flying
too close in certain situations was risky, so nobody budged.
Our plane flew on the deputy commander's left wing that day.
When we started letting down on the return, Predgen and I
decided to play smartasses.

"We'll show him what a *tight formation* looks like!" John
declared. We inched in on the officer until our wing was
almost in his waist window.

"Okay, wise guys," the deputy reacted, "open it up." That
was the last time he requested a tight formation. This man did
not last long in our ranks. I inquired about him at a reunion
years later and learned he was quietly reassigned. Good
riddance.

The vainglorious officer was not my sole problem during
that operation, and my patience was limited. I flew to Hamm
with a terrible head cold. Our crew was scheduled to leave for
an airmen's rest home the next day. I didn't want to be sent to
the infirmary rather than a resort, so I sucked up my misery
and joined the venture.

"I'll be fine," I stupidly thought. "One more mission and
I'll have a nice vacation."

I paid dearly for my poor decision. The sinus pressure was
unbelievable. I've never been in such excruciating pain in all
my life. My ears did not clear, and the episode was painful as
hell. Once we landed, I frantically ran to the medics with my

hands cupped over my ears. "Get me over to the hospital, fast!" I screamed.

The ambulance drivers must have thought I suffered a nervous breakdown. I probably resembled a madman as I approached. Horrendously, the remedies for my malady were as uncomfortable as the symptoms. For two hours at the base hospital, doctors attempted to fully clear my ears. Physicians shoved something akin to a baster up my nose and practically blew my head off. Blood ran out my nostrils like water from a faucet. Rather than occupy a hospital bed, I stumbled back to my bunk. I did not want anything to stand in my way of a leave. Yet the aches made me feel like crying myself to sleep.

While most of our comrades proceeded to battle over the likes of Lachen, Speyerdorf, Rheine, Hamburg, Clausthal-Zellerfeld, and Koblenz between October 3-9, the crew of *Rebel Gal* sought much-needed refuge at a "Flak Home." How did superiors determine if we needed time at such a getaway? A flight surgeon kept a close eye on us. If we were twitching, blinking, or ticking too much, we might be candidates for some R&R. I suppose our recent exploits rendered us more than eligible. Also known as "Flak Farms," the rest facilities were usually located at secluded hotels, clubs, estates, and coastal areas to afford battle-fatigued flyboys relaxation. Army psychologists were often on hand to assess shellshocked service members.

Our haven near the Irish Sea that October was the ornate Birkdale Palace Hotel, located at Southport, England. The Eighth Air Force and the American Red Cross appropriated this luxury resort for men in our strained condition. We enjoyed a quality menu, no discipline, and no uniform codes. The environment was designed to be a complete divorce from combat and military life. The boys savored the interlude. Activities were numerous and a nearby amusement park featured rollercoasters and shooting galleries. "Booze has been rationed as usual," wrote Predgen on October 9, "however, the crew has all the pub openings down pat. Crew would hit all at their various openings and get their daily ration fast!" The skipper referred to Southport as a playground for the British elite. "It's a lovely place, that is to go broke in," he quipped.[21]

Despite opportunities for seaside fun, I had more important business in mind. Escape from Halesworth and battle afforded me a precious moment to connect with family members. Just 150 miles across England was my father's hometown, Hull. He emigrated from his native land in 1923 and had never returned. Sensing a golden opportunity, I checked in at Southport and immediately planned a departure. The next day, I purchased a train ticket to seek out the grandparents I had never met. Anticipation grew with each passing mile over the rickety railroad tracks.

Spirits slackened a bit when I first pulled into the city. Hull was a vital seaport and had naturally been targeted by the Germans, especially during the Blitz. Over 1,000 citizens of the North Sea community were lost during the conflict. Although Hull had been spared destruction in 1944, damage was around every corner. The entire city center was destroyed.

After coming to terms with this bleak urban scape, I disembarked the train and initiated my genealogical quest.

The address for the family homestead was previously provided to me should this eventuality ever have arisen. Following some directions and searching, I came across the humble dwelling. I placed my bag down and knocked on the door.

The entryway opened . . . and there stood my grandmother, Anne. Her eyes widened, then swelled with tears. We embraced. She knew exactly who I was.

"You look just like your father when he left."

I cannot quite remember how long we hugged, but I do know this: No amount of medical attention or rest could have made me feel any better than I was at that instant. To greet my grandmother for the first time at age twenty, in a foreign country during a world war no less, was one of the most emotionally charged instances I've experienced. Words can hardly express the degrees of love, comfort, and safety I felt in that moment. Few actions are more consoling than being held by one's grandma. What else can I say?

The joy did not cease there. I was then introduced to my grandfather, Benjamin, and my dad's sister, also named Anne. My grandfather was a hulk of a man who had played on the city's rugby team in his younger years. For as quiet as he was, he was well-known in Hull's pubs for his spirited demeanor and love of stout. I witnessed his energy firsthand when I went on a pub crawl with the whole family that evening. Benjamin pounded down many a beer, but the thick, dark, and potent beverages eventually caught up with him. In fact, we had to haul him home and tuck the inebriated patriarch into bed. This brief interruption did not curtail the night's festivities. Once Grandfather was sound asleep under his covers, the rest of us continued the revelry into the early hours. Grandmother proved to be quite a heller who held her own when it came to liquor. She was a strong woman. Aunt Anne said whenever there was a bomb raid, my grandmother had thrown herself over her daughter to offer protection.

With each drink, more and more of my grandmother's Irish zeal emerged. Everybody sang and laughed in this lively setting. For just a few moments, the war faded from consciousness. This gathering was one of the genuine escapes I enjoyed while overseas. The previous July, Predgen enjoyed a similar visit to Walton-on-Thames, where he met his Aunt Annette. Strange how the war both separated and united us with family simultaneously.[22]

The next day, my grandmother started to cook for me. But rationing was severe, and I did not wish to be a burden. I asked my grandfather, still a bit groggy from the night before, where I might discretely acquire some rationed provisions. When he told me, I paid a visit to the black-market shops and purchased all manner of goodies. The only other times I participated in these illicit underground activities was when in pursuit of Scotch. I most often succeeded in these high-priority missions. (I resist the hard stuff these days, though I do enjoy a good lager beer around five every evening.)

We ate well because of my scrounging. Many cheery conversations were had around the dinner table. After spending several amazing days with my Hull family, time came for my inevitable return to the outfit. I boarded a train to Southport to rejoin my crew for a couple of days before we headed to Halesworth. Then back to business. I never saw my grandparents again.

When I reentered the combat zone on October 14, my recent travels through England seemed something like a dream. I had difficulty reconciling these two vastly distinct experiences. That week, I helped batter Cologne three times in four days. The city was considered a tactical target because it was occupied by the enemy and fortified. During the first of these missions, we used a new six-ship experimental formation designed to lessen the effectiveness of flak. The scheme worked. Enemy barrages were heavy, but no damage was inflicted.

The next day, we targeted the same marshalling yards with the same formation, but the results were drastically different. Our entire group was hit very hard. Twenty-eight aircraft were damaged. "The lead element ahead of us got no flak, but when we were right over the target, they opened up with everything," navigator J. G. Verplanck recalled. "Every ship that came back had holes." *Rebel Gal* was among those wounded birds. Her turret was struck yet again, and poor George Puska had plexiglass sprayed in his face a third time. He thought himself cursed.

"I'm not getting back in that damn thing," he declared after the mission. We ignored his protests and back in he went for the next round.

Cologne was home to five major railyards, and nothing was left to chance. Key infrastructure required demolition if the Allies were to tighten the noose around the Reich's neck. Our flight scheduled for October 16 was delayed and then scrubbed. We were supposed to fly *Lil' Cookie* that day. I should also point out that, by this time, most of France was in Allied hands. Advances on the ground meant we could fly to targets in western Germany and remain over friendly territory much longer. This development was a source of great relief.

October 17 marked our final flight to Cologne for a tactical mission. Planes were armed with a lethal mix of 500-pound general purpose bombs and incendiaries. The division line sloppily commenced out of England. "I followed them halfway across the Channel and the formation stunk," Col. Napier complained. "Everyone was all over hell, both in our wing and the others too." Regardless of any imprecision, Cologne was undeniably ravaged by 10,000 tons of ordnance over a mere ninety-six hours. Some 2,100 American aircraft contributed to this slaughter on October 17 alone. Ten times that number of city residents died resulting from Allied bombardments throughout the war. After the conflict, I remember seeing a photo of the Cologne Cathedral in *Life*. The majestic structure was surrounded by a ruined city. The caption read, "a testament to precision bombing." I don't think that description is entirely accurate. On several occasions, bombing took place through clouds, including on the day in question.[23]

The ruins of Cologne in 1945. The cathedral is seen on the far left.
Air Force photo. (31)

That cathedral took 600 years to construct. Allied bombs nearly obliterated it in no time. Months after my Cologne mission, American chaplain Philip Hannan observed of the scene, "The beautiful city I remembered had been reduced to an enormous pile of rubble. The only building standing was the cathedral, erect like a majestic symbol of the perpetuity of the faith." Today, the cathedral still stands as a testament to humanity's perseverance.[24]

With Cologne largely diminished to brick-and-mortar dust, we shifted focus to additional marshalling yards at Mainz on October 19. We woke up at 4 a.m. but takeoff was delayed due to poor weather over Germany. When we at last embarked, crews encountered clouds rising as high as 30,000 feet. The mission commander tried to avoid or go above the weather but could achieve neither. For a spell, we flew through clouds at scary altitudes far surpassing B-24 wing design capabilities. At this height, controls were "mushy" and flying in formation was hazardous.

This threat became even more evident when two ships, *Pregnant Peggy* and *Bomber's Moon*, collided thirteen minutes from the target. Only four crewmen survived. I saw a waist gunner bail out from a bottom hatch, pulling the rip cord too soon, catching his chute on the tail skid. I still don't know whether the man came out alive or not.[25]

Another damaged plane successfully hobbled to England, but crash-landed twelve miles southeast of the field, in the middle of a farm. All survived with a few minor injuries. The kindly property owner, a Mrs. Knight, emerged from the farmhouse the plane had just missed.

She approached the wreckage. "Would you gents like some tea?" she inquired. I always found the British to be this hospitable and charming. The busted-up crew followed her into the home for biscuits and bandages.

At that moment, our aircraft was snagged in quite a fix too. The ceiling was incredibly low when we returned to the field. Conditions forced us to let down over the North Sea until the water was visible. We thereafter headed back to base via our radio compass. Upon arrival, we spotted red flares arcing up from the end of the runway. The mission culminated in a hairy sideslip landing for us. Not far off, another plane crashed near the field. Once again, we sweated bullets.

This was my thirtieth mission. Five more to go until I became a ground-pounder. I think everyone onboard was ready to return to a Flak Home. Or better yet, our real homes. Airmen worried most during this stage of their tours. Fulfillment of mission quotas was just shy of our reach. Anxiety over "buying the farm" deepened when only a few flights separated crewmen from stateside rotation. Tensions lifted slightly with a generally uneventful return mission to the marshalling yards at Hamm on October 22. The next two days, we were briefed for flights to Essen and the Ruhr, but the advent of fall led to a deterioration of weather. The skies were dark and soupy.

A host of issues hindered our journey on October 25. Our primary aim was a synthetic oil refinery at Scholven, but we instead pushed toward railroad yards at Münster since our weather ship was late reporting target conditions. The mission was royally FUBAR from then onward. The group eventually dropped its bombs more than two miles from the intended destination. One ditched plane was lost on the way home—all for nothing. Poor guidance on this flight equated to poor results.

Ironically, I was promoted to first lieutenant when we returned to Halesworth. On a day otherwise afflicted by lack of tactical leadership, I was recognized for my ongoing dependability at the co-pilot's wheel. The silver bar pinned to my collar meant little to me at this stage of my duties. I was exhausted and merely wished to escape the madness before it destroyed me. I was so close to attaining that goal.

Notwithstanding incessant bloodshed and lethargy, some group members were in a carnival mood. A grand bash was slated for month's end to commemorate the unit's 100th mission. Superiors seemed all too willing to squeeze additional operations in the calendar to achieve that number before the scheduled gala.

One such mission was our October 26 passage to Minden, Germany. The target was the Mittelland Canal, where, by viaduct, waters coursed over the Weser River. Our load was four 2,000-pound bombs. When we salvoed loads that substantial, *Rebel Gal* literally jumped. Approximately 1,000 planes joined us on the raid. The target was bombed by radar due to complete cloud cover and was squarely hit, flushing the canal out onto farmland, sweeping barges into the countryside. Minden flooded and the Germans were forced to open lock gates to lessen the disaster. "The canal will not be able to carry traffic for a long time," one reporter surmised.[26]

Why attack something as seemingly innocuous as a canal? Why wreak such havoc on nearby German farmers? I read after the war that the enemy built super submarines capable of carrying more torpedoes with increased sea range. They were manufactured in sections and transported to coastline assembly by barge. Many natural resources were likewise ferried on this system—hence the significance of artificial waterways.

My thirty-third mission was now complete. This was when I became most apprehensive. I was playing the odds at that stage. On October 26, our flight engineer, Lou Wagner, joyously met his own quota. The final entry in his wartime log exclaims, "Well, that's all brother! My last mission of this tour!!" I was not far behind him.[27]

The 489th ended up one excursion shy of its aims by October 29—the day of its 100th mission party. The morale-boosting initiative was the brainchild of Col. Napier, who tasked key officers with collecting funds to underwrite the festivities: three pounds was provided by each colonel and major, two pounds from captains and lieutenants, fifteen shillings from sergeants and corporals, and ten shillings from enlisted men. The affair was a two-day open-house extravaganza with a carnival, bands, gypsies, vaudeville shows, tug of war matches, gym dances, and a massive cake. Ladies were invited from surrounding towns, beer was plentiful and, somehow, mountains of ice cream were procured. Ten thousand ice cream cones cost the group only six pounds. Two separate parties occurred—one for privates and noncoms and one for officers. The celebrations were colossal, drunken keggers. Any receptacle that could hold beer was filled. On the third morning, the CO finally laid down the law and declared, "It's time to send the women home! We still have a war to fight!" The party's energy eventually fizzled. The event was a perfect tonic for flyboy blues. What a grand time we had. Yet there was still so much war to be waged.[28]

Thankfully, for whatever reason, our crew was not scheduled to fly again for over one week. We had plenty of time to recover from the revelry. In the case of Predgen and Wagner, however, additional fun was had with passes to London for Lou's sendoff. As the two toured the city, Lou engaged in a verbal scuffle with an MP. The cop flagged him for being out of uniform on account of missing his hat. Wagner was reported to our commanding officer as a result. Still, the encounter did not prohibit plenty of drinking. When the skipper and engineer departed their hotel on the final morning, they decided to "kill" their last bottle by presenting it to a maid.

"I ain't a drinkin' woman," she declared, "but I'm not one to dilly-dally over a swig either." Wishing to move on with her chores, she emptied the bottle right then and there.[29]

During that first week of November, the exploits of fellow crews in the group were not as enjoyable. Rough missions were had over cities such as Gelsenkirchen, Bielefeld, Misburg, Metz, and Sterkrade. During this time, rumors about our stateside rotation began circulating. Scuttlebutt suggested we were bound for America to transport B-29 bombers to the South Pacific. As we pondered this possibility, the Battle of Peleliu raged on the other side of the globe. If nothing else, the bitter engagement demonstrated that the Japanese had not lost their will to fight. Were we destined for that theater of war? I had more immediate concerns at hand. Instinct led me to believe my thirty-fourth mission might be my final one. My stomach tightened when I was awoken at 3 a.m. for a flight to Metz on November 9. This was it.

Since late September, the heavily fortified Metz had been subjected to repeat attacks by Gen. Patton's Third Army. Germans fiercely defended the community, which was a key position during the Lorraine Campaign. Patton's fiery desire to seize the city was best articulated in a letter written some weeks earlier to Gen. Jimmy Doolittle. He declared, "This is to inform you that those low bastards, the Germans, gave me my first bloody nose when they compelled us to abandon our attack on Fort Driant in the Metz area. I have requested a revenge bombardment from us to teach those sons-of-bitches that they cannot fool with Americans." Patton asked for "large bombs of the nastiest type." We obliged his request for weeks on end.[30]

I was assigned to fly the November 9 mission with a different, much less-experienced crew. This sudden change threw me on edge. I kept a close eye on everyone and everything, lending no one any slack. I watched the crewmen like a hawk. I wasn't about to let rookies get me killed when I was so close to the finish line. No way in hell.

Our plane hauled one-ton general-purpose bombs to obliterate old Maginot Line defenses from World War I that the Germans had occupied. The attack was carried out through some broken overcast. Fortunately, I saw no flak or fighters.

Below, we could spot the zigzag pattern of enemy fortifications. From four miles up, the network resembled something like an ant farm.

"Bombs away," our bombardier announced.

And with that, I departed the combat zone for the last time. As I learned upon landing back in England, my journey to Metz was indeed my final mission. Patton complimented our "yellow-tailed B-24s" for supporting his advance that day, but no congratulatory note from any brass could match the exuberance I felt. Even now, I have difficulty describing the sensation of satisfaction and relief.

I survived!

My first order of business to celebrate the occasion was an immediate trek to the officers' club. I swaggered up to the counter and exclaimed, "Scotch!" My triumphant drinking binge surpassed that of even our unit party the week before.

I guzzled an endless stream of liquor until I was blotto. Nobody dared stop me. I had earned the privilege. Following this heavy bender, I haplessly stumbled through the small woodlot between the club and my quarters. Bewildered and practically blinded by dizziness, I walked smack dab into a tree.

In my dazed stupor, I was under the misguided impression that somebody had struck me. "You son of a bitch!" I snarled. My natural response was to return a punch at my assailant (the tree). My knuckles flung into the trunk and made an unpleasant crack. I howled and fell to the ground in pain. (Let this tale be a warning to any sloshed individual who dares to pick a fight with a piece of timber. You are unlikely to win.)

After releasing a string of verbal expletives unfit for print, I was lugged to the infirmary for bandaging and was then plopped into my sack. I fell into the deepest slumber imaginable. It was all a very loosening affair. My mind was cleared, and I awoke surprisingly refreshed. No hangover, bruised fist, or damaged ego could have possibly dampened my day. I was reassured. No more flak. No more fighters. I made it.

As a grand finale, I jumped in on a high stakes crap game atop the pool table in our officers' club. Men were throwing away English pounds like funny money. My temporary sense of invincibility did not get the best of me, and, after a healthy winning streak, I walked away with over one grand in cash (or $17,000 in today's currency). This amount was quickly stowed away for postwar plans.

I soon prepared to depart England, leaving the war to the next young batch of replacements in other outfits. Many of them saw the conflict through to its very end. My unit completed its final mission, appropriately enough, on the eve of Armistice Day 1944.

My story is not one of statistics, but numbers are quite revealing—and startling. During the conflict, the 489th Bomb Group boasted 3,000 sorties and dispensed hundreds of thousands of tons of ordnance over Nazi territory. The outfit flew 106 total combat missions, losing about fifty planes to battle and other hazardous conditions. Countless more returned to

Halesworth beaten and broken. For instance, my first mission on July 6 included 262 B-24s. At least 106 of these suffered damage. The next day, over one-third of the 373 planes sent over the sea were likewise impaired. In four months of combat, my planes suffered known battle damage on fourteen of thirty-four missions. Three of these episodes were considered critical and one of our planes, *Jo*, was scrapped. I flew approximately 24,000 miles back and forth over Europe.

On a broader scale, more than 2,000 Liberators were lost in the European Theater. Some 6,000 men of the Second Air Division were killed and many more were wounded or taken prisoner. Thirty-six of our group crews went down. In my unit history book, I tallied 184 men from the 489th who were killed in action. Some remain missing. I still mourn for them and their families. To me, these men are not black-and-white data figures. I knew many of them by name and appearance. They were bunkmates, drinking buddies, card players, pranksters, and—above all else—fellow aviators. That's how I remember them.[31]

Since I had attained thirty-four missions of the thirty-five required, Capt. Tanner jokingly suggested (I think) that I depart England with the group, master the controls of the B-29, and venture to the South Pacific to fly a single mission. I respectfully declined. I was eager to obtain a one-way ticket to the United States and complete my duties at domestic postings. There, in the comparative comforts of the home front, I was to encounter a whole new realm of wartime adventure.

CHAPTER 8

Home Alive by '45

The chilly English port was a flurry of activity. Southampton was alive with the bells, whistles, trucks, and tugboats of a bustling maritime hub. Its wharfs were a revolving door of soldiers and supplies both coming and going. Like Hull, the community had been heavily bombed during the Blitz and later served as a major point of embarkation for D-Day. Now I, too, prepared to depart the United Kingdom from that ancient city.

On November 14, 1944, just five days following my closing mission, I reported to Stone, England, to await transport to the States. The moment was quite bittersweet. My joy in returning home was counterbalanced by the dissolution of our crew. Over the previous ten months, we had endured the trying demands of war together. Through collective effort and no small amount of luck, every one of us survived our nearly three dozen combat missions. The experience forged a bond of kinship surpassed only by genuine family. I bid each of the men a fond farewell before we went our separate ways. Thankfully, this moment did not mark our final goodbyes.

When I reached Southampton by truck, I entered a bureaucratic process of "hurry up and wait." Standing within a mass of khaki and wool, I was again reminded of the Allied coalition's mammoth scope. Soon enough, I boarded an ocean-liner-turned-troopship named the SS *Brazil*. Among its tens of thousands of passengers during the war, the ship carried various notables including Medal of Honor recipient "Pappy" Boyington and cartoonist Charles Schulz. The vessel had crossed the globe many times, but I cared only about its next destination: New York City.

The *Brazil* sailed out of port to join a convoy on December 9. German submarines were not the threat they had been earlier in the war, but I suppose they were still menacing enough to warrant a well-protected flotilla. For a flyboy like me, watching the Navy go about its seafaring duties offered valuable perspective on the range of service.

Our "luxurious" accommodations were a stateroom originally designed for two. Twenty-one officers crammed inside the intimate suite. We were stacked floor to ceiling in flimsy bunks. Not only were we packed like sardines, but we began to smell like them too. The ship's freshwater supply was turned off the second day of our voyage and not switched on again until the last. We spent substantial time on the breezy top deck for obvious reasons. Interestingly, one of the lower decks included cages full of U.S. soldiers imprisoned for various offenses: desertion, rape, murder, and so on. The only time we saw these haggard inmates was when they were marched under armed guard to the mess for meals. Prisoners aside, all within the hall were abuzz with anticipation regarding our imminent homecomings. The ship's original civilian stewards, who served us food twice per day, did their utmost to make us comfortable despite the congested circumstances.

Passengers had plenty of time to kill during the two-week trip. We were supposed to be kept in the dark concerning our nautical location, but enough navigators were aboard to keep us informed. Many of them could peer into the sky and offer a solid course estimation.

None of us had to gaze as far to spot the nearest crap game. From the foot of every ship's stairwell echoed the sound of dice in tin cups. Warnings suggested that these games were run by seasoned Merchant Marines and were not necessarily on the up and up. I resisted the incredible temptation to gamble with my recently won earnings from Halesworth. Willpower persevered and my bundle of cash remained stowed away in my travel bag. Buddies onboard entrusted me with half their pay and demanded, "Don't give this to me under any circumstances!" Many of them inevitably returned, having lost their money, and requested the other half back. I witnessed many a small fortune squandered on the high seas.

And I truly mean high. During the first week of the trip, we encountered a severe winter storm in the North Atlantic with waves taller than I thought possible. When our ship crested one of these swells, the stern and props came right out of the water, causing the whole vessel to vibrate. Seasickness was pervasive among aviators unaccustomed to this type of turbulence. Painted numbers washed off the bow of an escort carrier and tankers temporarily disappeared into dark voids. From a distance, we could see only the bridges. My time on the ocean was limited up to that point, but I've never seen anything so powerful in nature before or since. We nervously envisioned the overwhelming force of the waves consuming our ship. I was one uneasy passenger.

A fellow 489th airman named John Rainey expressed similar trepidation of his return trip. "It seemed to me that the rivets holding the ship would pop," he observed. "The ship would then plunge into the chasm between the waves until the bow would become submerged in the following wave, and the deck was awash. This was my first ocean voyage. The plunging and the rocking made me sick, and I thought that surely the boat would sink."[1]

At night, we could see only a small stern light glaring from the ships. I thought, *How in the hell will they know the locations of each vessel?* I feared ships might inadvertently ram each other in the blackness. To my amazement, I awoke in the morning to find all vessels in the same positions as the night before. By our eighth day at sea, the weather turned balmy to the extent that we strolled the deck without coats, though we still sported lifejackets. I suspect we turned south and entered the Gulf Stream.

Promenade chatter turned lighthearted and optimistic. Lt. Chuck Bouchard waved around the photo of a pinup and boasted that "Miss Rheingold" was his girlfriend. Since 1940, Rheingold Beer chose an annual winner of a national beauty contest. I thought he was full of hot air. When we later reconnected in New York City, he arranged a double date to verify his claim. The model he brought along for me was as sharp as a doorknob, but his romantic boasts proved to be true: his date really was Miss Rheingold.

Chuck Bouchard at ease. "Pup" Dalgleish is in the bottom bunk. *John Homan photo.* (32)

A buddy reads on the deck of the SS *Brazil*. This photo was taken by Dalgleish. *John Homan collection.* (33)

Rough seas made me damn glad I had joined the Air Forces and not the Navy. I can't fathom how my father retained his sanity sweating away in a rocking boiler room below the waterline during the Great War.

Early on the foggy morning of December 23, the *Brazil* sailed into the calm waters of New York harbor. Lit by the gentle glow of sunrise, scores of us stood quietly on deck as the silhouette of the Statue of Liberty slowly emerged from the mist. All of us watched in humbled silence. Overcome with emotion, none of us uttered a word. As a New Jersey resident, I had seen Lady Liberty innumerable times. But I had taken the landmark and its meaning for granted. We coasted through the harbor in awe, perhaps like immigrants sailing to nearby Ellis Island. That morning, the symbolism of the Statue of Liberty rang true for me in a way it never had before.

Upon disembarking we learned that the Battle of the Bulge had commenced. Beginning December 16, three German armies punched through the wintry woodlands connecting Belgium and Luxembourg in a desperate gamble to reverse

Our convoy heads toward New York City.
John Homan photo. (34)

Allied advances. The ensuing struggle lasted over one month and set the stage for Germany's last stand. Thankfully, I was absent for what would become the largest battle in U.S. Army history. Still, I fully expected rotation to the Pacific. That looming prospect did not rest easy with me.

With unusual dispatch, we were transported from the docks of the Brooklyn Navy Yard to Camp Kilmer, New

Jersey. Given its proximity to New York City, the post processed over two million service members during the war. I truly appreciated the work ethic of base staff. They stayed at their desks and typewriters all night preparing orders for some of us to commence leave on Christmas Eve. Best of all, Kilmer was less than twenty miles from Parlin. Two bus rides placed me on my home street by mid-afternoon.

I could hardly believe I was back. The old neighborhood seemed far removed from all the world's turmoil. The place appeared as if I had never left.

Family members were initially oblivious to my return. I therefore decided to give them a holiday surprise. I walked up the front steps and knocked on the door. The entryway swung open. Mom's expression was one of brief astonishment, though she restrained her happiness. Always a stoical Englishwoman, she had a talent for concealing emotion. Acting otherwise was not her style. If she wept with joy that night, she did so in the solitude of her room. My arrival was a fine gift and was quickly followed by a call to Irene. It was time to be reacquainted.

I had missed Irene a hell of a lot. Her frequent letters mailed to England offered emotional boosts when my spirits were low. Her talents as a journalist were apparent on every page. Even so, each note read as if it was prepared for a newspaper editor. I had joked with her to quit writing so formally. She was sharing inner thoughts with her boyfriend after all, not newsstand readers! Regardless of decorum, mail from Irene reinforced why I had fallen for her in the first place. She was so cultured. The young woman was well-versed in art, opera, and museums, but also golf and baseball. When we visited horseraces at Monmouth before the war, she always bet two dollars to show and thereby earned more than me or any of our friends.

Her strong intuition similarly served her well as a reporter. When she attended her first prizefight (coincidentally the same week as my first combat mission) she was heralded by local media when she predicted a string of winners. Her newspaper declared, "When asked how she knew a certain pug would win, the little lady startled the ringside by explaining, 'I knew he'd win because he had such a nice look in his eyes.'"[2]

That was Irene—incredibly sharp and a good judge of people. No wonder she excelled at her job. Her wartime articles, now accessible online, demonstrate her range. Irene's pieces on rationing, food shortages, and local human-interest stories make for compelling snapshots of home front life. She likewise used her investigative skills when we developed a secret system to bypass censors scrutinizing my correspondence. I sneaked numbers into my letters, so she knew how many missions I had completed. But I never spilled details about combat. I wished to spare her that. Now home, I hoped to push memories of those battles behind me.

Enjoying creature comforts, relishing yuletide feasts, and reconnecting with loved ones was something like fantasy. That Christmas celebration will always remain close to my heart. I was home. But the war was never far removed from my thoughts. Between seasonal songs and specials, our radio broadcasted the ongoing miseries endured during the Battle of the Bulge. On the opposite side of the globe, combat raged in the Philippines. Where was I to be transferred next? I was soon to find out.

My leave concluded on January 21, 1945. That day, I reported to Atlantic City, New Jersey, where the Air Forces leased several major hotels as reassignment centers. Local businessmen simultaneously prepared for the postwar tourism boom. Large portions of the nearby boardwalk had just been replaced, but we dared not make use of the celebrated strip due to icy coastal winds.

The frigid intermission at Atlantic City was brief, and I soon found myself retracing footsteps at Moody Field outside Valdosta, Georgia. There, at Southeast Training Command, I mastered the controls of the B-25 Mitchell. My teacher had piloted that medium bomber in the Pacific and one day asked me to fly alongside him in formation. Once I got on his wing, he did everything in his power to shake me—turns, dives, and slow moves through cloud cover. Despite his best efforts, I stayed on his wing right to the landing pattern. We exited our planes and walked straight to the ready room without uttering a word. We merely nodded with subtle smiles. I had amply demonstrated my aviation skills. There was no need to boast.

The next day I transferred to Turner Field in Albany, Georgia, as an advanced flight instructor in B-25s. Several of my pupils were fresh from West Point, graduates with commissions but not pilot certifications. The enterprising officers sported gold bars on their shoulders but had yet to earn wings. That's where I came into play. At age twenty-one, I was likely younger than many of the students. To my delight, these rookie officers were smart, disciplined, and eager to learn. Unlike my former, high-strung deputy commander (also from the Academy), these young professionals were a pleasure. Even so, their energy matched their naïveté about the realities of battle. Their zeal was nonetheless understandable. For professional soldiers aspiring to long-term careers, proving one's mettle in warfare is a sure means of rising through the ranks.

The B-24 and B-25 were similar in appearance since both bombers featured twin tails. The former had four engines and the latter had two engines. B-25s gained fame three years prior when used with fanfare during the Doolittle Raids on Japan. I found the B-25 much simpler to operate. I could take off at fifty feet, pull one engine back, and still fly the plane. The Mitchell, so named in honor of aviator Billy Mitchell, was an incredibly dependable and versatile machine. Each engine had about 1,700 horsepower. The aircraft was lighter, faster, and easier to maneuver than Liberators. The Mitchell boasted more than adequate power and proved quite nimble, especially for someone like me who served as a "three-dimensional truck driver" over Europe.

In yet another twist of irony, I also attended survivor school during this stateside stint. These lessons would have been much appreciated a year earlier. Instructors showed us how to bail into water, survive poison gas attacks, and related tricks of the trade. Better late than never. I suspect we were being prepared for the unforgiving conditions of the Pacific. As we conducted drills and sessions, my mind once again drifted back to combat experiences. Why had I survived and so many others had not? I always arrived at the same conclusion: pure chance.

During down time, mentors like myself were permitted to sign out planes for "training flights." These brief escapes into the wild blue were pure joy rides. During one of these so-called exercises, fellow pilot Jim Kelleher and I checked out a B-25 and buzzed over the 700-mile Okefenokee Swamp toward the Naval Air Station at Brunswick, Georgia. We were gliding at 5,000 feet when we spotted a Corsair, a fast and modern Navy fighter, ahead and below us.

"Let's dive with full power," Jim deviously suggested. "When we approach, we'll feather one engine and shoot past him." I was certainly game for some interservice shenanigans.

We rapidly descended and darted past the naval airman so closely that we could see his startled expression. Immensely satisfied, we brought the engine back and headed home.

A short time later, the Corsair pilot exacted his vengeance. He scared the hell out of us by conducting a dramatic barrel roll right around our plane. One playful trick deserves another.

Perhaps we should not have operated our aircraft in such a lighthearted manner. After all, dreadful accidents could occur during even the most routine flights. We were reminded of this that summer when a B-25 crashed into the Empire State Building on a foggy morning. The accident claimed fourteen people, including the three crewmen aboard the ill-fated ship.

Near the end of training, I was surprised when asked my desired duty station. Weary of previous postings in mediocre English weather, I requested to remain in the sunny South. Subsequent orders fulfilled my hopes when I was relocated to instrument instructor school at Bryan Army Airfield in Texas with a ten-day leave. Pleased, I figured I had a smidge of wiggle room for leisurely travel within that week and a half period. This proved another incorrect assumption.

Believing we had a bit of time to spare, Kelleher and I hit the road for Jacksonville, Florida, located about four hours to the east. A result of my substantial wartime crap game winnings was the recent purchase of a 1942 DeSoto, a trusty automobile I drove for the next six years. The car was the newest model possible, for automotive manufacturers ceased production of civilian cars shortly after Pearl Harbor.

With a flair for spontaneous adventure, we boarded a train at Jacksonville and advanced up the coast. The intention was to spend some time at our respective homes. Our initial enthusiasm waned when we discovered there were no seats available. We thus stood or sat uncomfortably on chair arms all the way to Washington, DC. Our spunk was undercut by pure annoyance. Despite the ribbons on our chests, nobody on this train yielded their seats for even a few minutes as a gesture of thanks. By the time we reached Union Station in Washington, we felt a tad indignant.

After pushing through throngs of travelers, we spruced up in the station restrooms, enjoyed a hearty meal, and made use of amenities at the large USO lounge before continuing to New York and our homes. During my subsequent stay with family, Irene called, but I failed to connect with her in-person.

At the end of our leaves, Jim and I adjourned to the Savarin Bar at Penn Station for an eye-opener. Time was lost after we started downing large quantities of Bushmills Irish Whiskey. Meanwhile, our train left without us. Tipsy but undeterred after emptying many glasses, Jim called up an old flame and arranged an impromptu double date on the town that evening. I cannot even recall our boozy Big Apple adventures, but we ultimately boarded the subway to Jersey City for late-night lodging with Jim's family. There was no other choice since we had missed our train due to merrymaking.

We were off to a fresh start in the morning but again lacked reservations for our return to Florida. This time, we at least nabbed a single seat and took turns in it all the way back through Dixie. Aboard was an attractive young lady traveling with her mother. The former was being stalked by a pack of eager GIs in the car. Soon, the daughter approached me.

"I'm on my way to Florida to get married," she began. "I want to kiss one more man other than my fiancé before I can't anymore. Will you do me the honor?"

Who was I to refuse such a request? We quietly walked onto the enclosed platform connecting the cars and I happily granted her wish. Supposing she thought me to be the most attractive man aboard, I felt mighty spry after the brief encounter.

When Jim and I arrived in Jacksonville, we were a day behind schedule. What followed was an unusual road trip conducted as a madcap quest to avoid censure. To recover lost time, we jumped into my automobile and set out for Bryan, Texas. Our wanderings seemed interminable as there were few superhighways back then. In fact, the road that later became Interstate 10 was only a single paved lane with dirt shoulders. We frequently veered to the side when oncoming traffic approached. Progress was further hindered by unfenced farm animals who rested atop the pavement for warmth. I learned, oddly enough, that cattle had the legal right of way. Had we struck a cow, we would have been legally liable.

Jim and I felt as if the drive would never end. We had been on a train for twenty-four hours prior and started falling asleep behind the wheel. By the time we reached New Orleans, we could not proceed farther without rest. Given the city's robust role as a wartime manufacturing center, no decent hotel rooms were to be found at any price. After all, the Big Easy was famously home to Higgins Industries, a major producer of amphibious landing craft. The only accommodations available were at a grimy, third-rate establishment. When we carried our luggage up to the room, we spotted the biggest cockroaches we had ever seen. The insects were so big we could have mounted saddles on them.

Thoroughly unimpressed by our lodgings, we promptly left and ventured to the French Quarter. We made the rounds on Bourbon Street and were bolstered by some of that ever-present Mardi Gras spirit. The war certainly had not diminished the sizzling New Orleans ambiance. In the many saloons, scantily clad women swung seductively from brass bars bolted to ceilings. Dozens of brothels satisfied the urges of visiting servicemen and industrial workers. Amused by the various spectacles, we were revived, relinquished our infested hotel room, and hit the road once more.

The final logistical hurdle was encountered just beyond New Orleans. We had little difficulty procuring rationed gasoline, but tires were an entirely different matter. Wartime synthetic rubber was of extremely poor quality. After experiencing several blowouts, we had to plead with a local board to obtain ration tickets for four new tires. Our drive across the Deep South proved one hell of a ride. Jim and I arrived at Bryan Airfield a day late and completely worn out.

Nobody even noticed our tardiness.

At the Texas base, training consisted of nothing but instrument flying for six whole weeks. The plane made available to us was the North American AT-6, a single-engine, two-seater, all-metal aircraft. The advanced trainer bore a resemblance to the Japanese Zero and was later used for such depictions in war movies. To strengthen our instrument skills, the rear cockpit was temporarily covered with red plastic. The pilot, sporting green goggles, could not see out. Meanwhile, a safety pilot flew in the front position. Schooling consisted of all phases of instrument flying: takeoff, cross country, beams, glide path, and a new system called the Ground-Controlled Approach. This method allowed an operator to detect me on a radar screen and talk me through the landing pattern and onto the approach. The system later made the Berlin Airlift possible.

While conducting "unusual position recovery" training, the safety pilot ordered the rear pilot under the hood to cage his gyros (the compass and artificial horizon). The front airman then put the plane into a slight dive, turn, or climb before handing over the controls to the backseat aviator, who then had to level the aircraft. This difficult maneuver was done using only the altimeter, airspeed, needle ball, and compass.

During one session, I was scheduled to be under the hood and another officer was to be the safety pilot. Before takeoff, he confessed to persistent training hurdles and feared flunking out.

"Mind if we switch spots today so I can get some extra practice?" he asked. I agreed.

We ascended to approximately 7,000 feet and I instructed him to cage the gyros. I climbed to a safe altitude and decided to have a little fun. I put the plane on an unsustainable, full-power steep climb and told him he had the controls. "She's all yours," I announced.

And then the plane stalled out.

Black smoke erupted from the engine. I leaped into action.

"Get out from under the hood!" I shouted. "I got the controls."

There was nothing to do but cut power, kick full rudder, fall off on a wing, head straight down to pick up airspeed, and pull out.

The cockpit glass was now covered with streaks of dark brown oil. I couldn't see a damn thing. After leveling off, I pulled the slide canopy and stuck my head out for better visibility. All I got was a face full of very hot oil which, fortunately for us, splattered on my sunglasses and not my eyes. I ripped off the glasses and threw them in the plane. While anxiously wiping oil from my face, I put the plane in a slow glide with low RPM.

Five miles from base, I hopped on the radio and uttered something I never said before.

"Mayday! Mayday!"

The irony of surviving thirty-four combat missions and now facing my potential demise—in Texas of all places—was not lost upon me in that moment. Several veteran acquaintances met their fates during similar exercises.

Not today, I thought.

I placed the plane in a shallow dive toward the field while smoke and scorching liquid sprayed from the engine.

We neared the field, I notified the tower of our emergency, and an operator assigned us a landing pattern for a specific runway.

I cut him off. "Can't make it that far," I replied. "I'm coming in on the nearest runway. Clear the field!"

The landing was one of the most frightening of my career. I flew askew to line up with the runway and then looked sideways to gauge height. With black smoke still funneling out the engine and emergency vehicles chasing us down the runway, I braked hard, cut the switch, pulled onto the grass, and sprang from the plane. I then heard the blare of approaching firetrucks. Their crews apparently thought we weren't hustling fast enough and hollered, "Get the hell out of there, guys! Now! Run!" We eagerly complied as the firemen doused the maimed trainer.

Winded, filthy, and slicked with sludge, I staggered into the ready room to catch my breath. There, my chief instructor looked up and simply uttered, "Son of a bitch. I knew it would be you." For whatever reason, I suppose I had developed a daredevil reputation. Audacious or not, my luck persisted. I later learned an oil line in our plane had split and splashed oil on the hot radial engine cylinder heads, resulting in a very smoky fire. Another close call.

On April 12, we were startled by news of President Roosevelt's sudden death. For many of us, he was the only commander-in-chief we could remember holding office. Irene later told me she asked her priest if a mass could be held in honor of our fallen leader. The clergyman refused because FDR was not Catholic. Irene never went to church again. She stood trackside and watched Roosevelt's funeral train pass through New Jersey as it proceeded to New York.

Then, less than one month later, word of Nazi Germany's capitulation arrived. I was so thankful that hostilities in Europe had ceased, and I was proud of the small role I played in the endeavor. Back home, townspeople observed the rainy day with self-discipline and silence. The local newspaper recorded, "Virtually all places of business with the exception of the banks closed their doors." My brothers and their classmates were dismissed early from school and all the churches were opened. "Radio broadcasts were listened to with interest," the article continued, "but all comment carried the underlying theme that the war against Japan still remained."[3]

The collapse of the Third Reich made available three United States Air Forces in Europe for duties elsewhere. Various training programs were cut, and several bases were phased out. In fact, I recall some air personnel being shifted to the regular Army for the proposed invasion of mainland Japan. These grim projections sent chills down our spines. Few Americans were aware of the Manhattan Project's ongoing development of atomic weaponry, so a great deal of military reshuffling was underway for a vast, deadly effort. Servicemen often repeated sardonic quips about when they might at last conclude the war. These less than optimistic sayings were: Home alive by '45, Out of the sticks in '46, From hell to heaven in '47, and finally, Golden Gate by '48. Determining the ultimate costs and timeline of victory made for morbid calculations.

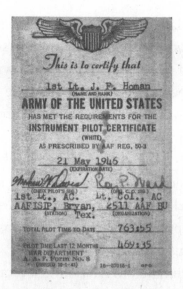

My Instrument Pilot certification from Bryan Airfield was valid for one year. *John Homan collection.* (35)

Amid reorganization efforts, I transferred to the Air Transport Command at Rosecrans Field in St. Joseph, Missouri. At this stage of the conflict, the base hosted many combat veterans awaiting their next stations. "Formality is scarce among these fellows," the St. Joe newspaper reported that May. "They've all been through their own private hells and respect each other for it. So, there's no snapping to when the guys with brass walk into a room." These flyboys were sometimes referred to as "ferrymen" since their specialty was airlifting people and supplies.[4]

I started training in a Curtiss C-46 Commando, the largest twin-engine, high-altitude transport in the military. Switching from the tricycle landing gear of a B-24 or B-25 to a conventional tail wheel configuration required personal adjustment. The plane proved rather difficult to set down. I landed nose-high in the bombers, but if I attempted the same in a C-46, the tail wheel hit first and caused me to "kangaroo" down the runway. The Commando was informally nicknamed "The Whale" due to its bloated size. "The Plumber's Nightmare" was yet another moniker since the transport's hydraulic valves for flap and wheel operation often stuck. A standard piece of equipment we kept handy in the cockpit was a rubber mallet for whacking troublesome valves.

As I grew acclimated to Missouri, several of us were suddenly flown on priority basis to Memphis, Tennessee, for a two-week crash course (so to speak) outlining the rules, regulations, and procedures of domestic flying. I visited the Memphis office of the Federal Aviation Administration to test for a single- and multi-engine pilot's license. I passed the exam with ease. I would undoubtedly be shuffling men, supplies, and planes to the West Coast for eventual deployment to the Pacific. But not long after my return to Missouri, the war abruptly ended with the dropping of two atomic bombs. I was astounded by the ferocity of these new superweapons.

Despite the astronomical loss of life and enduring controversies, I still approve of President Truman's decision to implement the bombs. Had he not used the technology at his disposal and instead sent tens of thousands of young Americans to die, the citizens of this country never could have forgiven him. Some of my comrades in the 489th Bomb Group, then equipped with new B-29s, undoubtedly would have been among the scores of Allied dead. The cost of the United States storming the Japanese mainland would have been an absolute bloodbath. The Japanese were prepared to defend their homes at all costs. We probably would have done the same were the roles reversed. As stark as the reality is, most Americans of the 1940s simply did not care if Axis civilians perished on a biblical scale.

Having witnessed fierce resistance and death in the skies over Europe, I feared the Japanese would eclipse the zealotry of even the Nazis. Dropping the bombs, from my perspective, was the only means of averting prolonged conflict in Asia. Our commanders were not interested in saving the lives of Japanese children. They were interested in saving the lives of *us*. Heavy American casualties sustained on Iwo Jima and Okinawa in the months prior further indicated that Japan was not going down quietly.

This opinion does not lessen my sympathy for civilian populations intentionally or inadvertently killed by our bombs. Even long after the war, I was under the impression my outfit bombed only military targets—sites of industry, stockpiling, and transportation. The problem was that enemy marshalling yards and plants were often located within or on the periphery of major cities. When our vast plane formations were even slightly off target, residential areas were inevitably struck.

But some instances of mass killing near war's end were quite purposeful. I was troubled when I later learned that the Air Forces deliberately bombed high population areas such as

Berlin in early 1945. When Gen. Jimmy Doolittle argued to Gen. Carl Spaatz that such missions would be acts of terrorism, his protests were ignored. These attacks commenced on February 3, killing thousands.[5]

Less than two weeks later, the RAF and AAF obliterated Dresden with incendiaries and high explosives. The British conducted this campaign in the name of retribution. I witnessed the destruction of London that prompted this vengeance. I agree with Gen. Doolittle's sentiments, however, that we Americans should have refused to participate in these retaliatory strikes. I am relieved I was rotated out of Europe two months before these missions transpired.

Some officers in my outfit later pondered the moral dimensions of the air war they waged. My friend Jim Davis unexpectedly confronted one bizarre reality at an airshow in the 1990s. He was introduced to a visiting German man in a wheelchair who was born in July 1944. "It seemed a strange feeling to realize that fifty-four years ago I had dropped bombs on Hanover where this man was a two-month-old baby," Davis confessed.[6]

Ludwig Lund, our official combat artist of the Second Air Division, likewise imparted harsh reckonings following a 1945 mission. "To see it all before my eyes was a revelation of the terrible destructiveness of modern war. This should be an object lesson to the world!" Lund wrote to his wife. "I could never gloat over anything like this—it is too horrible, too terrifying, too satanic. What a crime to have on one's conscience, I mean of course the crime of the Nazi leaders and the

Wehrmacht, and the fools who believed in them." Like Lund, I do not regret fighting the war, but I do lament that the war needed to be waged in the first place. The greater evil would have been to lose.[7]

When Victory over Japan Day finally arrived on August 14, though, our minds were far from the miseries of recent air campaigns. Our lives flourished in a moment of unrestrained exhilaration. I was signing out a C-46 for a training flight when word of the formal surrender arrived. I suddenly lost any desire to fly that day and instead set out in my DeSoto.

St. Joe had been the final home of outlaw Jesse James, but any Wild West excitement had long vanished by 1945. I needed to let loose. It was time to party.

Buddy Al Treylenik and I wash my new DeSoto at Bryan Field in 1945. *John Homan collection.* (36)

I sped all the way to Kansas City, about two hours away. Many celebratory hours were spent at the Muehlebach Hotel, which Missourian Harry Truman later used as a presidential retreat. Everybody was having a ball. There were kisses for everyone.

The hotel staff had to clear the lobby of furniture to make way for the mob. Young boys scaled construction scaffolding outside the hotel and jumped onto window canopies as if they were trampolines. Somebody pulled a fire alarm as a prank. When the firetruck arrived, the masses swarmed the vehicle and stripped it of its equipment. A half-naked man waved his shirt from the top of a lamppost. The August 15 edition of *The Kansas City Times* vividly chronicled the jolly pandemonium I witnessed that memorable evening. "Water cascaded from the upper floors of the Muehlebach and Philips hotels on the crowd below," the paper observed. "Now and then, someone would empty a pillow and the feathers and water gave merrymakers a drenched and woeful appearance. But that didn't dampen their exuberance." In the street, a plastered sergeant with plenty of ribbons on his chest dared the pranksters above to shower him with water. When the rains came, he lifted his bottle of Scotch, raised a toast, swallowed a massive gulp, and declared, "That's good dry likker!"[8]

I could surely relate to the boisterous sergeant. I drank until I could drink no more. I blearily headed back to base around midnight. (I should not have driven in my condition.) The war was over. I could hardly believe it. The lonely ride back to St. Joe offered plenty of time for introspection as I sobered up. The moment was marked with both joy and uncertainty. What was to come next?

My friend and former navigator, Chuck Reevs, married when he returned to Wisconsin. On the issue of veteran readjustment, his views were described by his hometown newspaper. I always knew Chuck was sharp, and the following report reinforces that notion: "Lt. Reevs says that most of the men he talks with think that the folks at home are going much too far in planning the future of the veterans. What they want . . . is an opportunity to return to normal civilian living." Veterans were best left to their own devices for reacclimating, "without a lot of well-meaning, but misguided, help," Chuck insisted. As I was to discover, so many of us simply needed breathing room as we returned to domestic life.[9]

Now that the war was over, the more immediate challenge was discharging millions of people in an orderly fashion. The method for prioritization was a point system based on time in service and combat actions. This system placed me near the top of the list. I ultimately concluded I was not the military type. In 1942, I assessed the situation as follows: "My country has been attacked. I have an obligation to serve." Three years later, I had fulfilled my commitment and possessed no desire to rise as a career officer. I didn't want brass barking at me to put on my summer uniform when it was cold and wear my winter uniform when it was hot. I hate taking orders blindly.

I wasted no time moving to the front of the line to muster out.
I had done my bit.

Consequently, my orders were cut to report to Wright and
Patterson Fields in Dayton, Ohio, for discharge processing. I
arrived there on November 2, 1945. One week later, the War
Department announced the two sites would "merge to become
the giant heart of the Army Air Forces research, engineering,
development, and educational training program." Postwar
transitions were already well underway.[10]

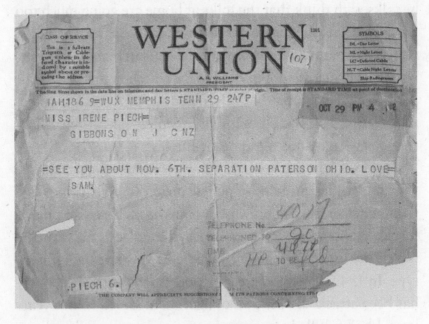

The telegram I sent to Irene with the anticipated date of my
homecoming. Sam was my nickname. *John Homan collection.* (37)

When completing separation, I was asked if I wanted to join the Reserves. My answer was a blunt no. I was then informed registration for the Reserves was a requirement.

"Do you want your status to be active or inactive?" I was asked.

"*As inactive as possible.*" I would not realize the importance of this decision until years later.

I was at last discharged on November 7—almost exactly one year since I had flown my final combat mission. With three days' travel time and twenty days' leave granted, my official discharge date was November 30. That made for thirty-five months in the service. I entered at age nineteen and departed at age twenty-one.

I hung up my uniform and embarked on the next chapter of my professional life. At the Hercules plant, to my pleasant surprise, I had devoted enough work time prior to the war to continue building my seniority—as if I had never enlisted in the first place. I immediately reentered the ranks of labor and was granted two weeks' paid leave that January. This development offered a dose of much-needed reassurance.

Most rewarding of all was my heartfelt reunion with Irene. She had waited for me after all, despite my insistence that she did not have to. She was as pretty as ever—spectacles and all. Irene remained very busy during my absence. When I returned from the war, she was a senior at the New Jersey College for Women and served as editor-in-chief of the school newspaper. Her academic distinction and drive fueled my ambitions to make use of the GI Bill and attend college myself. Soon enough, I would be enrolled in night classes again.

I only flew a few more times, mainly renting a Piper Cub to take friends and family for an aerial view of our town and neighborhood. Passengers included Irene and my mother. Showing off, I unsuccessfully attempted a loop with my girlfriend, who thought it was great fun. Flying was still a fine means of escape.

But not every aspect of readjustment was so smooth. I aged considerably during the war, although I didn't think so at first. Then Irene told me, "Compare yourself in the mirror with your high school pictures."

I was stunned. She was right. I had aged. I looked ten years older than I had two years earlier. My boyhood was gone. The conflict robbed me of my youth. I did not recognize this bleak fact until I reached home.

Irene had matured considerably herself. When I left her in 1943, I still perceived her as a cute high school kid. Now, she was a sophisticated young lady who radiated brilliance. She was a well-known regional columnist who penned witty articles for the Newark paper and others. I felt inferior when standing next to her. I had not seen or done anything civilized in three years. I sensed I was inadequate to suit her excellent standards. I felt like nothing more than a primitive sky jockey. Our relationship suffered as a result.

I felt adrift. I was detached from the world around me. When I sat with Irene and her friends at social functions, they discussed matters that were trivial or alien to me. My mind wandered as they spoke. It was as if their lips were moving but nothing was coming out. Nobody acted as if a war had been on. This, I couldn't understand. I needed to get away from it all. Meanwhile, thoughts of past battles occasionally sifted into my dreams. Everybody seemed ready to put the war behind them, but not all of us could.

Dana Andrews's performance in the 1946 film *The Best Years of Our Lives* resonates with me. The actor portrays a fictional Eighth Air Force captain named Fred Derry. The veteran returns home to a vivacious wife wishing to parade him as a hero from one nightclub to another. Fred demurs, wishing to pack away his uniform and leave the war in the past. Near the end of the movie, Fred comes to terms with his experiences by meandering through an airplane graveyard to mentally wipe his slate clean. While Irene was certainly not as pushy or impatient as Fred's spouse, I nonetheless felt equally out of place in a crowd. I simply couldn't keep up with Irene's standing as a dynamic social butterfly. I felt I had no option but to break up with her. After that, she told me later, she threw my ring in the fireplace.

Over the following months, I decompressed, settled into civilian life, and returned to a half-civilized state of mind. Maybe I kicked some of the war out of my system during that time. Realizing my grave error, I called Irene and suggested we get back together. Luckily for me, she consented. Perhaps she read me better than I read myself. I proposed in February, and we married on June 15, 1946, two days after her college graduation.

Irene and I wed. *John Homan collection.* (38)

Whereas I tend to be calm and deliberative, Irene's energy was boundless. She possessed a true zest for life that enriched my own. She was an empowered, cosmopolitan woman with deep interests in music, writing, theater, travel, sports, and politics. She read daily the *Wall Street Journal* and the *New York Times* while also having a longstanding subscription to the *New Yorker*. She was an active member of the League of Women Voters. If only a fraction of our citizens today were as well-versed and engaged in contemporary issues as she was, we'd live in a considerably healthier society.

While honeymooning at a resort near Burlington, Vermont, we devised a scheme to rent a plane and take in picturesque aerial views of Lake Champlain. At the local airport office, I asked the first man I saw if I could borrow an aircraft. He simply announced, "You can have mine." He called a ground crewman to show me the aircraft and check the fuel level and such. There were no questions, no check ride, and no asking for a license. Simpler times.

The plane was a major step up from a Piper Cub, with side-by-side seating and dual controls. I was so pleased by the opportunity for unique sightseeing. We had a great scenic tour and headed back to the airport when the engine quit without warning.

Not again, I thought. *Not now.*

My proven survival instincts automatically kicked in. All I could do was push the nose down to prevent a stall, take a quick look for an open ground area, and scan the instrument panel. I saw a carburetor heat knob, pulled it out, and pumped the throttle. The engine then restarted. I was fully prepared for an emergency landing on my honeymoon. Thankfully, I did not have to implement those skills as a newly married man. I still have no idea what caused the engine failure or if my corrective measures resolved the problem.

On the one-year anniversary of VJ Day, my hometown of Sayreville hosted a four-day homecoming celebration for local sons and daughters who served in uniform. The martial affair consisted of services, socials, speeches, and culminated in a downtown parade. I avoided the procession because I did not care to be in the spotlight, and I always hated marching. At Irene's suggestion, I was instead paid by the mayor to fly formation parade cover. Staying at arm's length from the festivities was fine with me. That 1946 parade was the last I ever participated in.

My final time at the controls was when a neighbor asked for a joyride in a front-and-rear-seat Piper Cub. As we flew over his house and conducted a very gentle turn, I looked back and noticed the poor man was going to be sick.

"Hold on!" I instructed him. "I'll set her down!"

Before I could reach the field, he vomited all over my shoulders.

Turning on the approach while the man's lunch ran down my jacket, I pulled the throttle back and the engine suddenly quit. Luckily, I had the plane in position for a dead stick landing and safely touched down. That unsavory experience, a lack of money, and new demands of life brought an end to my flying days. I simply lost the desire. My focus was required elsewhere. I hung up my wings to concentrate on earthly matters such as marriage, education, and building a profession.

At night school sessions, I had to boost my high school credits to become eligible for Rutgers University. Once accepted, I chose a dual major of Economics and Political Science. I didn't waste time. A pile of books always sat next to my desk. Even at the outset of class meetings as professors prepared notes and students settled down, I read. I cracked open books in the car while at stoplights. I remain a heavy reader to this day.

As was the case with so many universities, Rutgers was transformed by the war and its aftermath. By the early 1950s, temporary structures and mobile homes served as housing for many of us student veterans. In the classroom, one of our young professors of French was particularly engaging. Several of us who served in Europe could recall just enough dirty jokes and curse words in French to make him feel at home. Elsewhere, an Economics professor often held forums in a local pub with students to place them at ease in a less stuffy environment. So many of the faculty demonstrated empathy and went out of their way to make us feel comfortable.

Before college, I had helped organize a union, served on a bargaining committee, and then worked as assistant shop steward at the Hercules plant. During my upbringing, positions at Hercules were non-union jobs. I had higher expectations of my employers. This activist outlook was apparent in my college essays. In a course on labor and the law, I did not hold back views on the importance of unions in the American workplace. The professor flunked me. Not to be outdone, I requested an appointment and passionately explained my stance. Having heard my perspective and appreciating my ardor, he changed my grade to an A. I was obviously pleased with my persuasive power. But the professor had another trick up his sleeve.

"You're going to lecture the class," he announced. I did so and gained the professor's respect. Some of my instructors later informed me that those postwar years were the best of their teaching careers. Their veteran students were driven, focused, mature, and had a sense of a broader world.

I was twenty-four when I enrolled in college. A world of difference separated me from the seventeen- and eighteen-year-olds at my side in lecture halls. They had been too young to fight the war. They were insulated. They couldn't possibly grasp what I had seen and done while they were in high school. Yet I was now playing academic catch-up with these students.

Many of the youngsters seemingly had little control over their own destinies. They often lacked the autonomy a pupil should cherish at the university level. One of the worst things I saw in them was the inability to escape the expectations of their parents. So many of my classmates were the sons and daughters of physicians, lawyers, accountants, and other white collar professionals. Pressure was placed on them to follow in dad's footsteps so they could rake in cash. These expectations made students nervous wrecks.

College should be fueled by discovery and self-fulfillment, serving as a foundation for what *you* want to do with *your* life. Scholarly pursuits must gravitate toward what one enjoys. When my own children came of age, I never attempted to coerce their choices in curriculum. I granted them the same academic freedom I enjoyed in my own vocational interests. I could not be prouder of the paths they have chosen.

The first of those children, Kim, was born in 1947. After my freshman year, we moved into a trailer court off campus and did not live a very luxurious existence. In our mobile home, there was no running water and few amenities. We cooked with kerosene and restrooms were remote. I felt as if I was back in my Nissen hut in East Anglia. Irene sacrificed so much so I could attend college. She had already graduated and could have been out making a name for herself. Instead, she rode out my college years in a trailer in the pastures of New Jersey. That was true love.

Our fellow veteran neighbors used the intuition and improvisation they had mastered during the war to make life just slightly more bearable in those humble settings. We made ample use of a small community center at the trailer court to forge camaraderie and resolve challenges. Parties and dances there served as a welcome means of distraction on Friday nights.

Even so, we vets did not buddy around too much beyond the social hall. Our aim was to receive a top-notch education provided by the government and move on with our lives. The GI Bill of Rights, signed by President Roosevelt two weeks after D-Day, remains one of the greatest accomplishments of our nation. The legislation opened college doors to millions of service members like me who otherwise might never have had an opportunity to enter higher education. Our academic achievements subsequently helped construct a powerful post-war economy and a thriving middle class.

My service nonetheless had some strings attached. In my junior year at Rutgers, I received an official letter from the

Department of Defense declaring that men with my Military Occupation Specialty number were in short supply. Pilots with single-, twin-, and four-engine aircraft experience were needed over the battlefields of Korea. This request was more than I could stomach. "No thank you!" was my reply. I was quite glad I had opted for the "inactive" status in the Reserves during my separation process several years earlier.

Those who agreed to active reserve classification were tempted by the additional two weeks' pay and credit toward retirement. But they had no ability to decline deployment if they were summoned to fight. Several of our veteran neighbors were shipped out because of this reactivation process. Elsewhere, my former skipper John Predgen was sent to Korea as an Air Force pilot. The experience emotionally wrecked him, and I don't think he was ever the same. My decision in November 1945 meant Irene and I would never be torn apart by war again.

I worked so diligently my senior year that I was invited to attend graduate school. By then, I was twenty-seven and had already gained a job in the maintenance department at a local Johnson & Johnson plant. Irene and I were also expecting a second baby. Tim, our son, was born two days before my 1951 graduation. A daughter named Eve then joined our family in 1955. With all these fatherly obligations, I no longer had time for formal education. It was time to apply my learning to the outside world. I had lived in poverty long enough.

Over the following decades, my various industrial positions took me all over the Midwest and Mid-Atlantic. I was fortunate to have superiors who mentored me, and I used that guidance to advance through the corporate world. I was promoted to plant manager at a Johnson & Johnson facility in Cincinnati and then Decatur, Illinois. I remained there until my late thirties when I accepted a new job with the A. E. Staley Manufacturing Company, also located in Decatur. The company was prominent in the production of starches, corn, and cleaning products. Through hard work and persistence, I managed a promotion every two years throughout my career. The next point of advancement relocated me to a Staley plant in Bucks County, Pennsylvania, in 1970.

My professional exploits earned me an invitation to a black-tie gala with Queen Elizabeth II at the Philadelphia Museum of Art to commemorate the national bicentennial in 1976. The queen (who had visited many of our airfields during the war) expressed "sincere gratitude to the founding fathers of this great republic for having taught Britain a very valuable lesson" about freedom. That lesson was reinforced in the 1940s when our countries joined together in the struggle against Nazism.[11]

Fancy banquets aside, I never forgot my roots. I tried to remain true to the labor principles of my younger days. A satisfying reminder of these efforts is that I still receive cards from employees I managed fifty years ago. In the military, I learned to look after my people, and I always strived to do the same in the corporate world. There is no good excuse not to.

By 1977, I had accepted a position at a brand-new Staley plant in Lafayette, Indiana. The facility was very modern but poorly managed. I was entrusted with the task of transforming site operations. I oversaw thousands of employees and hundreds of millions of dollars in resources. I eventually took charge of four more sites in the region. This was the biggest responsibility of my life. I finally retired in 1985. I worked forty years following the war and raised three fine children. I've enjoyed nearly as many years in retirement since.

Irene and I certainly had no intention of slowing down after my departure from Staley. As my children grew, I embraced the pastime of sailing. Upon retirement, I successfully located a boat we could enjoy for leisurely excursions on the Chesapeake. During one of my early ventures, friends and I encountered a violent storm—one that reminded me of my voyage across the Atlantic four decades prior. We emerged safely from the treacherous waters, but I thought, "If I ever get my wife stuck in a storm like that, she'll divorce me." I therefore purchased a trawler, a heavier and slower vessel that served us well on many memorable journeys. In recognition of my days as an adventurous youth, I named the boat *Roamer.* We anchored her in Tolchester, Maryland, and, over time, veteran friends joined us when we sailed the waves.

In the 1980s, I finally had the opportunity to reconnect at a deeper level with old pals from the 489th Bomb Group and the Second Air Division. Reunions that followed allowed me to engage with the people, stories, and places of my past in profound and surprising ways.

CHAPTER 9

To Go Back Again

Serving as a B-24 pilot out of a rural airfield in East Anglia was perhaps the most memorable episode of my life. Even eighty years on, recollections of the conflict remain deeply ingrained in my mind. A decades-long quest to chronicle and comprehend my service is rooted in a sense of history. Devoted recordkeeping was driven by a concern that my children, grandchildren, and descendants might never know of my experiences.

My appreciation of the past was reinforced by a love of reading. Books analyzing the Great War and the Civil War filled my shelves as I attempted to contextualize my place within an extended military timeline. One of my realizations was troubling. I concluded that the costly bombing campaigns flown by the Eighth Air Force in Europe used essentially the same tactics as predecessors of the 1910s and 1860s. When we examine the combat of those earlier struggles, we might envision the slaughter of no-man's-land or sweeping assaults across open pastures. I survived comparable undertakings at 20,000 feet. I was part of mass bomber wings, flying formation in daylight, heading straight and level through murderous flak. We were attacked by fighters while carrying up to four tons of bombs and perhaps 2,000 gallons of fuel in a thin aluminum shell. We were, after all, the *Army* Air Forces. Early on, our generals refused to admit fighter escorts were necessary. These perilous trials reveal the shallow learning curves of war—and how easily we forget the price of error.

When considering our air campaigns, I am struck by the comparative obscurity of the B-24 in contrast to the celebrated B-17. The Eighth Air Force is practically synonymous with the powerful image of the latter aircraft. Wartime publicity efforts by the War Department and filmmakers decisively shaped this popular perception. But the B-17's indomitable status as the "Flying Fortress" fomented unsuspected problems. Some leaders initially believed the plane's ten heavy machine guns would negate the necessities of fighter support. Tremendous casualty rates from the beginning proved that assumption incorrect. My wife's brother, a B-17 bombardier, once told me of a mission in which two engines were shot out and several of his crewmates were left in a lifeless, bloody heap on the cabin floor. No plane is perfect or immortal, even when heavily armed.

I've endured my share of ribbing from friends who served in other branches. They jokingly claimed, "The Army went to the latrine, the Navy went to the head, and the Air Forces went to the powder room." I took their jests in good humor and modestly acknowledged that attaining victory was a genuine team effort. As articulated at the outset, this book in no way suggests I had a rougher time or achieved more than others who served. The uniqueness of one's experience should not diminish the contributions of another. Sadly, the war is rarely commemorated that way. For instance, will there ever be a motion picture about airplane mechanics or a ship's galley crew who saw to the vital needs of others?

Perhaps no cultural force carries more weight in shaping our historical memories than Hollywood. Movies about aviators were at their numerical peak in the 1940s and 1950s. Perhaps the finest of these depictions is *Twelve O'Clock High*, released in 1949. Actor Gregory Peck portrays an unsympathetic brigadier, fittingly named Frank Savage, who must transform a dejected bomb group into an efficient outfit. With each passing mission, Savage conceals the inner turmoil of ordering fine young men to their deaths. He finally snaps, revealing that nobody is immune to combat fatigue. The film offers fairly accurate depictions of air battles as it cleverly incorporates actual footage recorded by combat photographers. The movie offers a revealing glimpse of the burdens of command, although the screenwriter took creative liberties in condensing our actual organization systems. The representation of a general intimately involving himself in the functions of a single bomb group and coming to know its members on a first name basis is a stretch.

Hollywood is not done with our story. As I wrote this book, I learned Tom Hanks and Steven Spielberg had again partnered for a television miniseries about the Second World War. *Masters of the Air* depicts the harrowing exploits of the Eighth Air Force's 100th Bomb Group, fatefully known as "The Bloody Hundredth." I hope viewers sense the complexity of our operations. When I think back to those times, I am astounded by our ability to get 1,000 planes airborne and bomb multiple targets while evading bad weather and enemy fighters—all without the convenience of modern communications. The vast process required teams of unsung technicians, clerks, analysts, meteorologists, cooks, and doctors who never set foot in our planes. Our concerted efforts were tremendous.

For survivors among us, stories were enshrined on personal levels via friendships within our veteran communities. By the early 1950s, former officers of the Second Air Division launched a veterans' organization to perpetuate our camaraderie. "Now in peace we remember our associations of England," our former general Bill Kepner advertised in 1953. "We would enjoy meeting our buddies and hashing over old times." Address lists were created, networks were formed, and acquaintances were reestablished by telephone and mail. Annual membership dues were two dollars. "Let's tune up the motors, run through the check list, and get cleared by the missus and kids for a cross country mission to the next reunion," Kepner ordered. Hundreds answered his call.[1]

A newsletter was published, more reunions were hosted, the rosters grew, and international travels were planned—all as means of keeping our legacies and relationships alive. Seeking additional ties to the past, several men and their families ventured to our mostly abandoned airfield at Halesworth in the 1970s and beyond. They were surprised to discover that much of the property had been transformed into a giant turkey farm. The runways remained, but most other evidence of our presence was gone or repurposed for agricultural uses. Haystacks and pigpens were placed atop our old hardstands. The transformation of the pastures was an inevitable outcome of peace and the return to normality.[2]

Charles Freudenthal, a former captain of our headquarters detachment, was crucial in compiling the group's history and, unsurprisingly, revisited Halesworth perhaps more than anyone else. He wandered through the military ghost town in 1975, searching for tangible traces of a distant past. "The old shortcut through the woods took me up to the Combat Officers Mess, but it was filled with sugar beets, and nostalgia was temporarily snuffed out," he wrote. When the old captain encountered the dilapidated control tower littered with broken glass, memories swept back to "those who had stayed behind [and] stood to sweat out the returning birds."

Names of planes and their men likewise stirred in his thoughts. Inside a nearby Quonset hut, a panel with the words

"Training Status Board—845th Bomb Squadron" hung lonely on a flaking wall. In town, locals still recalled "Liberators roaring overhead before dawn." The visit proved bittersweet. "It's different," Charlie confessed of the site, "and I'm not sure I want to go back again."[3]

Despite the base "fading back into the countryside," Freudenthal did return four years later. "The place is losing the battle for existence, but it isn't giving up easily," he observed. "There were six of us there on June 4, trying to find some identifiable link to the 1944 days. Memories are pretty tricky after thirty-five years." The small squad of aged airmen then encountered a local gent named Mr. Bedser, who still cultivated the farm he resided on during the war. Back in the day, we could see the thatched roof of his home during takeoffs and landings. Bedser offered much-needed orientation and even gifted each American a bottle of SKAT insect repellent, left behind by Yanks when the field eventually closed.[4]

Little did I know that there was a simultaneous search for me as well. I had attended some small group reunions in the 1950s, but largely lost track of crewmates in the intervening years. Consequently, wartime friends were on the prowl for my whereabouts. In December 1979, our former engineer, Lou Wagner, wrote in the division newsletter, "Recently joined the Association. Heard about it from John L. Predgen (my pilot) and from Charlie Freudenthal. Would you believe that until then, I never knew we had such an organization! Hearing from 'Predge' has stirred up things! At last, the crew is getting together! We have made contact with 8 of the 10. Missing are John F. Homan (co-pilot) and John K. Dalgleish (bomb bay)."[5]

Their hunt was not immediately successful. The following March, Freudenthal announced to fellow veterans, "WE'RE LOOKING FOR: JOHN F. HOMAN and JOHN K. DALGLEISH, co-pilot and bombardier on John Predgen's crew. . . . Has anybody kept in touch or got any ideas?[6]

Like Wagner, I was unaware of the existence of this larger veterans' network. I was so pleased when Lou finally discovered me in 1981. Back in the circle once more, Irene and I eagerly set out for Nashville, Tennessee, for the 1982 reunion. Many years had passed since I last saw any of our men. At the social banquet, I was among fifty-six first-time attendees out of 700 veterans present. The best aspect of this splendid affair was reuniting with Wagner, Vernon Long, Marion Cochran, and Dick Bunch. It was wonderful to see these comrades again under less hazardous circumstances.

At the Nashville reunion, I had the sudden urge to procure a celebratory bottle of fine liquor to share with crewmates, just like old times. I walked to the hotel entrance, unsure as to how to accomplish my mission. The driver of a nearby city bus noticed how apparently lost I was and summoned me to his door.

"What are you looking for, buddy?" he inquired.

"I'm here with a veterans' reunion and I'd really like to invite my old crew to my room for a drink, but I have nothing to offer. Got any suggestions?"

"Hop in," he assured.

Nobody else was on the bus—only me and the Good Samaritan driver. The man hauled me to a downtown liquor store, waited as if he was a taxi operator with a running meter, and then returned me to the hotel. When I offered a tip, he declared, "You don't owe me nothing." The driver gave me a fine impression of Nashville. A charitable act goes a long way.

Bonds of brotherhood among crewmates were retained for the rest of their lives. Cochran and his wife attended several reunions with Irene and me. He candidly admitted, "If I ever knew the war was going to be like that, I wouldn't have volunteered." A chunk of hot flak striking his helmet and severing his mic cord all those decades prior undoubtedly led him to this conclusion.

Over subsequent years, our crew assembled to golf, sail, eat, and drink to our hearts' delight. We shared such fine times that other veterans of the group eventually joined the merrymaking. Dozens of airmen and families turned out for the shindigs—though none of these mini-reunions were as salacious as the group's 100th mission extravaganza in 1944.

It seems that our crew members never talked about the war except among ourselves. I encourage veterans of younger generations to maintain ties with their former brothers and sisters in arms. Communication presents therapeutic possibilities and outlets for support. I had wonderful times reacquainting myself with the crew. Joined by our wives, we embraced the present and simply had fun. I am fortunate that I never confronted severe challenges with what is now called Post Traumatic Stress. Regardless, knowing I had a network of friends with comparable experiences was a comforting thought.

Not all were as privileged. John Predgen suffered from acute psychological trauma inflicted by the Korean War. When I caught up with him decades later at a reunion, he had no memory of serving with me. I was at a loss for words.

Wide ranges of emotions were exhibited at reunions—joy, sorrow, relief, nervousness. In some instances, strange and unlikely encounters were witnessed. In 1944, a sixteen-year-old German anti-aircraft gunner shot down one of our planes and then snapped a photo of the aircraft. In adulthood, he attempted to identify the unit to which the ship belonged. A copy of the image was sooner or later forwarded to Freudenthal, who identified the bomber as a 489th plane. As a very magnanimous gesture, Freudenthal invited the ex-gunner to one of our reunions as a means of reconciliation and closure. Veterans within our association were very forgiving of their former foe, concluding they would have defended their homeland with similar tenacity.

"There is a psychological need to forget and a moral obligation to remember," historian Herman Knell says of the bombing campaigns. The suffering of both the bombers and the bombed must be understood as a conjoined tragedy. Furthermore, he insists there is "the human desire to forgive and the ethical necessity to warn of a possible repeat of disaster."[7]

I was eager to reflect on my war experiences in May 1987 when I returned to England for a Second Air Division reunion with Irene at my side. A genuine outpouring of gratitude was unleashed as soon as we landed. Escorts guided us to a hospitality room with refreshments and a big band. We boarded a special train to Norwich, where we were welcomed at the station by city officials, many supportive residents, and yet another big band. Over the next week we were treated to a series of fabulous ceremonies with much pomp and circumstance, for which the English have a special talent. One event was a moving memorial service in the old, beautiful Norwich Cathedral. Another was a formal dinner in the medieval Norwich Castle Museum, hosted by the Lord Mayor in his full regalia. The pageantry made us feel as important as visiting heads of state.

At Royal Air Force Coltishall, lunch was served for 700 in a massive hangar. Joining our group was a prominent barrister and liaison to the Second Air Division Association who frequently attended our stateside gatherings. The very dignified chap inquired about the lineage of we Americans seated at his table. I was surprised to learn how many first- and second-generation citizens were among us.

This pattern impressed the barrister. "They must have brought more than themselves," he observed with admiration. His sentiment was so thoughtful that I have never forgotten it. His implication was that we evoked an ancestral spirit of adventure, daring, and teamwork that ultimately helped save his country. I also then realized just how much the British valued our "special relationship." After lunch we were thrilled with a special demonstration by the Red Arrows, a precision flying group comparable to the Thunderbirds or Blue Angels.

Our travels grew somber with a pilgrimage to the Cambridge American Cemetery and Memorial. The lush patch of country-side was donated by Cambridge University in 1943 to accom-modate the interments of American airmen and sailors. Today, one can gaze out at 3,800 headstones arranged in a vast semi-circle. A subdued, rainy memorial service during our visit was a grim reminder of sacrifice. Each of us was presented with a name and flower. We dispersed into the burial grounds, paying small tributes to the fallen. The atmosphere was one of solitude and serenity. My reaction was one of sadness.

These poor bastards, I thought. I had grown into an old man. These boys never had that privilege.

Included on the Tablet of the Missing are two men from my squadron: Staff Sergeants Nicholas D. Bonitz and Loy M. Harvey, both of whom went missing in action on July 26, 1944. They have never been recovered. Nearby is a name etched in gold—that of Lt. Col. Leon Vance, our deputy group commander who posthumously received the Medal of Honor. His was the only such medal awarded to a B-24 crewman for an action flown from the United Kingdom.[8]

The Cambridge American Cemetery and Memorial.
American Battle Monuments Commission photo. (39)

Our final day touring England was no less emotional. Following a reception at the Chateaubriand Restaurant, we filled St. Peter's Church in Holton. The interior of the 1,000-year-old stone structure was adorned in our unit colors with yellow, white, and green flowers and ferns. The spectacle was awe-inspiring and rather beautiful. I never attended church while I was a young lieutenant, but I was glad to be in St. Peter's that cool spring day.

After services, local "Friends of the 489th" ushered us to our nearby airfields. On Halesworth's perimeter road, several gray-haired vets rolled out crinkled base maps and aerial photos atop the hood of a car and pointed in various directions, trying to reimagine their former stomping grounds.

"This was the Aero Club," one indicated.

"There was the mess for ground crews," another surmised.

"Here was Holton Hall."

"And Col. Napier's headquarters was there." The airmen effectively put their navigational skills to the test once more.[9]

Irene and I meanwhile set out to locate the site of my squadron quarters. As previously mentioned, squadron areas were widely dispersed in wooded areas, and I never knew where sister units were situated.

After hiking down some meandering country lanes, I halted near a lone house. "I think we are close," I informed Irene.

I knocked on the house door and a man with a thick Dutch accent answered.

"Good morning," I began. "I was in the 845th Squadron during the war and I'm trying to find my old quarters. Can you help us?"

Without hesitation the man responded, "Yes, my driveway was the squadron entrance." He immediately guided us through the woods to show me our old bomb shelter. This scene brought back vivid memories of standing on top of that shelter when distant British coastal gunners shot down incoming buzz bombs. The gentleman and his wife then graciously invited us into their home for coffee. Coincidentally, he had his own incredible military tale to share. During the war, he escaped the Nazi-occupied Netherlands, migrated to England, enlisted in the RAF, and was himself a bomber pilot.

Following this delightful conversation, additional warmth was conveyed at the dedication of a monument honoring the 489th Bomb Group. Located near the former runway, the unassuming marker stands in honor of all our personnel, but particularly those "who gave their lives in the cause of freedom and human dignity." Every Veterans' Day, villagers and service members from the nearest American air base still conduct a remembrance ceremony at the landmark. A very nice memorial museum is also located on the property.

The 489th monument dedication in 1987. *John Homan collection.* (40)

When the program concluded, we were informed that fresh flowers had mysteriously appeared every morning at the foot of the monument following its installation. Locals finally discovered that a ten-year-old boy named Tommy was responsible for the act of kindness. The youth and his mother were present at the dedication. We requested their company for the rest of the day and invited them to future events. The child's salute remains so meaningful to me. Young people tend to be classified as ambivalent or ignorant about history, but some of the most poignant acknowledgments of our service are undertaken by students.

I stood solitarily at the edge of the crumbling runway. The moment mirrored the haunting yet nostalgic opening of *Twelve O'Clock High*. I envisioned the base coming to life with predawn briefings, rumbling trucks, the din of 140 engines warming up, and the continuous roar of full-throttle 5,000-horsepower takeoffs. For a split second, I felt as if I was back in 1944.

The strip's deteriorated state afforded each of us a unique souvenir. Another local hauled a jackhammer to the site and carved out bits of pavement as mementos for us veterans. He took the time and effort to mount each piece of concrete on a small wooden base. My fragment proudly rests on my home office desk.

While many of us left with keepsakes, other airmen left emotional baggage behind. My friend Ted Harris departed Halesworth in a full body cast following a 1944 wreck in which he was the sole survivor. For the next half-century, he suffered from a terrible guilt complex. During his 1992 visit, Harris hoped to gain solace when a guide walked him to the crash location. For an hour, Ted explored the grounds weeping and talking to his dead comrades. "When he finally returned to the group," one veteran said of Harris, "he told his wife that he felt he had closure now."[10]

Our memorable English odyssey concluded with a lively pub night at a quaint country establishment called the Triple Plea—all with a typical dinner of bangers and mash. Swapping stories over beer was a wonderful way to end the trip. The beverages were cold this time.

Our old mess halls still stand at Halesworth.
2022 photo courtesy of Paul Starks. (41)

Reunions continued at a consistent pace over the following years: Colorado Springs, Hilton Head, Dearborn, Las Vegas,

My granddaughter Jessica Homan Clark and great-grandson James Killian
locate my name at the National Museum of the Mighty Eighth Air Force.
John Homan collection. (42)

and more. I am reminded of the moment I revisited the interior
of a B-24 at the Hilton Head reunion. I wiggled through the
tight confines of the catwalk and muttered, "This is smaller
than I remember." Without missing a beat, a woman behind
me replied, "Maybe you're just bigger now." Time can indeed
be cruel. I attended ten or so of these gatherings, each of which
diminished in attendance as the 1990s came and went.

Irene and I on our 65th wedding anniversary. *John Homan collection.* (43)

One of the most fitting reunion venues was the National Museum of the Mighty Eighth Air Force outside Savannah, Georgia. The institution offers a comprehensive overview of the airman experience during the war. Exhibits include enemy airpower, an immersive film about flying a mission, base culture, and prisoner-of-war life. Centerpieces are an actual B-17 and a P-51 (although no B-24 is on display). Outside, an extensive memorial garden and English-style chapel grace the grounds. There stands a black granite monument to the 489th Bomb Group, a plaque with my crew listed, and my name featured on a nearby wall of honor. I cherish a photo of my toddler great-grandson placing his tiny hand on my name.

As this moving interaction suggests, museums are compelling places to connect with history. Veteran and friend Jim Davis used to volunteer at the Midland Army Air Field Museum in Texas. He once recalled a young serviceman from the Norwegian Navy who saved hard-earned money to come view aircraft on display. After arriving in New York City, the aviation buff spent three days on a bus traveling to Texas. "He arrived in Midland and rented a room at a motel," Jim remembered. "The next day he walked twenty miles to the Midland International Airport and spent the whole day at the museum. It was an experience of a lifetime for him to see, touch, and crawl around the old airplanes that he had read and heard so much about." Museum staff members were so impressed that they purchased a return airline ticket to New York for the sailor.[11]

In October 2006, our division reunion in Arlington, Virginia, coincided with the dedication of the United States Air Force Memorial. The soaring, stainless-steel spires that compose the monument resemble the "bomb burst" contrails of three jets peeling away from each other. Irene and I were among the 30,000 spectators present for the opening ceremony. The memorial properly towers over the final resting place of so many airmen in neighboring Arlington National Cemetery.

By the early 2010s, membership numbers of the Second Air Division Association had dwindled to about fifty. We in the organization found ourselves with a large treasury surplus and little time to allocate the remnants. Our determination was that we had earned the right to spend those funds liberally. We thus treated ourselves to a luxury cruise to Bermuda on *Enchantment of the Seas*. Thirty-two veterans and guests set sail out of Baltimore in September 2011—right during hurricane season. The ship encountered a heavy storm the first night and at least one of our comrades was toppled by the turbulence. *Enchantment* thankfully handled the seas better than the SS *Brazil* during my homecoming voyage in 1944.

I long stayed in touch with my surviving crewmates but, one by one, they too succumbed to the passage of time. Lou Wagner died in 1991. Over three decades later, I still exchange Christmas cards with his widow. Between 2007 and 2017, Dalgleish, Predgen, Reevs, Leonard, and Long likewise passed away. When only two of us remained, we agreed that the last member standing would drink a champagne toast in honor of our crew. That sad responsibility was ultimately entrusted to me. I am the final man.

I felt a responsibility to impart our shared story not only with family, but with larger audiences. Interviewers from public television and the Library of Congress recorded my memories via the Veterans History Project. Scores of interested individuals turned out to hear me speak at the Pennsylvania Military Museum and the Eighth Air Force Archive at Penn State. Through these various engagements, I met my co-author for this book.

When Jared invited me to a World War II reenactor display at the Pennsylvania Military Museum, he likewise presented an opportunity to ride in his vintage Willys Jeep. To his surprise, I declared, "I've never ridden in one before."

"Well how did you get around base?" he asked.

"We walked or were trucked everywhere."

The last reunion of the Second Air Division in 2011 on *Enchantment of the Seas*. I am in the fourth row up on the far right. *John Homan collection.* (44)

He and a friend thereby satisfied my curiosity with a very bumpy spin around the property. It was my first Jeep ride and I'm fine with it being my last.

One day, I was reading on my back porch when I heard the very familiar growl of a heavy aircraft in the distance. *I know that sound*, I thought. Sure enough, traveling World War II aircraft were landing for public display at the local airport. I donned my Second Air Division Association jacket and set out with my son-in-law to inspect the B-17 that just landed.

Above: My first ride in a WWII Jeep, alongside reenactor Andrew Collins. *Jared Frederick photo.* Left: I explore a B-17 in my Second Air Division jacket. *Selden Smith photo.* (45 and 46)

When I informed the caretakers that I was a pilot during the war, they inquired if I would like to take flight once more.

"I'm not flying in that God-damned thing," was my gut response. I had risked my life in bombers on many occasions, and I wasn't about to do so again. Perhaps my apprehensions were well founded, as several well-publicized wrecks of World

War II planes have taken place in recent years. In November 2022, I was horrified to see on television a single-engine Kingcobra and a B-17 entangle in a ghastly mid-air collision at a Dallas airshow that claimed six lives. I witnessed plenty of fiery impacts over Europe and the tragedy in Texas served as a grim reminder of those episodes. Properly maintained aircraft from the era can indeed be flown, but the ventures are not without risk.

I have attended various demonstrations at WWII Weekend at the Mid-Atlantic Air Museum in Pennsylvania and think they are much fun. I am entertained by seeing youngsters become enthralled with the vintage planes I knew so well. But while flying can be fun, war is not fun. Those who recreate the 1940s should always remember this fact. If you want to accurately impart the Second World War experience to audiences, you need to discuss death and suffering as much as sleek airplanes, stylish cars, powerful weapons, and Glenn Miller music. Doing otherwise trivializes the truths of war. Everyday drudgery as a pilot was taxing on body and soul. Frankly, I am surprised I didn't suffer from acute combat fatigue. A sense of disbelief still lingers in my mind.

There's possibly some truth in the title of the "Greatest Generation." We entered and helped win the costliest conflict in human history. Then, empowered by the GI Bill, we forged a solid economy with a strong middle class. (The fact that so many countries were in industrial ruin undoubtedly made us financially dominant as well.) Even so, I don't embrace the phrase "Greatest Generation" to bolster my ego or denigrate younger generations. Young people are not the problem. They are not the ones who set policy or determine curriculum. If my generation was in fact "great," it was because we were not pampered and rose to the occasion when called upon.

To attain excellence, kids should be granted flexibility to be independent, creative, and curious. Build youngsters up intellectually as well as physically. Raise them to think not only of themselves, but others. Involve them in the community. If there was ever such a thing as the Greatest Generation, these were the building blocks that made it so. Any generation can achieve those aims with the proper spirit. As the old song proclaims, and as I often instructed my children, "Straighten Up and Fly Right."

All this said, I believe national service should be a requirement. The military is not for everyone, but we can nonetheless effectively instill the virtues of citizenship and service in our nation's youth. Modern equivalents of the Civilian Conservation Corps and related New Deal programs are perfect means to enhance our country's sense of civic health.

As I write these words, a horrendous war rages in Ukraine. Studies have shown that our world has gradually become more peaceful, but there is always the possibility of backsliding into the abyss if the wrong people are in power. Sadly, citizens have not always made the wisest decisions.

I and millions of others enlisted to ensure that authoritarianism could not threaten our system of governance. I am mightily pissed off by the insurrectionists who, on January 6, 2021, dared to undermine the way of life I fought to defend. As a longtime registered independent who has closely followed politics since the days of FDR, I had never seen our democracy in greater peril. Fascism again threatened us—and this time from within the White House itself. My plea to fellow Americans is to be watchful. Politically resist those who wish to divide and conquer. Bombs are not the answer; choose democracy. Vote to save the principles that I and millions of others risked our lives to maintain. Hold leaders accountable via the ballot box and our First Amendment rights. Remember that the Pledge of Allegiance is to the Republic and not to a single individual yearning for power.

If I were seventy years younger, I'd gladly sign up to fend off the forces of anti-democracy again. But others who are younger will have to resist in a different way this time. All I can do now is offer the lessons from my own life and hope readers take them to heart. My only regret in writing these thoughts is that they are not more strongly worded.

We are in a world of trouble. Pay attention to the big things. Don't be led astray by distraction and cable news carnival barkers. Elect leaders whose policies will nurture a sense of the collective good. Reflecting on the challenges of his own times, Franklin Roosevelt praised citizens for their unanimity and perseverance. "America will not forget these recent years, will not forget that the rescue was not a mere party task," he declared. "It was the concern of us all. In our strength we rose together, rallied our energies together, applied the old rules of common sense, and together survived."[12]

I don't see that togetherness today. But we can endure if we commit ourselves to the ongoing national experiment. As Gen. Eisenhower often declared to family, "*Be* for something." This is the noble task remaining for all.

Americans should be reading books, not banning them. Literacy is a key element of democracy. Every citizen should be required to study the book *The Rise and Fall of the Third Reich* by William L. Shirer. Only by recognizing the ruinous desires and tactics of autocracy can we avert them.

Even though my plane was called the "Liberator," I never thought of myself as a literal liberator during the war. We were attacked, plain and simple. I carried out my job, nothing more. I volunteered and did the best I could. Yet I now recognize that our efforts meant so much to so many.

At the conclusion of one of our English reunions, Jim Davis enjoyed an extended holiday in Switzerland. When he casually conversed with a European traveler and indicated he was an Eighth Air Force veteran, the other man unexpectedly rose from his chair and tearfully embraced Jim.

"Excuse me, but I owe you so much," the stranger sobbed. "I owe you my life."

The man was a sixteen-year-old Jewish boy in Poland when the Nazis invaded his country in 1939. The teen was taken prisoner and languished in slave labor camps for the entirety of the conflict. Five years into his incarceration, there was faint reason for optimism, he explained.

"As long as we could hear your planes, there was hope."

"He was the most grateful and gracious person that I have ever met," Davis remembered. "Until I met this gentleman, I never realized that just the sound of an airplane could give a person the will and courage to survive another day. I never regretted the effort and difficulty it took to survive a tour. Now it seems such a small effort compared to the untold millions who suffered so much in Europe during the war." Given this realization, I can only agree with Jim's sentiments. It was all worthwhile.[13]

Despite all we achieved, the war sometimes reemerges in my dreams. I'm back in the cockpit again, reliving my missions as foggy memories of long ago. The visions are not as vivid and cruel as they once were, but traces of those terrors remain. I can only be grateful I have lived a long and fulfilling life. So many were denied that chance.

The brightest aspect of that life was my marriage to Irene. After the war, we were happily together for seventy-two years. Irene passed away in 2018 at age ninety-three. Above all else, I miss our spirited conversations, her sense of humor, and her warm concern for others. She completed me.

Following her passing, I slowly delved into her personal belongings and discovered a secret drawer in the bedroom. Within the cabinet, I found all the love letters I penned to her while in the service—the communications I had so cleverly coded.

I was astounded. In our three-quarters of a century as a couple, she never once hinted about the fate of our correspondence. This hidden bundle of envelopes was her final gift to me, a demonstration of lasting love forged in wartime. Not even my children have read the folded, yellowed papers. Although some insisted that I incorporate this treasure trove into my memoir, I was simply unable to surrender them for public consumption. Their deeply personal contents will remain my secret until I am gone.

Age has dimmed some of my memories and enhanced others. When conditions are right, I can drift back to the days when I was a twenty-year-old flyboy soaring into the cold blue. I can see the faces of my comrades, I can hear their laughter, and I can listen to the roar of our planes. I have forgotten many things, but I can never forget those men. Remember them.

I hold my "crusher cap" from the war.
Jared Frederick photo. (47)

AFTERWORD BY THE CO-AUTHOR

I never had the opportunity to chat with my grandfathers about their roles in the Second World War. By the time I completed second grade, both were gone. This was especially tragic considering my budding love of history. In the nearly thirty years since, I have gained appreciation of my grandfathers' experiences vicariously through the testimony of fellow veterans of that conflict. John Homan's saga is among the most gripping and detailed of those personal reflections I have absorbed.

Throughout 2022, John and I sat together in his apartment for dozens of hours as he relayed his story. His meticulous records, sharp memory, insightful context, and notes made for enjoyable sessions. By the end of our detailed discussions, I had learned as much about life as I did about World War II. I value every conversation we shared.

From the outset, John was explicit in his demands that this book would not glorify war. In the text, we did our utmost to depict his combat episodes without sanitizing their horrors. His original mission logbook and annotations continually enabled us to place readers in his boots. The fact that John could remember weather conditions and technical problems for specific missions and then corroborate those details via his records repeatedly astonished me.

Especially helpful was the book *A History of the 489th Bomb Group*. Written by one of John's former superiors, Charles Freudenthal, the work is a 1989 self-published study that was generally made available only to veterans of the unit. Luckily, John owns two copies. Freudenthal's meticulous use of National Archives materials and personal records allowed us to connect the dots while crafting this narrative. Several other 489th veterans wrote their own, often underappreciated, memoirs in the last two decades. These works, listed in the bibliography, offered similar perspectives on life within the outfit. The same is true of the many articles written by veterans for the Second Air Division newsletter between the 1960s and the 2010s. We thank these men for their valuable firsthand accounts.

This book would not have been possible without Eve Homan, John's younger daughter. Over the years, she assisted him in collecting his thoughts on the war. Those files were foundational to this book and greatly assisted me in stitching together chapters of John's life. She and husband Selden Smith—both excellent editors—also aided with proofing and phrasing. Whenever my rhetoric or style strayed too far from John's, they were on hand to realign my route. Using the interviews and previous writings as my compass, I composed chapters and then forwarded each to the Homan clan for thorough scrutiny and review. Despite some early fumbles on my part, the family's tough love and encouragement remained steadfast throughout. This book is stronger and truer as a result.

Gratitude is also due to Dr. Vivian Rogers-Price and Heather Thies at the National Museum of the Mighty Eighth Air Force. Both these individuals were immensely helpful in procuring archival materials pertaining to John's crewmates. I invite readers to explore this incredible museum in Savannah. While stationed in that historic city, Capt. Brian Witty, a friend, Army officer, and fellow historian, ventured to the museum to make copies of the documents we required—all while preparing for transfer to a new base. His time and kindness are much appreciated.

John and I may never have crossed paths if it were not for the efforts of Sue Fox Moyer, historian with the Second Schweinfurt Memorial Association. Sue's father was wounded in a mission over Schweinfurt in 1943 and she has worked tirelessly to preserve and share stories pertaining to the Eighth Air Force. Her endeavors have included the facilitation of veteran presentations and memorial ceremonies. Sue's work along these lines led to my first meeting with John, and I am thankful.

We are indebted to our agent, Greg Johnson at WordServe Literary, who saw potential in this collaboration.

I sincerely hope that John's great-grandson, James—to whom this work is dedicated—will long appreciate the book as a poignant means of remembrance.

Aspire to the conviction John has expressed so often: "Straighten up and fly right!" We are all well-advised to heed such sound judgment.

Jared Frederick, Ph.D.
Altoona, Pennsylvania

APPENDIX

Lt. John Homan 1944 Mission Log: European Theater of Operations

Mission Date	Mission #	Mission/Target Location	Comments
Normandy Campaign			
July 6, 1944	1	Kiel, Germany	Shipyards bombed
July 7, 1944	2	Aschersleben, Germany	MT/SD
July 8, 1944	3	Nanteuil-sur Marne, France	Bridges targeted
July 11, 1944	--	Munich, Germany	Returned for oxygen mask
July 12, 1944	4	Munich, Germany	Tense fog landing
July 16, 1944	5	Saarbrücken, Germany	HD
July 17, 1944	6	La Houssoye, France	NOBALL targets
July 21, 1944	--	Led Formation Assembly	Flew *Lil' Cookie*
July 23, 1944	7	Juvincourt-et-Damary, France	MT
July 24, 1944	8	Saint-Lô, France	U.S. friendly fire
Northern France Campaign			
July 25, 1944	9	Saint-Lô, France	Operation Cobra
July 31, 1944	10	Ludwigshafen, Germany	MT/HD
August 1, 1944	--	Rouen, France	Aborted at takeoff

(Continued)

Mission Date	Mission #	Mission/Target Location	Comments
August 2, 1944	11	Avesnes-Chaussoy, France	MD
August 3, 1944	--	Avesnes-Chaussoy, France	Oil leak forced return
August 5, 1944	12	Brunswick, Germany	Plane plant bombed
August 6, 1944	13	Hamburg, Germany	Glenn Miller visited base
August 7, 1944	14	Bois de la Houssière, Belgium	Heavy rain and fog
August 8, 1944	15	Romilly-sur-Seine, France	Billy Conn visited base
August 15, 1944	16	Wittmundhafen, Germany	Jet training field bombed
August 16, 1944	17	Magdeburg, Germany	MT/MD
August 24, 1944	18	Waggum, Germany	MD
August 25, 1944	19	Rostock, Germany	Cochran's gun jammed
August 26, 1944	20	Ehrang, Germany	Bombed secondary target
August 27, 1944	21	Oranienburg, Germany	Mission scrubbed
September 1-9, 1944	--	Near Orléans, France	Supply runs for Patton
September 10, 1944	22	Heilbronn, Germany	Bombed railyards
September 11, 1944	23	Magdeburg, Germany	Inaccurate salvos
September 18, 1944	24	Groesbeck, Holland	HD at Drop Zone

Mission Date	Mission #	Mission/Target Location	Comments
Rhineland Campaign			
September 27, 1944	--	Led Formation Assembly	Flew *Lil' Cookie*
September 28, 1944	25	Kassel, Germany	MD
October 2, 1944	26	Hamm, Germany	MT/HD
October 14, 1944	27	Cologne, Germany	New formation tested
October 15, 1944	28	Cologne, Germany	SD
October 17, 1944	29	Cologne, Germany	Heavy cloud cover
October 19, 1944	30	Mainz, Germany	30,000-foot clouds
October 22, 1944	31	Hamm, Germany	MT
October 25, 1944	32	Münster, Germany	Premature bomb drop
October 26, 1944	33	Minden, Germany	Mittelland Canal
November 9, 1944	34	Metz, France	Lorraine Campaign

Abbreviations Key:
SD: Slight Damage
MD: Moderate Damage
HD: Heavy Damage
MT: Mechanical Trouble

BIBLIOGRAPHY

Archival Materials
392nd Bomb Group Website — www.b24.net

Second Air Division Association Newsletter Digital Collections (1950-2012).

National Museum of the Mighty Eighth Air Force

John L. Predgen Letters [A 2017.0097.0001 Letter] / National Museum of the Mighty Eighth Air Force, Pooler, Georgia.

John L. Predgen Log [A 2017.0097.0003 Log] / National Museum of the Mighty Eighth Air Force, Pooler, Georgia.

Chuck Reevs Memoir [A 2012.0154.0228 Memoir] / National Museum of the Mighty Eighth Air Force, Pooler, Georgia.

Lou Wagner Memoir [A 2012.0154.0245 Memoir] / National Museum of the Mighty Eighth Air Force, Pooler, Georgia.

Period Newspapers

For complete bibliographic information on the dozens of historical periodicals used, refer to full citations within the Notes.

Published Books

Ambrose, Stephen. *The Wild Blue: The Men and Boys Who Flew the B-24s Over Germany*. New York: Simon & Schuster, 2001.

Astor, Gerald. *The Mighty Eighth: The Air War in Europe as Told by the Men Who Fought It*. New York: Dutton Caliber, 2015.

Atkinson, Rick. *The Guns at Last Light: The War in Western Europe, 1944-1945*. New York: Henry Holt, 2013.

Bodle, Peter, and Paddy Cox. *The 489th Bomb Group in Suffolk: A Pictorial History of the USAAF's 489th Bombardment Group at Halesworth during WWII*. Norfolk, United Kingdom: Liberator Publishing, 2010.

Davis, James M., and David L. Snead. *In Hostile Skies: An American B-24 Pilot in World War II*. Denton, Texas: University of North Texas Press, 2007.

Dorr, Robert F. *Mission to Berlin: The American Airmen Who Struck the Heart of Hitler's Reich*. Kenilworth, New Jersey: Zenith Press, 2011.

Freeman, Roger A. *The Mighty Eighth: A History of the Units, Men, and Machines of the U.S. 8th Air Force*. London: Cassell & Company, 2000.

Freudenthal, Charles. *A History of the 489th Bomb Group*. Self-published, 1989.

Fussell, Paul. *The Boys' Crusade: The American Infantry in Northwestern Europe, 1944-1945*. New York: Modern Library, 2003.

_____. *Wartime: Understanding and Behavior in the Second World War*. Oxford, United Kingdom: Oxford University Press, 1990.

Hansen, Randall. *Fire and Fury: The Allied Bombing of Germany, 1942-1945*. New York: NAL Caliber, 2009.

Imperial War Museums. *Somewhere in England: American Airmen in the Second World War*. London: Imperial War Museums, 2016.

Kaplan, Philip. *With Wings as Eagles: The Eighth Air Force in World War II*. New York: Skyhorse Publishing, 2017.

Knell, Hermann. *To Destroy a City: Strategic Bombing and Its Human Consequences in World War II*. New York: Da Capo Press, 2003.

Miller, Donald. *Masters of the Air: America's Bomber Boys Who Fought the Air War Against Nazi Germany*. New York: Simon & Schuster, 2007.

Overy, Richard. *The Bombers and the Bombed: Allied Air War Over Europe, 1940-1945*. New York: Penguin Press, 2015.

Perret, Geoffrey. *Winged Victory: The Army Air Forces in World War II*. New York: Random House, 1997.

Peterson, Brian W. *Paper Doll*. South Forty Publishing, 2021.

Plate, Wilmer. *The Storm Clouds of War: Reflections of a WWII Bomber Pilot*. Self-published, 2014.

Reevs, Charles. *Remembrances of the 489th*. Self-published, 2006.

Ryan, Cornelius. *A Bridge Too Far*. New York: Simon & Schuster, 1974.

Sayreville Historical Society. *Images of America: Sayreville*. Charleston, South Carolina: Arcadia Publishing, 2001.

Sutherland, Earl. *Just an 18-Year-Old During World War II*. Morrisville, North Carolina: Lulu Publishing, 2008.

Turnham, Keith. *Death Denied*. Fairdale Publishing/CSN Books, 2007.

For complete bibliographic information pertaining to additional articles, refer to full citations within the Notes.

NOTES

Prologue

1. "42 U.S. Craft Lost in Fierce Aerial Fight," *The Baltimore Sun*, July 8, 1944, p. 1.
2. Freudenthal, *A History of the 489th Bomb Group*, 86.

Chapter 1: Roamer

1. Royal Navy Registers of Seamen's Services. ADM 188, 362 and 363. The National Archives of the UK, Kew, Surrey, England. www.ancestry.com.
2. Sayreville Historical Society, *Sayreville*, 86-87.
3. "Flaming Ruins After Kenvil Blast Resemble Scene of War Inferno," *The Philadelphia Inquirer*, September 13, 1940, p. 3.
4. "Definite Action to Eliminate Bund Camps Urged in House," *St. Louis Dispatch*, September 15, 1940, p. 19.
5. U.S. School Yearbooks, 1880-2012: "The Oriflamme," South River High School, 1941. www.ancestry.com.
6. Charlie Freudenthal, "Green, White, and Yellow Research," *Second Air Division Association Journal*, Vol. 28, No. 2, Summer 1989, p. 25.
7. "Bund Camp Site Given Mortgages," *Central New Jersey Home News*, June 4, 1941, p. 1.
8. "Change Made in Membership of Next Contingent," *The South Amboy Citizen*, January 15, 1943, p. 4.

Chapter 2: High into the Sun

1. "Government to Pay for Land in Dix Area," *The Daily Record*, January 18, 1943, p. 3.
2. George R. Averill, "Here and There," *The Wakefield News*, April 2, 1943, p. 3.
3. Ibid.
4. "500 Prisoners of War to Pick Cotton, Nuts," *The Huntsville Times*, August 29, 1943, p. 2.
5. Graham Aviation, *Southern Field – Americus, Georgia*, 2.
6. Plate, *The Storm Clouds of War*, 47.
7. "Air Cadet Death Toll Shows Drop," *The La Crosse Tribune*, January 16, 1944, p. 2.
8. Charles T. Lucey, "Mars Rides the Rails," *El Paso Herald-Post*, June 2, 1943, p. 8.
9. "Vaudeville," *Chicago Tribune*, January 16, 1944, p. 8, 9.
10. Turnham, *Death Denied*, 40.
11. Ambrose, *The Wild Blue*, 78, 80.
12. "Gulf Pump Station Accidentally Bombed," *The Austin American*, April 29, 1944, p. 1.
13. "3,000 Planes Turned Out," *The Windsor Star*, March 25, 1944, p. 9.
14. Sutherland, *Just an 18-Year-Old During World War II*, 97.

Chapter 3: The Wash

1. "6,000 Warplanes Carry Offensive Through 9th Day," *The Morning Call*, May 28, 1944, p. 1.

2. "Credit is given merchant ships," *The Leader-Post*, May 30, 1944, p. 3.

3. Turnham, *Death Denied*, 86.

4. John L. Predgen Letters [A 2017.0097.0001 Letter] / National Museum of the Mighty Eighth Air Force, Pooler, Georgia.

5. Reevs, *Remembrances of the 489th*, 1-2; Chuck Reevs Memoir [A 2012.0154.0228 Memoir] / National Museum of the Mighty Eighth Air Force, Pooler, Georgia.

6. Reevs, *Remembrances of the 489th*, 5.

7. Ibid., 4.

8. "Nazis Vow to Scorch Earth Before D-Day," *Abilene Reporter News*, May 31, 1944, p. 1.

9. Charles Freudenthal, "Doesn't Seem Like 34 Years," *Second Air Division Association Journal*, Vol. 16, No. 2, June 1978, p. 5.

10. Reevs, *Remembrances of the 489th*, 6-7.

11. U.S. War Department, *A Short Guide to Great Britain*, 20, 24.

12. John L. Predgen Letters [A 2017.0097.0001 Letter] / National Museum of the Mighty Eighth Air Force, Pooler, Georgia.

13. Dr. Bryce Evans, "Ireland during the Second World War," 1940s Society, accessed September 11, 2022, www.1940.co.uk/acatalog/Ireland-in-WW2.html.

14. John L. Predgen Letters, June 30, 1944, [A 2017.0097.0001 Letter] / National Museum of the Mighty Eighth Air Force, Pooler, Georgia.

15. "Notes from the Air Force," *Stars and Stripes*, July 10, 1944, p. 4.

16. Plate, *The Storm Clouds of War*, 85.

17. Freudenthal, *A History of the 489th Bomb Group*, 38-39.

18. Ibid., 36; Plate, *The Storm Clouds of War*, 93-94.

19. Freudenthal, *A History of the 489th Bomb Group*, 36.

20. "Hash Marks," *Stars and Stripes*, July 17, 1944, p. 4.

21. "Faithful Service of Forces Mascots," *Lincolnshire Echo*, April 22, 1944, p. 4.

22. "Former Anti-Sub Man Is Now Pilot," *Fort Worth Star-Telegram*, November 6, 1944, p. 8.

23. Mineral Wells High School, Texas, *The Burro 1937*, 49, www.ancestry.com.

24. Charlie Freudenthal, "Just 'Facts' Don't Tell the Story," *Second Air Division Association Newsletter*, Vol. 10, No. 4, September 1972, p. 4.

25. "Soldier Pays Tribute to Doc. White," *Wellsboro Gazette*, March 16, 1944, p. 9.

26. Charlie Freudenthal, "Halesworth: 489th Notes," *Second Air Division Association Newsletter*, Vol. 49, No. 2, Summer 2010, p. 9.

27. "More interest in religion overseas," *Lincoln Journal Star*, January 27, 1945, p. 2.

28. "America in Action," *Brown County Democrat*, April 7, 1944, p. 6.

29. Jacob T. Elias, "Reflections," *Second Air Division Association Newsletter*, Vol. 19, No. 1, March 1980, p. 14.

30. David J. Hastings, "The Norwich Blitz from a Schoolboy's Perspective," *Second Air Division Association Newsletter*, Vol. 50, No. 1, Spring 2011, p. 13.

31. "Classics v. Swing," *The Birmingham Mail*, May 19, 1944, p. 4.

Chapter 4: Hell After Breakfast

1. Jim Davis, "Thoughts and Night Sounds," *Second Air Division Association Newsletter*, Vol. 42, No. 4, Winter 2003/2004, p. 20.

2. Charles Freudenthal, "Danny's 489th Diary 30/9/44," *Second Air Division Association Newsletter*, Vol. 23, No. 3, September 1984, p. 7.

3. John Steinbeck, "Steinbeck Explains What Flyers' 'Superstition' Is," *The News and Observer*, July 1, 1943, p. 9.

4. "Bugs Baer in the Army," *The Honolulu Advertiser*, January 22, 1943, p. 4.

5. Charles Freudenthal, "Danny's 489th Diary 30/9/44," *Second Air Division Association Newsletter*, Vol. 23, No. 3, September 1984, p. 7.

6. Alfred Segal, "Parachutes and Flak Vests: Dressmakers Who Make 'Em Get an 'E' for Lives Saved," *The Cincinnati Post*, August 30, 1944, p. 19.

7. "Sergeant Describes Battle Experiences; Lions Shown Equipment," *Arizona Daily Star*, November 19, 1943, p. 3; Margaret Bean, "La West Invades Stage and Critics Go to Town," *The Spokesman-Review*, August 27, 1944, p. 4.

8. Plate, *The Storm Clouds of War*, 122.
9. Will Plate, "The 'Luxurious' B-24 Bomber," *Second Air Division Association Newsletter*, Vol. 50, No. 1, Spring 2011, p. 26.
10. Plate, *The Storm Clouds of War*, 86-87.
11. "They Just Won't Let Boys Be Boys!" *Brownsville Herald*, June 4, 1944, p. 38.
12. John L. Predgen Log [A 2017.0097.0003 Log] / National Museum of the Mighty Eighth Air Force, Pooler, Georgia.
13. Additional insights on the particulars of prop governors and feathering were gained from an email interview with aviator Jason Capra on October 16, 2023.
14. William Stewart, "Canadian Troops Keep Moving Fast," *The Montreal Gazette*, September 6, 1944, p. 16.
15. Joe E. Tarpley, "Rookie Too Green to Know Fear," *Second Air Division Association Newsletter*, Vol. 37, No. 1, Spring 1998, p. 38.
16. Walter Cronkite, "How Yanks Bomb Germany," *The Detroit Free Press*, February 27, 1943, p. 2.
17. Mel Pontillo, "Flying the Unfriendly Skies of Europe in 1944," *Second Air Division Association Newsletter*, Vol. 47, No. 3, Fall 2008, p. 12.
18. Roger Freeman, "Mid-Air Collisions," *Second Air Division Association Newsletter*, Vol. 11, No. 2, June 1973, p. 8.
19. Fussell, *Wartime*, 48.

Chapter 5: The Nut House

1. John L. Predgen Log [A 2017.0097.0003 Log] / National Museum of the Mighty Eighth Air Force, Pooler, Georgia.
2. Miller, *Masters of the Air*, 216, 293-294.
3. "Victorian Tells of Parachute Fall," *Victoria Advocate*, July 17, 1944, p. 1.
4. Pete Henry, "Men of Gallantry," *Second Air Division Association Newsletter*, Vol. 16, No. 2, June 1978, p. 10.
5. Neal Sorensen, "489th Notes," *Second Air Division Association Newsletter*, Vol. 39, No. 3, Fall 2000, p. 19.
6. "Mosquito Bombers Blocked Germany's Kiel Canal Traffic," *St. Cloud Daily Times*, July 6, 1944, p. 11.
7. Freudenthal, *A History of the 489th Bomb Group*, 84.
8. Ibid., 84-86.
9. "1500 American Planes Attack Nazi Industry," *Spokane Chronicle*, July 7, 1944, p. 2.
10. Jim Davis, "Thoughts and Night Sounds," *Second Air Division Association Newsletter*, Vol. 42, No. 4, Winter 2003/2004, p. 20.
11. Lou Wagner Memoir [A 2012.0154.0245 Memoir] / National Museum of the Mighty Eighth Air Force, Pooler, Georgia.
12. "Sergeant Paul Redden Dies in Air Battle on Flight to Germany," *Corvallis Gazette-Times*, July 21, 1944, p. 2.
13. John L. Predgen Log [A 2017.0097.0003 Log] / National Museum of the Mighty Eighth Air Force, Pooler, Georgia.
14. Freudenthal, *A History of the 489th Bomb Group*, 94.

15. Lou Wagner Memoir [A 2012.0154.0245 Memoir] / National Museum of the Mighty Eighth Air Force, Pooler, Georgia.

16. Freudenthal, *A History of the 489th Bomb Group*, 95-96; John L. Predgen Log [A 2017.0097.0003 Log] / National Museum of the Mighty Eighth Air Force, Pooler, Georgia.

17. Freudenthal, *A History of the 489th Bomb Group*, 96.

18. Turnham, *Death Denied*, 113.

19. Charles A. Freudenthal, "I Remember, I Remember," *Second Air Division Association Newsletter*, Vol. 14, No. 4, November 1976, p. 3.

20. "NOBALL Targets," 416th Bombardment Group, accessed October 12, 2022, www.416th.com/missions/Mission_NOBALL_Targets.html.

21. "Cpl. Tom Wilcox Vividly Describes Blitzed London, Cosmopolitan Center of Europe's Freedom," *Wellsboro Gazette*, April 27, 1944, p. 1-2.

22. Freudenthal, *A History of the 489th Bomb Group*, 87.

23. "Fly Bomb's Return," *Stars and Stripes*, July 17, 1944, p. 4.

24. Sutherland, *Just an 18-Year-Old during World War II*, 81.

25. Plate, *The Storm Clouds of War*, 114.

26. Davis and Snead, *In Hostile Skies*, 99.

27. Freudenthal, *A History of the 489th Bomb Group*, 87.

28. Ibid.

Chapter 6: SNAFU

1. Freudenthal, *A History of the 489th Bomb Group*, 110.

2. Ibid., 110-111.
3. Ibid., 113.
4. James M. Davis, "489th Notes," *Second Air Division Association Newsletter,* Vol. 36, No. 1, Spring 1997, p. 20.
5. Mel Pontillo, "489th Notes," *Second Air Division Association Newsletter,* Vol. 46, No. 4, Fall/Winter 2007, p. 20.
6. Freudenthal, *A History of the 489th Bomb Group,* 37.
7. John L. Predgen Log [A 2017.0097.0003 Log] / National Museum of the Mighty Eighth Air Force, Pooler, Georgia.
8. Ibid.; Bill Roland, "10 Bombs An Acre," *Sunday Pictorial,* July 30, 1944, p. 12.
9. Arthur W. White, "GIs Sleep on Floors, Chairs in London," *Stars and Stripes,* March 13, 1944, p. 1.
10. Lou Wagner Memoir [A 2012.0154.0245 Memoir] / National Museum of the Mighty Eighth Air Force, Pooler, Georgia.
11. Turnham, *Death Denied,* 121.
12. Ibid., 127.
13. Larry Hobbs, "Being Jewish Was An Extra Risk For This Kassel Survivor," *Second Air Division Association Newsletter,* Vol. 35, No. 3, Fall 1996, p. 7.
14. Freudenthal, *A History of the 489th Bomb Group,* 127; Lou Wagner Memoir [A 2012.0154.0245 Memoir] / National Museum of the Mighty Eighth Air Force, Pooler, Georgia.
15. Lou Wagner Memoir [A 2012.0154.0245 Memoir] / National Museum of the Mighty Eighth Air Force, Pooler, Georgia.
16. Freudenthal, *A History of the 489th Bomb Group,* 128.

17. Lou Wagner Memoir [A 2012.0154.0245 Memoir] / National Museum of the Mighty Eighth Air Force, Pooler, Georgia.

18. Frederick A. Meyer, "489th Notes," *Second Air Division Association Newsletter*, Vol. 22, No. 1, January 1983, p. 3.

19. James Hoseason, "Can You Remember? Glenn Miller's AAF Orchestra," *Second Air Division Association Newsletter*, Vol. 10, No. 4, September 1972, p. 8.

20. Charles H. Freudenthal, "I Remember, I Remember," *Second Air Division Association Newsletter*, Vol. 14, No. 4, November 1976, p. 3.

21. Freudenthal, *A History of the 489th Bomb Group*, 133.

22. "Two Thrusts on Paris," *The Daily Telegraph*, August 11, 1944, p. 1.

23. "Jet Ultra-Fast Fighters," *Liverpool Daily Post*, August 17, 1944, p. 4.

24. Steve Birdsall, "Time to Remember: The Little Friends," *Second Air Division Association Newsletter*, Vol. 17, No. 1, March 1979, p. 8.

25. Freudenthal, *A History of the 489th Bomb Group*, 146.

26. Plate, *The Storm Clouds of War*, 89, 120.

27. Davis and Snead, *In Hostile Skies*, 73.

28. G. K. Hodenfield, "Paris Remains City in Dream," *Stars and Stripes*, August 27, 1944, p. 5.

29. Freudenthal, *A History of the 489th Bomb Group*, 147.

30. "Oil Supplies of Nazis Blasted," *The Cincinnati Enquirer*, August 25, 1944, p. 8.

31. Freudenthal, *A History of the 489th Bomb Group*, 150.
32. Ibid.
33. Ibid., 151.
34. John P. Zima, "Our First Mission: Ludwigschafen!!! 8-26-44!" *Second Air Division Association Newsletter*, Vol. 25, No. 4, December 1986, p. 20-21.
35. John W. Archer, "Small Unit—Big Operation," *Second Air Division Association Newsletter*, Vol. 15, No. 2, June 1977, p. 10.
36. Freudenthal, *A History of the 489th Bomb Group*, 152.
37. Ibid.
38. "Helping Front Liners," *The Rhinelander Daily News*, August 16, 1944, p. 3.
39. Lou Wagner Memoir [A 2012.0154.0245 Memoir] / National Museum of the Mighty Eighth Air Force, Pooler, Georgia.
40. George A. Reynolds, "Truckin'," *Second Air Division Association Newsletter*, Vol. 14, No. 4, November 1976, p. 9.

Chapter 7: Out of Darkness
1. Freudenthal, *A History of the 489th Bomb Group*, 163.
2. Overy, *The Bombers and the Bombed*, 303.
3. Dorr, *Mission to Berlin*, 20.
4. Freudenthal, *A History of the 489th Bomb Group*, 165.
5. John L. Predgen Log [A 2017.0097.0003 Log] / National Museum of the Mighty Eighth Air Force, Pooler, Georgia.

6.   Charlie Freudenthal, "489th Mailbag – Aborts & Bogies," *Second Air Division Association Newsletter*, Vol. 18, No. 2, June 1979, p. 7.

7.   John L. Predgen Log [A 2017.0097.0003 Log] / National Museum of the Mighty Eighth Air Force, Pooler, Georgia.

8.   Ibid.

9.   John L. Predgen Letters, September 16, 1944, [A 2017.0097.0001 Letter] / National Museum of the Mighty Eighth Air Force, Pooler, Georgia.

10.   Ryan, *A Bridge Too Far*, 363.

11.   Ibid., 365.

12.   Lou Wagner Memoir [A 2012.0154.0245 Memoir] / National Museum of the Mighty Eighth Air Force, Pooler, Georgia.

13.   Collin Allan, "Details of the Crash of 'Heaven Can Wait,'" *Second Air Division Association Newsletter*, Vol. 50, No. 2, Summer/Fall 2011, p. 14.

14.   Freudenthal, *A History of the 489th Bomb Group*, 170.

15.   Ryan, *A Bridge Too Far*, 368.

16.   Higginbotham, Adam, "There Are Still Thousands of Tons of Unexploded Bombs in Germany, Left over from World War II." Smithsonian.com, Smithsonian Institution, January 1, 2016, www.smithsonianmag.com/history/seventy-years-world-war-two-thousands-tons-unexploded-bombs-germany-180957680. Accessed November 6, 2022.

17. Ed Johnson, "Land Short and Roll Out," *Second Air Division Association Newsletter,* Vol. 31, No. 1, Spring 1992, p. 24.

18. Freudenthal, *A History of the 489th Bomb Group,* 179; "Nazi Air Force Still Far From Eliminated," *Baraboo News-Republic,* September 30, 1944, p. 1.

19. "Lt. Edward C. Piech Member of Crew Which Narrowly Escaped After Action," *The Central New Jersey Home News,* August 22, 1943, p. 8.

20. "2200 American Bombers Blast Nazi Railroads," *The Tampa Tribune,* October 3, 1944, p. 4.

21. John L. Predgen Log [A 2017.0097.0003 Log] / National Museum of the Mighty Eighth Air Force, Pooler, Georgia; John L. Predgen Letters, October 12, 1944, [A 2017.0097.0001 Letter] / National Museum of the Mighty Eighth Air Force, Pooler, Georgia.

22. John L. Predgen Letters, July 26, 1944, [A 2017.0097.0001 Letter] / National Museum of the Mighty Eighth Air Force, Pooler, Georgia.

23. Freudenthal, *A History of the 489th Bomb Group,* 197; Douglas Werner, "Cologne, Other Axis Areas, Hit by Deluge of Bombs," *The Greenville News,* October 18, 1944, p. 5.

24. Guise, Kim. "In the Ruins of Cologne." The National World War II Museum, March 4, 2020, www.nationalww2museum. org/war/articles/ruins-cologne. Accessed November 6, 2022.

25. John L. Predgen Log [A 2017.0097.0003 Log] / National Museum of the Mighty Eighth Air Force, Pooler, Georgia.

26. "Another Big German Canal Wrecked," *Manchester Evening News*, October 27, 1944, p. 1.

27. Lou Wagner Memoir [A 2012.0154.0245 Memoir] / National Museum of the Mighty Eighth Air Force, Pooler, Georgia.

28. Freudenthal, *A History of the 489th Bomb Group*, 201, 204, 208.

29. John L. Predgen Log [A 2017.0097.0003 Log] / National Museum of the Mighty Eighth Air Force, Pooler, Georgia.

30. Atkinson, *The Guns at Last Light*, 345.

31. Mel Pontillo, "489th Notes," *Second Air Division Association Newsletter*, Vol. 46, No. 2, Spring 2007, p. 27-28.

Chapter 8: Home Alive by '45

1. John H. Rainey, "My Trip on a Liberty Ship," *Second Air Division Association Newsletter*, Vol. 33, No. 3, Fall 1994, p. 31.

2. "Fistic Expert," *The Central New Jersey Home News*, July 8, 1944, p. 4.

3. "Rain Curbs V-E Day Observance," *The Central New Jersey Home News*, May 9, 1945, p. 5.

4. Lucille Walker, "Every Man in Ferrying Division at Rosecrans Field Is a War Story in Himself—All Are Combat Veterans," *St. Joseph News-Press*, May 27, 1945, p. 11.

5. Perret, *Winged Victory*, 369.

6. James M. Davis, "489th Notes," *Second Air Division Association Newsletter*, Vol. 37, No. 4, Winter 1998-199, p. 6.

7. Ludwig Lund, "The Terrible Bombing Damage of Germany," *Second Air Division Association Newsletter*, Vol. 50, No. 3, Winter 2011, p. 27.

8. "The City Is Wild," *The Kansas City Times*, August 15, 1945, p. 3.

9. "Wants Suggestions," *The Rhinelander Daily News*, November 18, 1944, p. 2.

10. "Wright and Patterson Fields to Be Merged," *The Star Press*, November 10, 1945, p. 10.

11. "Queen Admits George Erred," *Valley News*, July 7, 1976, p. 6.

Chapter 9: To Go Back Again

1. "Dear Old Gang," *Second Air Division Association Newsletter*, June 15, 1953.

2. David Stoker, "The Airfields 30 Years After," *Second Air Division Association Newsletter*, Vol. 11, No. 4, December 1973, p. 8.

3. Charles Freudenthal, "The Angel is Alive and Well," *Second Air Division Association Newsletter*, Vol. 13, No. 1, March 1975, p. 9, 12.

4. Charles Freudenthal, "Halesworth Revisited: Where Did My Hardstand Go?" *Second Air Division Association Newsletter*, Vol. 18, No. 3, September 1979, p. 7.

5. Louis J. Wagner, "Letters," *Second Air Division Association Newsletter*, Vol. 18, No. 4, December 1979, p. 17.

6. Charles Freudenthal, "489th Pot Shots," *Second Air Division Association Newsletter*, Vol. 19, No. 1, March 1980, p. 13.

7. Knell, *To Destroy a City*, 2-3.

8. Freeman, *The Mighty Eighth*, 261.

9. Charles Freudenthal, "Green, White, and Yellow Tales," *Second Air Division Association Newsletter*, Vol. 26, No. 3, Fall 1987, p. 25.

10. Plate, *The Storm Clouds of War*, 120.

11. James M. Davis, "489th Notes," *Second Air Division Association Newsletter*, Vol. 39, No. 2, Summer 2000, p. 28.

12. *Public Papers of the Presidents of the United States: F.D. Roosevelt, 1936*, Volume 5, p. 231.

13. James M. Davis, "The Roar That Gave Them Hope," *Second Air Division Association* Newsletter, Vol. 36, No. 2, Summer 1997, p. 8.

INDEX